THE

BOURNE SOCIETY

Village Histories

4. WARLINGHAM

Editor: Dorothy Tutt

Series Editors - Roger Packham & Gwyneth Fookes

ISBN 0 900992 47 6

Acknowledgements

These few words of thanks encompass not only those people who have provided help and information recently but also many others over the years. What can only be called an accumulation of detail has been invaluable in the compilation of this village history. Some early scenes derive from the work of C H Goodman, others from the postcard collection of Roger Packham and access to these sources is gratefully acknowledged. A number of the illustrations are my personal photography, and some are from my own collection of postcards.

I am greatly indebted to Roger Packham, Mary Saaler and Brian Thomas for the excellent coverage of their specialised subjects and to Gwyneth Fookes for the range of maps, essential to illustrate the areas described. Finally, very sincere thanks are expressed to Robert Warner who has given many hours of his time welding the material together to create this the fourth in the Bourne Society Village History series.

Dorothy Tutt

Cover photograph by Gwyneth Fookes
– *The White Lion* public house in 1999

CONTENTS

Unless otherwise indicated, chapters were written by Dorothy Tutt

Introduction 1

1. Prehistoric and Roman Times   *by Mary Saaler* 3

2. The Manor and its People   *by Mary Saaler* 5

3. Local Administration from 1800, including Beating the Bounds 13

4. Westhall 21

5. Well Farm, Dr Tuzo's Development and Tydcombe 29

6. Beyond Tydcombe to the Parish Boundary 35

7. Crewes 41

8. All Saints' Church 49

9. The Atwoods and Wigsells 60

10. Warlingham Court Farm and Batts Farm 63

11. Hamsey Green 69

12. From Hamsey Green to *The Leather Bottle* 75

13. Enclosure of the Common on the North-East of Limpsfield Road 81

14. North of the Green and Farleigh Road 89

15. Warlingham Green 99

16. The West side of the Green 105

17. South and East of The Green – The Wards and the Methodist Church 111

18. School Common and the Vicarage 119

19. Charities 127

20. Celebrations, Organisations and Personalities 135

21. Technical Progress Brings Change 147

22. Sport in Warlingham   *by Roger Packham* 155

23. Birds and other aspects of Natural History   *by Brian Thomas* 165

Illustrations

Page No.

2   Bourne Society Area

Chapter 1 – Prehistoric & Roman Times

3   Vessel of Patch Grove Ware, found at Marks Road

4   Location of Finds

Chapter 2 – The Manor & Its People

5   Bermondsey Arms

7   Coat of Arms of Sir John Gresham

Chapter 3 – Local Administration from 1800 including Beating the Bounds

12   Boundary of the Civil Parish in 1880, including Common land

12   'Dorincourt' as seen from near the Parish Boundary in the Valley

16   Beating the Bounds 1908 – Starting Point near *The Hare & Hounds*

17   Beating the Bounds 1908 – near the Old Barn in Whyteleafe

17   Caterham & Warlingham Urban District Boundary Marker near the Old Road

19   Candidate's Letter to the Voters, Parish Council election 1925

20   Map of the Modern Civil Parish

Chapter 4 – Westhall

23   Sketch map and Detail from Wm Chapman's Survey 1761

24   Westhall Road 1901

24   Sale of land 1905, Westhall Park

24   Farm Cottage – a painting by C L Lockton

25   'The Laurels', 1897

25   'Bayards', 1931

25   'Woottonga', 1978

26   'St. Erth', demolished 1985

26   'Court Lees', 1950

26   'Kooringa', 1950s

27   William Gilford's Signature

Chapter 5 – Well Farm, Dr Tuzo's Development and Tydcombe

28   Map of the Westhall Area

29   Well Farm in 1960

29   'Hillside Cottage' at the corner of Godstone Road and Well Farm Lane in 1960

30   Jacob's Ladder photographed in about 1905

30   'Ravenscroft' in about 1902

32   Tydcombe Farm in about 1900

32   Leas Road before 1919

32   Westhall Road in May 1986

Chapter 6 – Beyond Tydcombe to the Parish Boundary

34   Map – Tydcombe to the Parish Boundary

34   St Christopher's Church, 1998

36   'Portland Cottages' and shops in about 1920

36   'Newland Cottages', photographed in 1962

36   'Rutherford Cottages', photographed in 1967

37   Paddock, Mayes Place in 1981

38   St Ambrose Roman Catholic Church, 1999

39   Advertisements from 1950s

Chapter 7 – Crewes

41   Extract from Tithe Apportionment 1844

42   Kennel Farm

42   Kathleen Quinn in March 1977

42   Rear Living Room in March 1977

44   Warlingham Park Hospital, about 1908

44   Harrow Road in 1903

44   Harrow Road in 1907

45   *The Harrow* Inn in 1908

46   Crewes Lane in the 1960s

47   Crewes Farmhouse in 1910

47   Crewes Farmhouse in the 1930s

47   Crewes Place in 1967

Chapter 8 – All Saints' Church

50   All Saints' Church, 1893 from the field

50   -do- with Hayward tomb

50   -do- showing vestry added in 1857

53   North side of church in 1959

54   Church interior, looking West, Edward Hassell 1829

54   Interior, looking west 1930

56   Elizabethan cup and paten, 1569

57   Vicar & Wardens 1907

58   Church bell, being returned in 1970

59   Churchyard consecration 1927

Chapter 9 – The Atwoods and Wigsells

61   Atwood livery button

Chapter 10 – Warlingham Court and Batts Farms

63   Map of area

64   Batts Farm about 1905

65   Tithepit Shaw Lane before widening

66   Approach to Court Farm, 1904

66   Court Farm about 1904

66   Wedding Hemsley/Taylor outside Court Farm

67   Pleasure Grounds

67   Battalion of Royal Fusiliers at Court Farm

67   Canteen, Empire Battalion, Royal Fusiliers

68   Souvenir Jug *(Courtesy of Bob Davidson)*

Chapter 11 – Hamsey Green

69   Map of area

70   Top of Tithepit Shaw Lane about 1910

70   Hamsey Green Farm in 1901

71   James Bex's premises

71   Hamsey Green Pond in the 1960s

72   View towards Hamsey Green Parade in 1950

Page No.

73   Lower Barn Farm

74   Adveriesments from the 1930s

Chapter 12 – *From Hamsey Green to* **The Leather Bottle**

75   Map of the area

76   Kingswood Lane 1970

76   Gardner's Aerodrome

76   Hamsey Green Gardens 1934

77   Flint Bungalow

78   The Millstone outside the library

79   Mill House – *The Leather Bottle* 1906

Chapter 13 – *Enclosure of the Common on the North-East of Limpsfield Road*

81   Map of the area

83   Village Club in 1904

83   Third Methodist Church, Limpsfield Road

83   'Hazel Cottage' in Bond Road in 1961

84   Bus Garage in 1962

85   The Wheelwright's in about 1905

86   Farleigh Road School

87   Blanchard's Forge in about 1905

87   Final Resting Place of the Bellows

87   'Forge Cottage' in Farleigh Road

88   Advertisements of the 1930s

Chapter 14 – *North of the Green and Farleigh Road*

89   Map of the area

90   Cottages opposite *The Leather Bottle*

91   The Green 1904

91   Mrs Read and Children

91   Church Hall

92   Ringer's Stores

93   Church Activities Club in the Church Hall

94   C L Lockton Reconstruction Picture

Page No.

95	*The White Lion* in about 1890
95	*The White Lion* in about 1910
95	*The White Lion* 1930
96	*The Horseshoe* in about 1905
96	*The Horseshoe* 1999
96	'Horseshoe Cottages'
97	'Box Cottage' early 1900s

Chapter 15 – Warlingham Green

99	The stone marking the division of the ways
100	Service on the Green 1916
100	Dedication of the War Memorial
100	The Howitzer on the Green
102	Aerial View in the early 1930s
103	Remembrance Day Service 1949
103	The Green 1963

Chapter 16 – The West side of the Green

104	*The Leather Bottle* in about 1887
105	Nalder & Collyer plaque
104	Adjacent Cottages
106	*The Leather Bottle* in about 1905
106	*The Leather Bottle* in about 1936
107	View Across the Green in the early 1900s
107	View Across the Green in 1986
108	*The Hare & Hounds* in 1998
109	Advertisements in the 1930s
110	Tom Sales & 'Vicarage Cottage'

Chapter 17 – South and East of The Green – The Wards and the Methodist Church

111	Map of the area
112	1839 Chapel
113	Second Chapel 1871
113	Ann Sarah Windross

113   Household Accounts 1921

115   'Aberdeen House' 1905

115   'Aberdeen House' 1980s

116   Cottages near the Chapel, 1901

116   Looking towards Bradford Buildings, 1963

117   Only the chimney of 'Yew Tree Cottage' is still visible

Chapter 18 – School Common and the Vicarage

118   Map of the area

119   School Common in about 1911

121   The School in the 1960s

122   Vicarage and Barns in 1890s

123   A Sale of Work in the Vicarage Garden June 1905

123   Vicarage 1925

124   Guide Hut & Barns 1998

124   Old House which faced the Common. Demolished in 1898

Chapter 19 – Charities

126   Workhouse – diet 1873

127   'The Plantation' 1901

128   Hillbury Road in 1967

128   View across the Valley 1914

129   Henry Smith Charity letter 1896

130   Almshouses

132   Almshouses

134   23rd June 1997 – unveiling plaque

Chapter 20 – Celebrations, Organisations and Personalities

136   1902 Coronation Celebrations Programme

137   1902 Coronation Celebrations – Comic Cricket Match team

138   Sir Alan Cobham's display team airborne at Hamsey Green

141   Festival of Britain Pageant

141   Festival of Britain Pageant performers

Page No.

142	Festival of Britain Week – Baby Show
143	Coronation Party 1953
144	Warlingham May Queen 1958
145	Harry Leppard and his Spots
146	Salute the Soldier Week 1944

Chapter 21 – Technical Progress Brings Change

149	Dr Epps' Pond, 1903
149	Warren Park – Drainage
150	Plaque on Post Office Sorting Office
151	Fire Brigade 1905
152	Succombs Hill 1969
152	Narrow Lane 1969
153	Westhall Road

Chapter 22 – Sport in Warlingham

156	Warlingham Cricket Club cartoons 1932
158	Warlingham Football Club cartoons 1932
159	Members outside Warlingham Golf Club, early 1900s
161	Members of the Archery Club in action 1952
163	Warlingham Sports Club advertisement 1932

Chapter 23 – Birds and other aspects of Natural History

165	Map of wildlife strongholds in Warlingham
167	Katy & Sam on the Leas above Halliloo
167	Buzzard
168	The Dobbin and Court Farm
169	Meadow Pipit
169	Blackcap
170	Red Kite
170	Stonechat
170	Song Thrush
172	Slines pond on Limpsfield Road

INTRODUCTION

Dorothy Tutt needs little introduction to this Village History of Warlingham – the fourth in the Bourne Society's series.

Paradoxically, she is a native and a resident of Caterham but her heart is very much in Warlingham, especially its history. She was closely involved in village life during 54 years' residence at Hamsey Green and at Warren Park.

The history of Warlingham has commanded Dorothy Tutt's attention over many years. She has herself captured, photographically, many of the changes for over 50 years; additionally she has written two volumes of *Warlingham in old Picture Postcards* for the European Library and innumerable articles on Warlingham in various volumes of the Bourne Society's annual *Local History Records* and its quarterly bulletin. She has also lectured – with a wealth of historical slides – on Warlingham, researched Warlingham, worshipped in Warlingham and no doubt still dreams of Warlingham.

This fund of knowledge has been made available to local history groups, women's groups, luncheon clubs, Local Authority evening courses, schools and everyone wishing to learn about this historic east Surrey village.

She has also found time to serve on the Bourne Society's council for over 30 years and enthusiastically carried out the roles of membership secretary, honorary secretary, vice-chairman, chairman, vice-president and president. To a large number of local people, Dorothy Tutt *is* the Bourne Society.

This village history of Warlingham has been arranged in a different style to its predecessors. Great care has been taken to explain how and why Warlingham has evolved and Miss Tutt has systematically examined the different locations to consider the sequence of landowners, their demise and subsequent development and this is reflected in the chapters.

With Miss Tutt's vast knowledge of the subject, the normal methodology of the series has also been varied, in that the large team of researchers gathered to work on the earlier volumes did not seem to be appropriate in this case. Only three other experts were invited to participate – Mary Saaler, Roger Packham and Brian Thomas – and their chapters make a very valuable contribution to the whole.

Anyone with even a passing interest in Warlingham will find in this volume a fascinating amount of historical information which will explain the village as it is at the dawn of the new millennium.

Gwyneth Fookes

Roger Packham

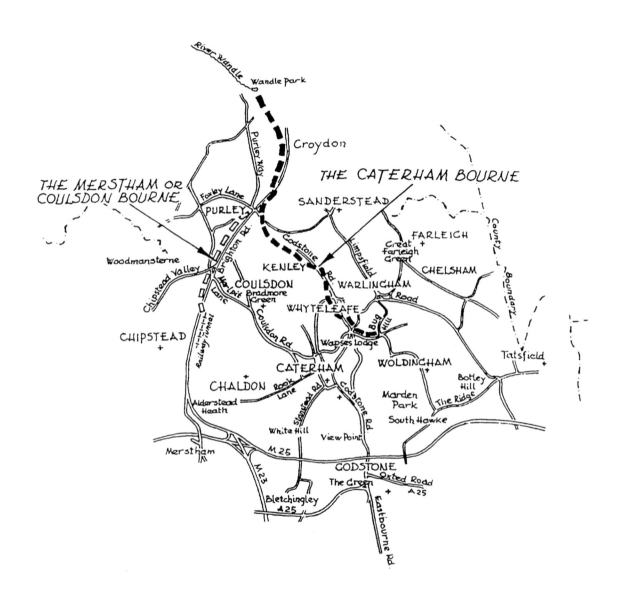

The Bourne Society Area

Chapter 1

Prehistoric and Roman Times

by Mary Saaler

The areas of chalk and clay with flints that stretch across the North Downs attracted people in the past who needed the flints to make their tools and weapons. As a result, Warlingham, like many other local places, produces surface scatters of worked flint, providing evidence for activities in the past. Many of these were collected in the early part of the 20th century and placed, with other local items, in a cabinet in the Church Hall, which became known as 'Warlingham Museum'. When the East Surrey Museum opened in Caterham in 1980, the collection was deposited there.

The earliest evidence for the use of flint in Warlingham dates to the Mesolithic period (10,000–4,000 BC), in the form of an axe which was found near Ridley Road. However, most of the worked flints can be attributed to Neolithic times (4,000–2,000 BC), including an arrowhead, found when Searchwood Road was being constructed in 1908, and an axe from the garden of 'Stonebanks', in Marks Road at the junction with Limpsfield Road. Polished axes have come from Succombs Hill and Rogers Lane, while scatters of worked flint have been found near St Christopher's Church; close to the junction of Eglise Road with Farleigh Road, and along the bridle path that links Limpsfield Road to Tithepit Shaw Lane. Flint implements continued to be used during the Bronze Age (2,000–500 BC) and such finds from Warlingham include three arrowheads and a flint dagger. A number of bronze axes were found at Chelsham in the 1890s and two of these were deposited in the Warlingham Museum.

Three storage pits of Iron Age date (500 BC–AD 100) were found in the Whyteleafe Recreation Ground during the construction of a gas-pipe trench; pottery and burnt clay were associated with these. In addition, pottery dating from the late Bronze Age or early Iron Age was found at Marks Road, where there was also a number of Romano-British vessels, two of which contained cremated bones, including the bones of a child. An account of the discovery of these items records—

> 'In the spring of 1909, while some ground was being trenched for garden purposes, pieces of pottery were found, together with a few burnt bones. The site was about 200ft north of the Westerham Road and midway between the village and *The Hare & Hounds*.'

One of the vessels, of a type usually known as Patch Grove ware, was decorated with a band of herring-bone slashes. The concentration of finds around Marks Road, along the 200m contour,

Vessel of Patch Grove ware found at Marks Road
(Courtesy of Surrey Archaeological Society)

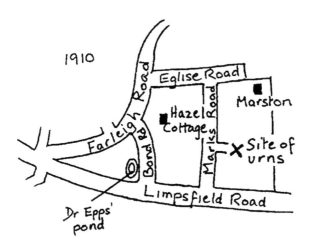

Sketch-map showing location of finds of urns

suggests that this part of Warlingham was close to an early settlement site. As well as these items, a bronze brooch, a ring and eight Roman coins in poor condition were found at 'Whiteleaf', Warlingham, in the 1890s. Although the line of the Roman road from London to Portslade has not been firmly established, it may run through the western part of Warlingham, now known as Whyteleafe on or near the present A22. The line of the road first becomes visible in Caterham, where it runs along the side of the valley.

SOURCES:

BIRD, J and D (eds.) *The Archaeology of Surrey.*

FARLEY, M (1967) *Bourne Society Guide to Local Antiquities.*

Notes, *Surrey Archaeological Collections* **24**, (1911) 178–179.

Parish Notes, *Warlingham and Chelsham Parish Magazine.*

Chapter 2

The Manor and its People

by Mary Saaler

The Middle Ages

There is no definite reference to the manor of Warlingham in the Domesday Survey of 1086 and, from time to time, the name of Warlingham has been confused with that of Woldingham, which was sometimes written as 'Waldingham'. However, Saxon settlements probably existed in both places before the Norman Conquest, since place-names ending in -ham suggest a Saxon origin.[1]   Although Warlingham is not mentioned in Domesday the manor was probably held by Robert Watteville from his overlord, Richard of Tonbridge. Certainly, Watteville held the nearby manors of Farleigh and two manors in Chelsham, later called Chelsham Watteville and Chelsham Court, from the time of the Norman invasion, and we know that in 1144 his descendants, William and Robert Watteville, gave their manor of Warlingham to the monks of the Cluniac priory of St Saviour in Bermondsey.[2]   By this grant the income from the manor went towards the upkeep of the Priory, which was founded in 1085. The Priory attracted such grants because of its size and prestige. It was often used for meetings between kings and their ministers on matters of state.

The grant of 1144 was followed by another in 1158, when William, 'with the consent of his children', also gave the churches of Warlingham and Chelsham to provide further income for the monks of Bermondsey. This grant was later confirmed by various monarchs until the middle of the 15th century.[3]   The manor of Warlingham was, therefore, managed by the officials of Bermondsey Priory which became an abbey in 1399.

The Domesday Survey shows that the adjoining manor of Sanderstead was in the hands of the Abbot of Hyde Abbey, which lay in Winchester. For many years the officials of both establishments were in dispute about the use of the common land that lay on the boundaries of both manors. The first record for the dispute dates from 1272 when the Abbot of Hyde brought charges against John, Prior of Bermondsey, about unlawful use of the boundary area. Further records of the case in 1275 give us the earliest known names of some of the people of Warlingham

BERMONDSEY: party azure and gules a border argent.

(Blue and red, with a silver border)

at that time, including Walter the Bailiff, who managed the manor for Bermondsey Priory, William Atteful and John Hamond. Other local men named were: John of Selsdon, John Flore of Godstone and Thomas of Stonham, from Caterham. The case continued the following year when the abbot accused the prior of setting up a gallows within the manor of Sanderstead, while the prior claimed that it was in Warlingham.[4]   Unfortunately, as in many such cases, there is no record of the outcome, but the disputes about use of the common land on the boundaries continued for the next 300 years.

In 1318 the Prior of Bermondsey granted the manor to Robert de Keleseye as a sub-tenant, and the tax returns for 1332 show him as the leading tax-payer. While the poorest people did not pay tax, the list shows that there were at least 14 households in Warlingham prosperous enough to be taxed, including that of the miller, John atte Mulle, who was also a tenant of the manor of Chelsham Watteville. The names of the tax-payers were—

Robert de Keleseye
Robert Russel
Stephen atte Frith
Roger le May
Geoffrey le May
John Cockes
John atte Mulle

Walter Athelard
Thomas Lacy
John Stephen
Ralph Aleyn
Thomas Randulf
John Hamond
The Prior of Tandridge
(for land at Westhall)

These men were taxed on the value of their crops (wheat, oats and barley) and on the value of their animals, mainly oxen and sheep. Some of the names, such as Mays, Cok(mans), Stephen (or Stevens), Lacys and Westhall, remained as place-names in Warlingham for many years afterwards, some until the present day.[5] Sometime before 1352 the Prior of Bermondsey had leased out land, later known as Crewes, to the Carew family of Beddington. The land took its name from the Carews and was administered by their officials.

Fifteenth Century

The first half of the 15th century was a time of great unrest, culminating in the south-east in Jack Cade's rebellion in 1450. The rebels, who included a large contingent from east Surrey, marched on London, expressing their discontent against central government, county administrators, tax collectors, local bailiffs and officials who were demanding excessive sums of money. The rebels chose as their spokesman, Thomas Cook, a merchant and citizen of London, who had property in London and Essex and was also lord of the manor of Chelsham Watteville. Cook was a good spokesman whom the early 16th-century chronicler, Fabyan, described as 'a man of great boldness in speech and well-spoken and singularly witted and well-reasoned.' However, as the rebellion lost its momentum, the rebels asked for pardons and their names were recorded in the Pardon Rolls of 1450. Among those from Warlingham who received pardons were—

William Wooden
John Planesfeld
John Valentyne
Laurence Wanegate
William Maye
Thomas Knot [6]

Since the protest was about high levels of taxation, these men were not the poorest in the community, but were among the better-off people who had more to lose. This is the first reference in Warlingham to the family with the surname 'Wooden', formerly 'ate Wodeden', which had already been resident in Chelsham for over 100 years. Several wills of the 1480s also show the relative prosperity of a few local people who left money for the benefit of the rest. For example, William Ewston gave 12d for the 'premying' of All Saints' Church, which probably refers to putting the first coat of paint on the walls (priming). William Stephens gave 6s 8d for the bell-house on the church and left 6d for repairs to the road, known as East Street, while his widow, Joan, gave 6d for the upkeep of the high altar.[7]

Sixteenth century

Bermondsey continued to own the manor until the Dissolution of the Monasteries, when the Abbey estates were surrendered to the Crown in 1538. Three years earlier, Thomas Cromwell, the King's chief minister, had carried out a valuation of church property which reveals some details about Warlingham. The manor itself was worth £20 and it contained 12 acres of woodland, worth 12s 0d. The vicar was Thomas Ipswell, who held the vicarage and 16 acres of glebeland, worth 16s 0d. The list of tithes that were payable to Bermondsey gives us clues about the products of the manor at that time, listing milk and calves, rabbits, wool and lambs, piglets, geese, flax and hemp. The Prior of Tandridge still held the lease of land at Westhall, valued at £4 13s 4d.[8]

Following the Dissolution, the manor was sold to Sir John Gresham, a highly successful businessman, who was Lord Mayor of London in 1547 and bought up the manors of Warlingham, Sanderstead, Woldingham and Titsey, making his home at Titsey Place. He married Mary, daughter of Thomas Ipswell, the vicar of Warlingham, and had 11 children by her. After Mary died, he married a widow, formerly Catherine Sampson.

From the time when Gresham purchased the manor, we have records of the manor court which tell us about the local people and their properties. It was usual for a new lord of the manor to ask for information about the property he had just bought and, as a result, the record for 1544 gives us a list of his tenants and their lands and some clues about previous owners—

> William Comport was tenant of Stephens, consisting of a house and 30 acres of land, and a croft called Rydons.

The arms of Sir John Gresham, who acquired the Manor of Warlingham in 1539

> Richard Wooden was tenant of a house and garden called Frenches, and also held properties known as Allards and Conys.

> John Wooden had married widow Stephens and took over her property, known as Cokmans. Thomas Wooden was tenant of a house and 40 acres of land, one toft of 16 acres called Hobblockes, a house and 30 acres called Whytemilkes and Eggs (sometimes called Sweetmilk and Eggs), nine acres called Mannys or Mannyngs, one acre called Crouchacre and a piece of land known as Godewyns. John Valentyne held 30 acres called Butlers, a toft with 18 acres (formerly held by Peter Hamond), a cottage and 16 acres of land, a toft called Cottishill (Cottarshill), an acre and a half formerly held by William Stephens and four acres once held by Agnes Hoo. Thomas Lambe, tenant of Lacys, held two crofts called Douce (two) Annottes and two gardens. He also took over a garden called Hoberdsyshawe, paying the lord of the manor a fee of two capons for it.

Hoberdsyshawe took its name from a family called Hoberd or Oberd which had been living in Tatsfield since at least 1401. Four tenants, named as John Valentyne, Richard Wooden junior, Thomas Lambe and Thomas Saunder, were ordered to make repairs to their properties.[9]

The men who were listed in 1544 were the direct tenants of the lord of manor and would have sub-let much of their land in small parcels to poorer families. While this is the earliest detailed evidence we have for tenants and their lands in Warlingham, it also shows the dominance of the family with the surname Wooden. Because there were so many local inhabitants with this surname, they had to be identified in the records by extra information; for example, there was a John Wooden 'of Batts', (Batts Farm), another of 'Court Lodge', a third John Wooden was described as 'alias Palmer', probably taking his mother's name. There was also a John Wooden 'of Slines' and yet another 'of Frenches'. In addition, William Wooden was the bailiff and ran the manor for the Greshams. There is also evidence of a family dispute in 1553, when John Wooden of Frenches assaulted his brother, William, with a stick. He broke the stick and went home to find another one to continue the assault, but was arrested and fined 3s 4d for his offence.

Apart from recording changes in tenancies, the manor court was also responsible for managing the local community and the environment. The leading local residents and tenants formed the jury of the court and issued orders, made decisions and settled disputes; for example, the jurors of the court ordered local people to clear the mud from North Street Lane and East Street Lane, and to make repairs to these roads. They told all tenants with land facing East Street Lane to cut back overhanging trees. They ordered Richard Heath to open up the footpath that he had blocked between Warlingham and Farleigh and they fined William Wooden of Batts for cutting down the lord's trees to repair his property, without permission. The court also put restrictions on the number of animals allowed to graze on the common, which was known as Warlingham Heath, or the Upper Common, to distinguish it from the common at Warlingham Bottom (now part of Whyteleafe). In addition, Peter Hamond, who had a brewhouse in Croydon, was fined for overcharging for his beer and William Ownsted, a local man, was similarly fined for charging too much for ale and for selling it in unauthorised measures. The ale taster, John Gawton, was responsible for supervising the price and quality of ale and beer and he reported Ownsted as a frequent offender.

The manor court also kept watch on the price and quality of food and fined Thomas Hurlock, a baker, for selling bread containing adulterated flour. Other offences included catching rabbits with illegal traps and enclosing parts of the common land for individual use. In particular, John Wooden had enclosed two acres, known as Edmond's Close, that lay within the Upper Common, while John Wooden of Batts fenced off the pond at Hamsey Green for his own use and put a pigsty there. Unfortunately, others followed his example and, eventually, all tenants were told to remove their pigsties from Hamsey Green and Warlingham Heath. Tenants were also ordered to repair the village stocks and the archery butts, which had been in a state of decay for a year. In a move to encourage men to practise archery, which could be used for the defence of the realm, Parliament had banned games like football, handball, quoits and bowls. However, the ban was not particularly effective and, in 1553, the manor court fined Robert Nightingale, John Wooden of Frenches, William Ownsted, John Taylor and others for playing bowls, 'in secret'.

The dispute about the use of the common land on the boundaries of the manor that was first recorded in 1272 had continued through the years until, in 1575, an attempt was made to divide up the common and allocate specific areas to the tenants of Warlingham and Sanderstead. Since both manors were held by the Greshams at this date, it was probably easier to organise a settlement than when they were in separate ownership. The officials of both manor courts decided that the tenants of Sanderstead should have 20 acres on the north side of the common at Hamsey Heath, while the tenants of Warlingham should use the rest of Hamsey Heath and a piece of woodland known as the Hassocke (or Riddlesdown, or Scrubbes) lying on the south side of the path called the Broadway which led from Hamsey Heath to the three dikes. These dikes are probably the earthworks that are still visible between Riddlesdown Road and footpath number 124, leading to Famet Close, on the north-west edge of Riddlesdown. To make sure that the agreement was permanent and to avoid trouble in the future, the tenants were ordered to mark the divisions clearly with boundaries or hedges.

While the local manor court, probably held at Warlingham Court Farm, dealt with minor offences, more serious cases went to the assize courts at Croydon, Guildford, Reigate or Southwark. In 1581, there was a case of highway robbery by 'gentlemen of London' at Riddlesdown, where they stole money from a draper of Eastbourne, and in 1584, William Rixon of Warlingham, with others, assaulted John Wooden, 'in the highway', at Warlingham and stole his money and his cloak. Rixon was found guilty but escaped from prison.[10]

National and international events also had repercussions in Warlingham; in 1558, as the English garrison at Calais fell, the Marquess of Winchester, Lord Treasurer of England, ordered a muster of men and weapons in every parish, to ensure that all able-bodied men would be ready to defend their country. A muster roll for Warlingham for the year 1569 has survived, which lists the able-bodied men as: Richard Holman, Michael, Richard and William Hayward, and a member of the Ownsted family. They were equipped with arquebuses (hand-guns), pikes, breastplates and helmets. The parish also had its own hand-gun and helmet, to be used by a man too poor to provide his own. When the Spanish Armada threatened in 1588, men were summoned from Surrey to defend London, but returned home when the threat did not materialise.[11]

Seventeenth Century

By 1594, John Ownsted, who was already lord of the manor of Sanderstead, had purchased the manor of Warlingham and meetings of the manor court continued as before. However, increasing amounts of parliamentary legislation extended the powers of the manor court, using it to combat poverty and overcrowding. We can see the results of this policy during the first half of the 17th century when Ralph Jackson and Mary Wood were charged with having lodgers without permission and Thomas Heath was ordered to demolish a cottage he had built, without the statutory four acres of land considered necessary to support the occupants. An increase in population had also brought pressure on the common land, and the manor court was forced to regulate the number of animals on common land and the building of hovels by the poor. As a result, tenants were fined for allowing their geese to spoil Warlingham Heath, for putting too many sheep to graze on it and for building sheds there.

A will of 1602 also shows the sad fate of an unmarried mother, who brought shame upon her family. Agnes Bromfield, 'a maiden', of Warlingham, was driven out by her relations just as she was about to give birth—

> 'First she exclaimed against her sister who would not let her stay, but thrust her out of
> doors so that she went longer than her time, which was the cause of her death'.

The witnesses of her will included a midwife, Margery Woodstock; the reference to her role is an indication that women worked as nurses within the parish, looking after the sick and the dying. Generally, each parish would have one or two women who did this work, often paid for out of the parish rate. [12]

In contrast to such distress and poverty, some families continued to prosper. In 1581, the jurors of the manor court granted John Wodden of Warlingham permission to pull down a house, called 'a gatehouse', on condition that he carried out repairs on his dwelling house. When he died in 1614, an inventory of his possessions indicated that he still held two houses. One of these was his main dwelling and contained a hall, parlour, bedchamber and kitchen, while the 'old house' contained a furnace and other stuff, suggesting that this second 'house', with its furnace, was probably a brewhouse, with a cauldron for brewing beer. [13]

During the second half of the 17th century, when Harman Atwood was lord of the manor, John Batt was charged with putting a cottage on Warlingham Heath, and the residents of Chelsham, Coulsdon, Farleigh and Sanderstead were fined for grazing their animals on the same common without permission. In effect, the fine became a licence granting them permission, which limited the use of the land to wealthier people. With so much pressure on the use of the commons, there was a corresponding increase in the number of stray animals because poorer residents could not afford to pay the fines for putting them on the common. Sometimes they resorted to force to recover their stock that the bailiff had impounded. In fact, there were so many strays that the tenants asked the lord of the manor to repair the pound, which was in a state of decay. As part of the same process, wealthier tenants fenced off their property to protect it; for example, Mary Mills was brought before the court for putting a fence and a gate on the road leading from le Cross gate to Crewes Corner, causing annoyance to other residents. Similarly, John Newton of Coulsdon had blocked the road from Riddlesdown to the common fields and enclosed the land for his own use. The lord of the manor also enclosed part of the common to build almshouses.

During the period of the Commonwealth, all Englishmen aged 18 and over were required to take an oath, swearing to uphold 'the true Reformed Protestant Religion' of the Church of England, and lists of those who took the oath, or refused to do so, were compiled in every parish for the year 1641-2, known as the Protestation Returns. In Warlingham there were no refusals, and 30 heads of households and 17 youths took the oath. The list suggests that there were about 30 families in Warlingham at this time, and there is confirmation of this number in the Hearth Tax Returns for 1662-4.

At this date the government devised a scheme to raise money by imposing a tax of 2s 0d a year on every hearth. It was a highly unpopular tax and so difficult to collect that it was soon abandoned but, as with the Protestation Returns, the lists also give us information about the size of the community and, in addition, about relative wealth. In Warlingham there was a total of 32 dwellings. About two-thirds of these paid the tax, the rest being excused on grounds of poverty. This proportion was typical across north-east Surrey, except for Farleigh and Chelsham where only half the inhabitants were considered chargeable. In Warlingham, Christopher and Elizabeth Hayward lived in the house with the largest number of hearths (eight); they probably needed space for themselves and their eight children. Widow Mills had six hearths, while William Heath had five and Henry Phillipps had four. At the lower end of the scale, Thomas Farley, Richard Woodstock, Richard Green, Widow Ives and several others, with just one hearth each, paid nothing. We can account for the slight difference in the numbers of households given in the Protestation Returns and the Hearth Tax records – widows were included in the Hearth Tax, but the Protestation Returns listed only males.[14]

From Tudor times onwards, matters relating to the supervision of trade, particularly the sale of alcohol, gradually moved away from the local manor court to the quarter sessions, administered by Justices of the Peace. For example, in 1661 two retailers from Warlingham were summoned to appear before the justices at Croydon 'for various Offenses', and Thomas Farley of Warlingham was fined at the Reigate sessions in 1663 for keeping an ale-house without a licence. [15]

Eighteenth Century

During the early 18th century, we can see how more of the common land passed into private control when the lord of the manor and his tenants agreed to enclose Warlingham Bottom, which is now part of Whyteleafe. The men who took over the land were John Hayward, Thomas Rumsby and Nicholas Stacey. The court roll for 1728 lists their holdings in detail. John Hayward had two acres in Barking Bottom and the house and land known as Stevens. Thomas Rumsby had four acres in Middle Hill, three acres in Barking Bottom, Longlands Close, Bourne Croft, part of Yewtree Bottom, part of Five Acres, Understepshill and Coney Crook, which together amounted to 13 acres, for rent of 18s 0d a year. In addition, Nicholas Stacey took over common land in Sotteswood (Searchwood) Bottom, Middle Hill, Scalled Field, Barking Bottom, Road Piece 'lately divided into three parts', Black Bush, and an acre and a half on the road from Warlingham to Godstone through Nine Cornered Field.

By 1739, John Atwood, lord of the manor, had also taken over some of this land, described as Chantry Hill, Barking Bottom, Woodmans, No Man's Bush, Nine Cornered Field, Lambercroft and Longcroft. From then on the common land was restricted to the 'Upper Common' and Hamsey Green.

Most local people worked on the land, but during the 18th century the records begin to give us some information about different occupations. For example, Richard Sharpe was a blacksmith, William Cullingham was a gardener and, in 1742, Edward Gatland, a butcher, became tenant of two houses, brewhouses and various outhouses. In 1760 Gatland's widow, Elizabeth, married Thomas Frame, described as 'a shopkeeper of Warlingham'. Since married women could not hold property in their own right, Frame gained possession of one of Gatland's houses and a brewhouse by his marriage. He was later fined for keeping his sheep on the Upper Common, which he should have kept on the Parsonage lands, while five other tenants were also fined for putting horses to graze on the common, and Benjamin Quittendon had to pay 3s 4d because he had put his geese there. Another trade mentioned for the first time was bricklaying, as William Morris of Chipstead, wheelwright, took over the property of his father, also called William, who was described as a bricklayer. Morris's house was called Butler's but he was also tenant of other properties, including Little Broadfield, Great Broadfield, Burton Ridden, with the adjoining field, and the land known as The Little How. The records of the manor court for the year 1786 list the jurors as William Lucas, John Peake and James Frame, who noted three changes of tenancy and named two as Stevens and Cockmans, while the third consisted of a total of 44 acres abutting on to Limpsfield Road. From then on, the manor court continued to meet, but on a reduced scale, dealing chiefly with transfers of property. Matters relating to local disorder were considered by magistrates.

SOURCES

1.	BLAIR, J (1991) *Early Medieval Surrey*, Alan Sutton & Surrey Arch. p. 45.

2.	MORRIS, J (1975) *Domesday Surrey*, Phillimore **19**, 7-8.

3.	LUARD, H *Annales Monastici* **3**, 437; 440.

4.	*Calendar of Close Rolls 1272-9*, 39; 226.

5.	SRO. 2575 box 3F.

6.	*Calendar of Patent Rolls Henry VI* pt. 2, p. 359.

7.	*Surrey Wills, Spage Register,* Surrey Record Society No. 17, 17-18.

8.	*Valor Ecclesiasticus* **2**, 58-59.

9.	LEVESON-GOWER, G 'Notes on the Family of Uvedale', *Surrey Archaeological Collections* **3**, 137-46.

10.	COCKBURN, J *Surrey Indictments, Elizabeth I.*

11.	Surrey Musters, *Surrey Record Society* No. 10, pt. 2.

12.	Surrey Wills, *Herringman Register,* Surrey Record Soc. 5, No. 7, p. 156.

13	PRO HW 1614.

14.	PRO E179/258/4; Carter, H, 'Surrey Protestation Returns' *Surrey Archaeological Collections* **59**, 35-68.

15.	POWELL, D & JENKINSON, H *Surrey Quarter Sessions 1658-68,* Surrey Record Society.

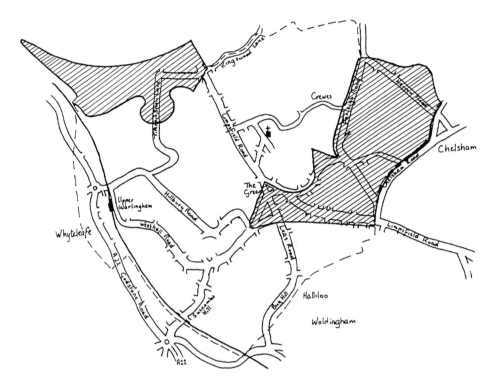

The boundary of the Civil Parish is outlined, and the shaded areas
indicate the common land enclosed in the 19th century

'Dorincourt' stands out on the
hilltop in this view taken from
across the valley in about 1905.
The parish boundary went along
the valley, just above the road.

Chapter 3

Local Administration from 1800

— including Beating the Bounds

At the start of the 19th century Warlingham was entirely rural. The civil parish, some 1703 acres, was small compared to the adjacent parishes of Caterham, Coulsdon, Sanderstead or Chelsham, and the census of 1801 provides the information that there were 187 people living in 56 houses. Most of the people gained their living in some aspect of agriculture. The common land, known as Warlingham Bottom, which is now Whyteleafe, had been enclosed in the previous century, but there was still a large area of open land on the hilltop above, including Hamsey Green. Beyond a band of cultivated land lay the upper common, which extended right to the parish boundary with Chelsham and north-east to Farleigh.

In 1805 a County Surveyor named Malcome wrote—

> '... let any man accustomed to good roads follow me through Limpsfield, Titsey, Tatsfield, Addington, Warlingham, Chelsham, Woldingham...during any of the Spring months, and he would be ready to conclude that he was got into some of the most inaccessible and uninhabited parts of Ireland... If we want to go from Warlingham to Limpsfield or Tatsfield we must enquire all along the road, for we see no post to inform us...The public houses on the bye-roads, and sometimes on the high roads, are frequently so bad and so occupied by licentious people that it is dangerous to put one's head into them. They are the haunt of the smuggler and the riotous.'

The same writer also mentioned the superabundance of flints which were collected from the fields and used for the repair of the turnpike and parish roads.

Local administration, in the form of the church-based Vestry, had been evolving over previous centuries. Male residents who paid dues such as the poor rate were eligible, and indeed if elected by their fellow Vestry members, were more or less obliged to fulfil a year in one of the positions of responsibility in the administration of the parish. In Warlingham it was probably the same small group who took turn and turn about, with the occasional addition of a newcomer, such as Dr Epps, who had an interest in helping the community.

In large churches this gathering of local people must have originally met in the Vestry, but at All Saints' Church in Warlingham, which did not have one, the meeting was held in the nave. The incumbent, who in Warlingham was a vicar, was officially the chairman of the meetings. Appointments to be decided included the churchwardens, sexton and the parish clerk who, amongst other duties, took the minutes of the meetings. The Vestry put forward names for the positions of constable, responsible for law and order in the parish, the waywarden or surveyor of the highways who was concerned with local roads, and the overseers of the poor who collected and administered the Poor rate. These appointments had to be approved by the justices of the peace. Some parishes also appointed a beadle who had various small duties, such as helping the constable or calling the people to attend parish meetings.

There were long spells in the 18th and into the 19th century when the rector of Sanderstead was also vicar of Warlingham, and although Warlingham had a resident curate it does seem that in course of time things did become rather slack. The Revd John Courtney, who held both livings after Thomas Wigsell died in 1805, wrote an open letter addressed to 'such of the inhabitants of Warlingham and Chelsham as neglect altogether or very seldom attend Divine Service'. He not only rebuked his parishioners for neglecting church but asserted that their Sundays 'were profaned by drunken riot and revelry in houses of public resort.' Further evidence of slackness is apparent with regard to the Elizabethan cup and cover, the story of which is given in the chapter on

All Saints' church. The parish chest was lost along with any existing Vestry minute books and other early parish records in the late 1830s when Simon Baker, overseer, who had the chest in his private possession, emigrated to America. Apparently this did not come to light until the Parish Council came into being in 1895. One cannot help but wonder if this is the whole truth of the matter. Thankfully the parish registers remained, but the only Vestry minute book extant starts in the early 1840s. The interesting information it contains, though it could with advantage have been a little more detailed at times, makes one greatly regret the loss of earlier records. It was during this time when the activity of the parish church was at a low ebb that the Wesleyan Methodists became established in the village.

The Bounds of the Parish

One of the duties of the Vestry was to arrange a perambulation of the bounds of the parish. It was necessary about every four or five years to check that the boundary markers were in order and that there were no encroachments or other irregularities. It was important that the parishioners knew where the boundaries were. With the creation of the detailed Ordnance Survey maps in the 19th century this walk around the bounds became unnecessary, but continued occasionally in some parishes just to keep up a tradition.

One of the earliest entries in the Vestry minute book reads—

'On Holy Thursday in the year of our Lord 1844 the bounds of the parish were perambulated (after a lapse of many years). Present the Reverend Mr.J. Dalton, the vicar of the parish and the overseers of the poor, accompanied by two aged poor and infirm parishioners who were taken to show the bounds'.

Some encroachment was found on the Farleigh side, and also at Hamsey Green where it would seem that James Bex, whose house was just over the boundary in Sanderstead, had extended his holding to enclose a piece of the common.

Following an Act of Parliament in 1861 the area within which the City of London could levy tax on coal and wine coming into London was extended to the boundary of the then Metropolitan Police area. Iron posts were erected wherever a road, railway or canal crossed the boundary, and some of these 'City' posts are on the civil boundary of Warlingham parish. The ecclesiastical district of St Luke, Whyteleafe, was formed in 1866, comprised of portions of Caterham, Warlingham and Coulsdon parishes, but this did not alter the boundary of the civil parish. The 1861 census shows there were then 602 people living in 118 houses, and 20 years later in 1881, just before the development at Westhall started, the population of the parish had grown to 1147, of which 366 lived in Whyteleafe.

At a vestry meeting held on 24th March 1892, it was proposed and agreed that there should be a beating of the bounds of the parish. The date chosen was 15th July, and the School Board granted the children a day's holiday. The group consisted of the vicar, Revd F R Marriott; churchwarden, W Stiff; overseers, T E Taylor and H Jarrett; schoolmaster, J D Clarke, and the 20 boys who had maintained the best attendance at school during the previous quarter. All wore a red and white rosette and carried a willow wand. It is difficult to tell which of the adults wrote the following report, but he had a sense of humour –

" One fine morning last July, a gallant band of 20 of the biggest boys attending the Board School all armed with long osiers, with our popular Schoolmaster at their head and accompanied by the Vicar, Churchwarden and two Overseers, might have been seen marching through the village. I am told we looked a very formidable party, each with a stick in his hand and a rosette on his breast but our object was a peaceable one; we were going to 'beat the bounds'.

We marched straight down the road to our first boundary post – the iron milepost at the corner of Chelsham Lane. I may remark that these fifteenth mile posts generally mark the parish boundary on its eastern and southern sides. We now turn sharp to the right through the old recreation fields of Upper

Mays, and there our trouble begins. A steep bank and rail fence has to be negotiated. One of the Overseers, being rather stout and shortwinded, has to be pushed through, and we find ourselves in the 'Firs'. After some difficulty we put the Overseer in a perpendicular position, and away we go through the lovely wood, then in all its glory, the boys whooping and scampering in their glee. "Hello, what's this?" – exclaims a boy – and we find a snake about three feet long curled up asleep in the sunshine just at the margin of the wood. As this was the first snake that many had seen it was an object of curiosity. We now find our next boundary – the iron post on the top of Bug Hill – and away we all scrambled down to Wapses Lodge.

We now turn to the right, parallel to the Godstone Road, to Well Farm and here occurs one of the peculiarities of boundaries; a barn being built on the line so that it is in two parishes. The only way of going along the boundary lies through a small window; somebody must go through. The Vicar is suggested, then the Overseer. Eventually a small boy is lifted through, and the circuit is completed. Now we go through private grounds, and some of the people come out to discover the cause of the invasion.

We now take a diagonal line from the fifteenth milestone on the Godstone Road, across the Caterham Railway, and here find a tall fence and stiff hedge which are but slight obstacles for the boys, and after the Overseer has been lifted over and pushed through we are all across the line and away through Whyteleafe. Here somebody has thoughtfully planted a line of trees to mark the boundary. Now over the line again and the Schoolmaster looks more satisfied now that he has got his charges clear from danger from any passing train. I must say we should have got over this part sooner, but the Vicar was botanising – he says he found some interesting specimens among the wild strawberries.

We now go through the chalkpit and up onto Riddlesdown. Here our parish runs out in the form of a long wedge, the acute angle of which is our westernmost boundary. Here we have to hunt for the post, and someone must be bumped. "We have no Beadle – it won't do to bump the Vicar – how about the Schoolmaster? Or the Overseer? Oh, he's too heavy. Shall we try?" Just at this juncture we fortunately found a wagonette half-full of sandwiches, cake and buns, with some dozens of gingerbeer, lemonade etc. So we sat down on the turf for refreshment and we thought we had fairly earned it. I know we enjoyed it; I never saw cake and buns, not to mention sandwiches, vanish more quickly, but I must say that though I am of a forgiving nature I have only just forgiven the man who forgot to put in the beer.

Our provisions being finished and the last bottle of gingerbeer (after some dispute) emptied we turn our backs on the pretty view from the heights of Riddlesdown and make our way to Hamsey Green. About here the boundary is plainly marked by a hedge till we get into the Sanderstead Road which we cross, and find the boundary posts in the shrubbery a few yards off the road. In that shrubbery our clothes and tempers were much tried. The line then takes a turn to the north up Kingswood Lane to near the Lodge where we turn to the right, through fields and woods to Farley, finding boundary posts on the way. Now past the Harrow Inn, through the woods opposite, and out on the road at Chelsham Green. Then straight on through Mill Green to the post we started at in the morning, and our task is completed. The next scene takes place on the lawn at the Vicarage where 20 tired and hungry boys are seated at a long table and speedily demolishing meat pies, cakes etc. with the conviction that they have deserved a good feed. When the meal is over three hearty cheers are given for the Vicar, and we all go home tired, but well pleased with our day's outing 'beating the bounds'."

Sixteen years later, in 1908, it was decided to perambulate the bounds of the civil parish again. The date chosen was 11th August, and the group numbered 31, Whyteleafe being well represented. The Warlingham boys were Will Peters, Will Botting, Percy Quittenton, Cyril Kirk, Arthur Hankins, Frank Tamplin and Len Lancaster.

Whyteleafe was represented by A Cole, H Odd, E Hewett, A Eagle and T Rapley. They all carried long wands decorated with red, white and blue ribbons. The officials, who wore rosettes included –

Overseers, Messrs F Bushby and J Quittenton
Parish Councillors, Messrs Hewett, Quinn, Goodwin and Simmons
Godstone District Councillor, Mr Vincett
The Revd G R Macaulay, Vicar of Warlingham
Churchwardens, Messrs Goodman and Lockton
Parish Clerk, J Davis
Messrs Clarke and Waterson, Schoolmasters
School manager, Mr Kirk
Clerk to the Parish Council, Mr H Jarrett and his assistant
Mr Hodgson, Postmaster
Mr Cheeseman, Captain of the Whyteleafe Fire Brigade, carrying a coil of rope
and Police Constable Payne.

As before, a start was made from the iron post at the top of Chelsham Road, near *The Hare & Hounds*, at 10.00 a.m. They carried maps and followed the boundary shown as closely as possible. From above Bug Hill Farm just a few walked diagonally across the field to the viaduct, while the rest went round by the road. At Well Farm all the boys managed to get through the small window of the barn, and also a few of the adults. The railway companies sent officials to ensure everyone crossed the lines safely. Mr & Mrs Bushby provided lunchtime refreshments at their home in Godstone Road, then at 1.30 p.m. it was time to tackle the next stage of the route.

11th August 1908. Beating the Bounds. The starting point at
the top of Chelsham Road, near *The Hare & Hounds*.

11th August 1908. Beating the Bounds. The group pose by the old barn in Whyteleafe, before the ascent to the hilltop, for which Mr Cheeseman's rope came into use.

This involved crossing the line and up the steep face of the cutting. This was where Mr Cheeseman's rope was put to use, and no doubt the boys enjoyed the adventure. Those who did not want to 'play the monkey' went over the footbridge. The stump of the crab apple tree, which is marked on the 1869 OS map at the extreme limit of the parish, was located. As described in the previous chapter the boundary between Warlingham and Sanderstead parishes in this area was defined by the Manor Courts in the 16th century. The return route was past Riddlesdown Farm, and then along the north side of Hamsey Green to the Sanderstead Road. The iron boundary post found here would have been one marking the limit of Croydon Rural District. Crossing the road they then turned back and emerged opposite 'The Elms' in Kingswood Lane. Further on, beyond a stile on the right, was the path to Farley Green. Near *The Harrow* Inn was the first of the coal and wine 'City' posts on this side of the parish. On then to Kennel Farm by 5.00 p.m. where a splendid tea was provided. The starting point near *The Hare & Hounds* was reached at 6.20 p.m. and the day concluded with the singing of the National Anthem.

A Caterham and Warlingham Urban District Council boundary marker near the old road as it turns away from Hamsey Green towards Riddlesdown. It could not be placed on the exact line because crops were being grown in the field.

In the 1950s 'beating the bounds' took place several times in Chelsham and Farleigh parishes, but no further occasion is recorded for Warlingham.

The Parish Council

County councils were established following the Local Government Act of 1888. Another Local Government Act, in 1894, provided for the establishment of parish councils. These took over the civil functions of the Vestry. As the population of Warlingham was more than 300 the members of this new council had to be proposed, and elected at a parish meeting. This was held at the board school on 4th December 1894, and the nine members of the new parish council met for the first time on 9th January 1895. Rural and Urban district councils were also formed at this time, Warlingham coming within Godstone Rural District. In 1913 the number of parish councillors was increased to 12. The chairmen between 1895 and 1929, when this council ceased to exist, were—

1895 -	T E Taylor	1916 - 1919 R A Price
1896 - 1900	Revd F R Marriott	1919 - 1929 Joseph Underhill
1900 - 1916	P W Hewett	

The clerk to the council throughout its existence was H T E Jarrett.

Initially the Councillors were elected annually, but from 1900 the election was every three years. 1925 is probably typical of the later years. There were two Polling Districts –

1. The Parish of Warlingham ex Whyteleafe.
2. The part of the Parish of Warlingham known as Whyteleafe.

Polling Day was Saturday, 4th April, and the polling stations were the Infants' School on the Common, Warlingham, and the village hall in Whyteleafe. The 12 seats, four for Whyteleafe and eight for Warlingham, had attracted 20 candidates.

Those living in Whyteleafe were—

Edward Albert Borer	Master Plumber
Joseph Paul Hart	Railway Clerk
Eli John Bird Marwood	Builder
Oswald Facer Odell	Chartered Accountant
George Robert Waterson	Retired Schoolmaster
John Thomas Woodland	Retired Railway Officer

The Warlingham candidates were—

Robert Arthur Card	Laundry Proprietor and Freeholder
John Cooper	Gardener "Retired"
Robert Feetham	Stockbroker
Charles Langton Lockton	Justice of the Peace
William Lawrence Morgan	Company Secretary
Richard Arnold Price	Surveyor
Edward George Quinn	Contractor and Farmer
George Reed	Qualified Dispenser
Edward Swann	Insurance Broker's Clerk
Edward Herbert Terry	Retired
William Stanley Russell Thomas	Medical Practitioner
Joseph Underhill	Stockjobber

Robert Woolley Walden .... Knight

and one lady –

Adelaide Ann Rea .... Married Woman

This list shows a wide range of occupation and status in the community. At this stage the powers of the parish council were limited, and all items of real importance to the community, such as the need for main drainage and the state of the roads, had to be referred to the Godstone Rural District Council.

Warlingham,
31st March, 1925.

WARLINGHAM PARISH COUNCIL ELECTION,
Saturday, 4th April, 1925.

Candidates' letter to the voters. Parish Council election, 1925.

Dear Sir or Madam,

A poll having been demanded at the recent Parish Meeting, voting by ballot will take place on Saturday, 4th April.

We, the undersigned members of the late Warlingham Parish Council, together with Mrs. Rea, one of our representatives on the Godstone Rural District Council, desire to obtain confirmation of our election that was recorded by show of hands on that occasion.

The sanitation of the village of Warlingham is the most urgent question before the parish, and main drainage is the only satisfactory method of dealing with it.

Should any of our number be re-appointed to the Joint Drainage Committee, we shall make every effort to secure more frequent meetings in order to arrive at an early and definite conclusion.

Pending the adoption of main drainage, the present system of cleansing cesspools should be completely reorganised, so that ratepayers may receive equal and regular attention.

We are of opinion that an attendance register of members of the Parish Council, Parochial Committee, and all other Committees should be published annually for the information of the electors.

We regard the Housing Question and the Regulation of Motor Traffic through the villages of Warlingham and Whyteleafe as subjects that call for the strongest representations of local opinion to the higher authorities.

If our views meet with your approval and we are re-elected, we shall do our best to retain your confidence.

We are, dear Sir or Madam,

Yours faithfully,

J. COOPER,
R. FEETHAM,
C. L. LOCKTON,
E. J. MARWOOD,
R. A. PRICE,
A. REA,
J. UNDERHILL,
R. W. WALDEN.

P.S.—In order to avoid any confusion as to the names of those you may decide to support, it is suggested that you have this letter with you when recording your Vote at the Polling Station on Saturday next.

Printed and Published F. J. Holbrook, 47 Croydon Road, Caterham Valley.

Caterham and Warlingham Urban District Council

In 1929, to improve general administration, Warlingham and Whyteleafe were moved from Godstone Rural District to join Caterham, and the Urban District of Caterham and Warlingham came into being on 1st October. Caterham had become an Urban District in 1899. Initially, Warlingham and Whyteleafe constituted one ward with six representatives, two of whom retired each year. As time passed there was a number of changes affecting the wards. It was usual for some compensation to be paid, and Godstone Rural District put in a claim for £29,030. In 1933 Woldingham and Chaldon were also transferred into the Urban District, and, as with Warlingham, this meant the end of their parish councils. A northern area of Tandridge Parish (detached) had been absorbed in 1910. In 1956 the District was comprised of 10 Wards, with 27 representatives on the Council.

Tandridge District Council

As a result of more recent reorganization of local government, Tandridge District Council came into being on 1st April 1974. Under this new designation Godstone Rural District and Caterham & Warlingham Urban District were combined, recreating the ancient administrative 'Tandridge Hundred' with the addition of Burstow and Chaldon. The parishes that were in Godstone Rural District have retained their parish councils throughout, and at the time of writing a movement to reinstate the parish councils in the northern part of Tandridge District is well advanced.

Currently Warlingham civil parish consists of the two wards, Warlingham East and West. Boundary changes, the first of which was in 1929, have resulted in the loss of many acres. On the other hand, on the Woldingham and Chelsham side the boundary now includes the hillside along the Halliloo valley, sweeps round and up to include Slines pond, crosses Limpsfield Road and returns passing behind *The Hare & Hounds* to meet the old boundary line at the top of Sunny Bank. Before World War II many Councillors described themselves as Independent, but nowadays party politics rule. Following the Local Government Act 1992, subsequent consultations have now resulted in several recommendations by the Local Government Commission for England. That which affects Warlingham is the proposed addition of Chelsham and Farleigh to the East Ward for electoral purposes.

This book is based on the Warlingham which evolved within the bounds of the ancient civil parish.

SOURCES

TATE, W E (1969) *The Parish Chest*. Third edition, Cambridge University Press.

GOODMAN, C H *Parish Notes*.

Warlingham & Chelsham Parish Magazine.

The bounds of Warlingham civil parish as defined by the political wards in the early 1990s

Chapter 4

Westhall

In the 1086 tax assessment, known as Domesday Book, Chertsey Abbey is given as holding two hides of land in Tandridge Hundred with William de Wateville as principal tenant, and a further threequarters of a hide from which the Abbey retained the benefits, placing a tenant of its choosing to work the land. Land measurement varied according to its quality, and the size of the smaller piece ties in quite well with that part of Warlingham parish cultivated around a farmhouse which in time became known as Westhall. Just over a century later, in 1198, William de Hamme was given a grant of land from Chertsey Abbey for himself and his heirs for ever at a rental of 20 shillings a year. By his marriage to Margaret de Lucie, Odo de Dammartin acquired the northern part of Godstone parish which included Marden. He was the founder of the Hospital of St James, which after about 25 years became Tan(d)ridge Priory. The Warlingham land was adjacent to the north of Odo's land, and it may be that the grant to William de Hamme was just a necessary step in a legal transfer. Whatever means Odo used to obtain the land he did not keep it, as a Deed of Endowment dated to around 1200 shows—

> '...Be it known to you all that I have given and granted, and by this my present charter have confirmed ... to God and the Hospital of St. James in the Ville of Tanregge, and three priests in perpetuity, there serving God, and Confraters of the said Hospital; all my land at Warlinggeham, in pure and perpetual alms, for the support and maintenance of the sick and poor, and wayfarers needing a refuge; together with a windmill, with all its pertinents without restriction; in crofts, pictlakes, woods, plain, meadows, pastures, cornlands, ways, waters, marshes, hedges, enclosures, in common pastures and in all liberties; To have and to hold entirely, peaceably, and free from all service and secular exaction due from me to the heirs of William de Hamme, that is, twenty shillings sterling and two gilt shoes of the price of six pence...'

This is a very early reference to a windmill. The top of the hill on which it must have stood retained the name of Windmill Field right down to the later 19th century when the house 'Dorincourt' was built. A pictlake was a small enclosure of land. In the early 16th century a lease was granted to William Comporte for 'a tenement with all lands, meadows, feedings and pastures at Westhall in Warlyngham' but there are few surviving documents.

Tandridge Priory was one of the first to suffer following the Act of Dissolution of the Monasteries passed in 1536. The King, Henry VIII, wanted the Oatlands Estate, Weybridge. He took that estate from the Rede family, and in exchange gave them Tandridge Priory and all its possessions of land, rents etc. In the 1570s the Rede estates were split, part going to Richard Bostock of Tandridge, while Westhall was amongst the lands sold to Henry Hayward, Alderman of London. It remained in the possession of the Haywards until 1713 when it was sold to Sir Joseph Jekyll. After his death in 1738 Westhall was sold, along with the Manor of Garston (Bletchingley) to the Claytons of Marden Park.

The survey of Sir Kendrick Clayton's estate carried out by William Chapman in 1761 provides names and acreage for the fields. When comparing this to the 1869 OS map the outline of the landholding is unchanged but some hedges have been removed. The names Waterfield, Homefield and Court Bush(es) have survived. Luckhams is now Succombs. Mumleys, now divided by the railway, changed to Mumblers, now Mumbles. This may have been Mumbleleys, that is, meadows with sticky soil – due to the Bourne flow at its lowest level.

The year 1884 brought major change to Westhall. Sir William Robert Clayton sold Westhall farm to William Gilford of Redhill who planned an exclusive housing development. The following notice appeared in *The Croydon Advertiser* of 25th October 1884—

WESTHALL FARM, WARLINGHAM, SURREY.

The whole of the Live and Dead Farming Stock, Hay, Straw, Mangolds, and Swedes, moveable Buildings and effects which

Messrs. C & F RUTLEY

are instructed to Sell by Auction, on the premises on

MONDAY NEXT 27th OCTOBER at 10.30 o'clock.

COMPRISING nine home-bred cart horses and colts, young and unusually good and suitable for London work, eight milch cows and calves, pigs and poultry, 130 Down ewes and lambs, well bred and in good stock order, and one ram from Mr. Chandler's flock.

The valuable modern IMPLEMENTS and machinery, iron and turnwrist ploughs, sets of iron duck's foot and wood harrows, iron cultivators and horse hoes, iron cylinder hand rolls, Cambridge's roll, Crosskill's clod crusher, Garrett's 12-coulter corn drill, two turnip and manure drills by Reeves & Smythe, one-horse gear with chaff-cutter and corn mill, Hornsby's mowing and reaping machine, Wood's mowing machine, two iron horse rakes, Smith's haymaking machine, two stack cloths with poles and ropes, capital road and harvest waggons, dung cart, spring market cart, shepherd's house, weighing machines, iron sheep and water troughs, oil cake crusher, turnip cutters, winnowing machines, capital sets of harness, dairy utensils, garden frames and lights, garden seats, two lawn mowers, and numerous effects.

Ricks of hay, wheat, oat and barley straw off 60 acres, six acres of mangolds and swedes, three-quarter acre of underwood, quantity of poles, rods and faggots, the wood and zinc roofed fowl house 8ft.6in. by 5ft.6in., the wood and capitally roofed cowhouse 35ft.3 in. by 20ft.6 in., with stall divisions and lean-to at end, the wood and asphalt roofed toolhouse 8ft.6in. by 5ft.6in.

Luncheon will be provided. Catalogues may be had of Mr. Hodgson the Bailiff at the place of sale, and of Messrs C.& F. Rutley Auctioneers and Land Agents, 11 Dowgate Hill, E.C. and Birchwood Farm, Caterham, Surrey.

It is interesting to know the range of farm implements in use a hundred years ago. 'Capital' in current parlance meant 'top quality'. The shepherd's house was a small moveable hut providing shelter when he was out overnight with the sheep.

The farmland was divided into large and small plots to be sold by private contract. Purchase money could be paid over eight years by half-yearly instalments. Each purchaser had to sign a deed of covenant which included items such as the value of the house to be built which must not be less than £500, contributions to the upkeep of the road until adopted by local authority, building lines, frontages and fences etc. Some later sales of land were by auction. The only existing road was Westhall Lane from the village to the farm. From there the parish road, now called Narrow Lane, led to Succombs Hill. From near the farm a straight length of road was laid out across the field, slightly to the south of an existing footpath, then to the right and through Westhall Wood. Beyond the wood the Trustees of the Arkwright Estate gave permission for the road to continue through their land and down to the valley. Other new roads were Homefield, Landscape, Westview and Southview off Succombs Hill.

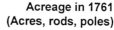

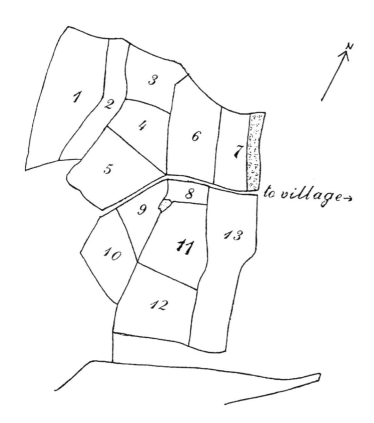

Acreage in 1761 (Acres, rods, poles)			
1. Wood Piece	12.	3.	20
2. West Hall Wood	6.	0.	26
3. Chalk Field	6.	1.	20
4. Chalk Field	5.	0.	12
5. Water Field	9.	2.	8
6. Water Field	10.	2.	9
7. Hollow Field & Shaw	5.	2.	38
8. West Hall, farm buildings, yard etc.			
9. Four Acres	4.	2.	26
10. Windmill Field	6.	3.	24
11. Barn Field	9.	3.	26
12. Home Field	11.	1.	9
13. Broom Field	16.	0.	5

> The 1869 O.S. map indicates that hedges have been removed between 3 & 4, 6 & 7, and 11, 12 & 13. West Hall Wood has spread towards the west, consequently Wood Piece is narrower.

Copied from William Chapman's Survey of 1761. This shows the northernmost part of the West Hall section of the Clayton Estate that was the land bought by William Gilford in 1884.

Westhall farmhouse was advertised along with stabling cottage and a range of farm buildings including those put up for auction but not sold. It changed hands several times, farm outbuildings were demolished, and in 1902 it was described as—

'An exceptionally attractive and convenient old-fashioned Freehold residence known as "West Hall" with stabling for three horses and gardener's cottage.'

Sale documents provide some detail of the interior of the house but no known exterior view exists. C L Lockton did paint a view of the cottage. When William Charles Rudkin bought the premises in 1910 they were demolished, and the present house, which carries the date 1911, was built.

In 1898, when C L Lockton had his house 'Teeton' built on what became the corner site of Westhall and Ridley roads, a thatched cottage which had stood there was demolished. It is recorded in one of Lockton's paintings. The house built by the Rudkins, replaced the old Westhall property, but apart from these two sites the houses were built on former farmland. As they were built gradually over some years it was not so great an impact on the village community as happens today when whole estates are planned and constructed within months.

Above: Westhall Road in May 1901. Beyond the hedge the road continued through Arkwright Estate land. The footpath coming up on the left, which originated in the valley, continued along the boundary. Part was made into Searchwood Road, but the stretch between Westhall and Searchwood Roads still exists.

Left: November 1905. Notice of an auction sale to be held by C & F Rutley. Westhall Park Road was laid out on this land. The gas lamp is outside 'The Laurels'.

Right: The Westhall farm cottage, where Louis H Emm, local grocer, was born in 1899, is depicted in this painting by C L Lockton. It was on the road frontage, near the cart shed. Lockton gives some indication of a house behind the trees, but no view is known of the old Westhall house.

This view of 'The Laurels' dates from about 1897. It was built for Timothy Neems in 1887 (demolished 1985), and stood on the corner site, Narrow lane to the left and the newly laid-out stretch of Westhall Road to the right.

'Bayards', completed in 1898, stood in grounds of just over eight acres, previously called Hollowfield and Hollowfield Shaw. This view, dated 1931, is from the south-east. The stable/garage, with accommodation over, became separate premises called 'Temple Belwood', and this has survived the demolition and redevelopment that started in 1977.

'Woottonga' was built for J L Travers on a large plot of land with access from Homefield Road. The name was changed to 'Overhill' by Sir Joseph Swan. This view taken in 1978 shows modern additions. Demolished in 1983.

'St. Erth' was built on what had been the further end of the grounds of 'The Laurels'. The name was changed to 'Lanka' and then to 'Guernsey'. Demolished in 1985.

'Court Lees' was built on a large corner site, with frontage to Westhall Road and Homefield Road. This view was taken in 1950. Demolished.

Built in the early 1900s, 'Kooringa', altered and extended by later owners, had grounds of about 4½ acres. These were terraced and landscaped to fit into the hillside site, which included a long-disused chalk pit. This house has also been demolished and the site redeveloped. The view dates from the early 1950s.

Redevelopment

Over the past 40 years or so, many of the houses built in the early years of the development of Westhall have themselves been demolished, and the sites redeveloped. While the structures usually remained sound they had become outdated in design. Many were much too large for a modern household without live-in servants, and extremely expensive to maintain. Some have survived, the premises being divided up to provide accommodation for two or three households. A few have become residential homes, and there are others which remain as built.

Of the few illustrated here 'The Laurels', built for Timothy Neems, was one of the first erected. It stood on the corner of Narrow Lane and Westhall Road, close to 'Westhall' where Neems had once lived. 'Bayards' stood in eight and a half acres, with frontages on Westhall and Hillbury Roads. 'Overhill', which was originally named 'Woottonga', had even larger grounds, and 'Kooringa' in Westview Road had four and a half acres. Other properties which have gone include 'Teeton'; 'Outspan' renamed 'Hillbury House'; 'Waterfield'; 'Clovelly'; 'Monowai'; 'Eriskay'; 'Horton'; 'Ashwood' originally called 'Sywell House'; 'Burfield' originally 'Nateby'; and not forgetting 'Dorincourt' built on Windmill Hill for William J Stuart in the early 1890s.

SOURCES

HEALES, Major A (1885) *History of Tandridge Priory.*

MANNING & BRAY (1809) *History and Antiquities of the County of Surrey.*

Sale particulars.

10th July 1888 Indenture of Conveyance made between the said William Gilford of the one part and the said Frank Goodingham of the other part.
10th July 1888 Indenture of Mortgage made between the said Frank Goodingham of the one part and the said William Gilford of the other part.

Signed Sealed and Delivered by the abovenamed William Gilford in the presence of
Annie Gilford
Ridgway Road
Redhill

William Gilford

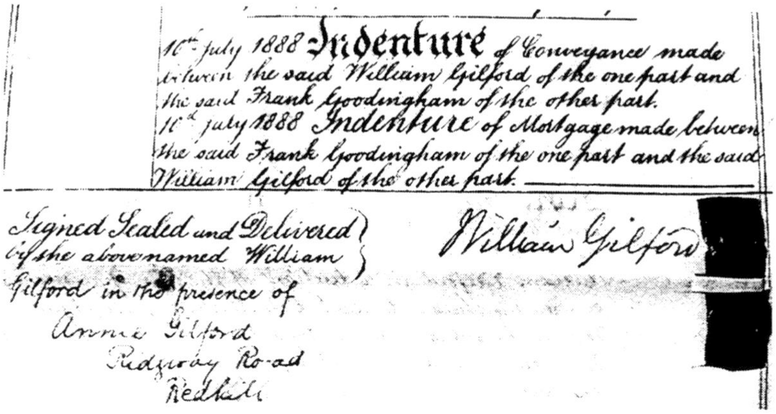

William Gilford's signature on an Indenture concerned with land in Westhall Road purchased by Frank Goodingham. The house he had built was named 'Hilminster'.

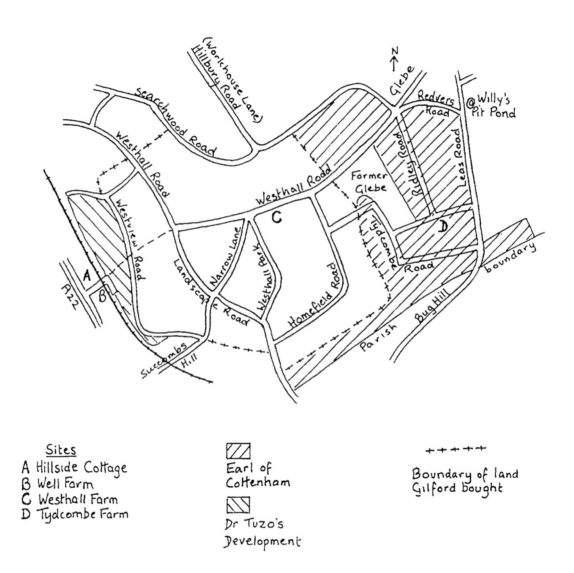

Sites
A Hillside Cottage
B Well Farm
C Westhall Farm
D Tydcombe Farm

Earl of Cottenham

Dr Tuzo's Development

Boundary of land Gilford bought

Map of the Westhall Area

Chapter 5

Well Farm, Dr Tuzo's Development and Tydcombe

The survey of the Clayton Estate, made by William Chapman in 1761, clearly defines the extent of the West Hall land which Sir Kendrick owned. There was an area of 30 acres, much of it hillside, tucked in between the parish boundary along the valley and a 12 acre field named Wood Piece on the western edge of the Clayton land above. To the north was Barking Bottom, a large expanse of hillside sweeping down to the valley, and down which Westhall Road now runs. To the south was Court Bush and Succomb Field. In 1842 Sir William Clayton leased this plot of 30 acres abutting his land. His tenant was John Woods. When the main common was enclosed in 1866 Sir Wm Clayton was allotted a narrow two acre strip alongside the 15 acres allotted to the Earl of Cottenham.

Well Farm, photographed in 1960. It stood well back from the Godstone Road, approached along a leafy drive parallel with Well Farm lane.

Well Farm stood just inside the parish boundary. The location, very near the lowest level of the valley, had a well which never lacked water, and in times of drought it was a useful source. On the other hand, when there was an excess of natural water the Bourne flooded the valley. The construction of the railway line through to Oxted commenced in the 1860s, and an embankment was built to carry the line across what had been meadow between Well Farm and the hill behind. Elsewhere on this stretch a way had to be carved through the chalk hillside, leaving a scar visible for many years afterwards.

The line lay abandoned, unfinished, for ten years and during this time the hillside area became the property of Ippolito Leonino. He was a naturalised alien, a merchant with business interests in London and Milan. He and his wife, Hannah, had four sons and a daughter, and their home in Surrey was across the valley at 'The Ellery' by Bligh's Wood, off Salmon's Lane. In June 1877, while visiting Milan, Leonino died. In his will he left 'Bleak House' (also near Bligh's Wood) and

'Hillside Cottage' stood at the Godstone Road end of Well Farm Lane. Demolished 1966.

land to his son, Edward, and 'Magenta House' near the foot of Salmon's Lane, to son Charles. His sons Charles and Arthur were the executors of his will, and in accordance with his wishes began to sell local assets. In 1878 they sold the land between the, as yet, unfinished railway line and the Clayton owned land above, to Dr Henry Tuzo. 'The Ellery' was renamed 'Blizewood', and within a very few years the Leoninos had left the district. When Arthur died at Middle Wallop, Hampshire, in 1886, his brother Charles, an executor, was described as 'a landed proprietor in Milan.'

Jacob's Ladder in about 1905.

In contrast to William Gilford's much larger but more random development, that created by the Tuzos was planned to suit the site. Well Farm Lane, set on a causeway to raise it above possible flooding, led, as it still does, to the bridge provided under the railway. Beyond, the old track went up the hillside to Westhall Farm, passing through Westhall Wood. The steps known as Jacob's Ladder were established on the route of this old footpath. The last section, through Gilford's land, was slightly diverted to emerge at the corner where Landscape Road meets Westhall. The plan was to build in the central area of the hillside, and other properties spaced out in a semi-circle around. The Caterham builders Christie were employed to do the work.

To allow for building on the hillside the land had to be terraced in the central area. The first house in which the Tuzos lived was named 'The Bush', a very apt name if it stood, as seems likely, on the open hillside by Jacob's Ladder. The name was shortlived, and the building was probably incorporated into 'Hillside' which was completed in 1885. A boarding school for young gentlemen was established there in 1886, and with various tutors lasted until 1900. 'Grosvenor Mount', later called 'Picton Mount', 'Le Chalet' and 'Hill Brow' were all occupied by 1889. The second centrally positioned house, intended to be named 'Hillview' was not complete when Dr

When built this house was named 'Hillside'. The decorative features made it very distinctive. This view, *c.*1902, shows the young ladies of Eden College. The name was soon changed to 'Ravenscroft'.

Eden College, Warlingham, Surrey
Photo Tourists Association, Turnham Green S.W.

Tuzo died in 1890. Said to have a large number of bedrooms it seems probable that it was intended as an expansion of the boarding school. In 1895 Mrs Laetitia Tuzo moved from 'Hillside' to the new property, and named it 'The White House' . This was also the name of her daughter's home in Ottawa. After 1900 'Hillside' became a boarding school for young ladies, first as 'Eden College', and then as 'Ravenscroft'. This school continued into the 1930s, and two sisters who were educated there for a time while their parents were abroad, recalled the head's (Miss Rheam) strict regime with little pleasure.

Mrs Tuzo remained at 'The White House', and took an active part in both Warlingham and Whyteleafe affairs. She subscribed generously when funds were needed for local matters such as the enlargement of All Saints' church. Latterly she was at 'Brightside', a small nursing home on Westhall Road, and died in 1930, aged 89. Her son, John, had been killed in World War I, and not until her grandson, Harry, came of age were the trustees of her will able to finalise matters regarding her estate. Then The White House Naturist Club, which had occupied 'The White House' since 1933, became official owners of the property, and still remain there. 'Ravenscroft' was demolished nearly 30 years ago, and there is modern development in this area.

Court Bushes Road was laid out along the parish boundary. The original houses, 'Court Bushes', 'Kinnoull', and 'Dunnottar' have all been demolished and the sites redeveloped. Well Farm, rebuilt in the mid-19th century, was restored in 1919 when Sir David Prain, a director of Kew Gardens, came to live there. He made the garden into a show place, with many rare shrubs and other unusual plants. From the early 1960s this stretch of land by Godstone Road was gradually turned into an office and factory area. Well Farm, and 'Hillside Cottage' nearby were both demolished, and Godstone Road was widened in 1966.

Until obliterated by housing there was a footpath which climbed from the valley and along the boundary between Barking Bottom and the Clayton lands. One section still remains, connecting Westhall Road with Searchwood Road. Searchwood Road was laid out along the route of this old path, passing the top of Upper and Lower Searchwood fields, to the junction with Workhouse Lane (renamed Hillbury Road in 1904). This lane was little more than an access to the Searchwood fields and those lower down the valley, but after 1856 it was widened and made into a more useable route. Improvements to Hillbury Road were made when the house building of the 1930s was in hand, but it was not until 1969 that the upper section was widened and the bend opened out. Lower Barn Farm was built in Barn Field, opposite the junction with Tithepit Shaw Lane, and the next field along towards Whyteleafe was one of the two hillside fields that had the name White Leaf.

Titcombe or Tydcombe

On the east side of the Westhall land were two copyhold properties, Stevens and Cockmans. These had been farmed together for some years by a family called Matthew, long enough for the lane along the eastern boundary, which led to Bug Hill, to be identified in a document as Matthews Lane. In October 1818 Giles Long took the tenancy of these properties, part of the Wigsell Estate, which totalled about 45 acres. The yearly rent was 6s 8d for Stevens, and 4s 6d for Cockmans.

In 1832 Giles Long borrowed £1100 to buy land on the western side of the main road, previously part of the Crewes Estate. George Smith had acquired all the rest of Crewes Estate. £150 of the loan was repaid quite quickly, as Giles Long sold about 11 acres, called Colonel Close, which was situated near *The Leather Bottle* public house. This land came into the possession of Francis Tummons, and further detail appears in another chapter. The remainder, just over 28 acres, was in the vicinity of Workhouse Lane. The greater part was near the top, with one frontage on Westhall Road. Giles Long then borrowed a further £600 to buy another piece of freehold land on the further side of Matthews Lane. This was eight acres, half of a holding previously known as Young Mays.

How Sir William Weller Pepys, of Tandridge Court, Tandridge, became involved is obscure. Maybe he had expressed an interest in acquiring some hilltop land. Giles Long died in 1834, and his son, also Giles, inherited

Titcombe – or Tydcombe – Farm in about 1900. Two of the three visible farm buildings are thatched.

Leas Road, towards the top of Bug Hill. 'Bug' can mean a goblin, but here it is more likely a 'bugbear', referring to the hazards of the steep, narrow road. Most of Fir Tree Wood was cut down in 1919.

This view in Westhall Road was take in May 1986, and shows the frontage of the former Glebe land that was sold to the East Surrey Water Company. The houses built here obscure the view of the reservoir.

the capital debt, any interest due having apparently been paid each year. In May 1838 Sir William repaid all the money owed, and added the freehold land to his estate. He also paid £700 to Giles Long the younger, who subsequently relinquished the tenancies only recently granted to him. Sir William was then admitted as tenant at the Manor Court. At this time James Atkins held the freehold land on a 21 year lease, which had started in 1825. His annual rent was £30. He was also a tenant of the Clayton Estate, the land being some 67 acres of hillside and lower ground in the vicinity of Bug(s) Hill and Mumbles. He lived at 'Maples' on Godstone Road, later known as Rose Cottage (demolished in 1993). Nearby he had three fields covering a stretch from valley to hilltop, and an adjacent piece on the upper level called the Goss, or Gorse. The chalkpit, opposite *The Rose and Crown* Inn, was started around 1805, and work ceased in 1969.

William and Ellen Titcombe came to Warlingham from Chelsham, and for some years were tenants of the Pepys, later Earls of Cottenham. William died aged 42, but Ellen remained at the farm until the end of their tenancy in 1853. The next, and last tenant, was Richard Jarvis, who farmed 'Titcombes', as it was now known, for almost 50 years. Searchwood Coppice, which had been allotted to the holding in the 18th century when the lower common was enclosed, lay at some distance and remained woodland.

When the main common was enclosed in 1866, the Earl of Cottenham was allotted two plots. One was a strip adjoining 'Titcombes' land along which Redvers Road was made in 1900. The other was 15 acres near the parish boundary with Chelsham. The fourth Earl of Cottenham was still an infant when he inherited in 1881, and trustees managed the estates until 1896. By deed of enfranchisement, dated 4th May 1895, the freehold of 'Titcombes' was purchased for £496. The land now promised a good profit if sold for house building. At some time the spelling was changed to 'Tydcombes'. In 1900 Arthur Leonard Pike bought land for housing along the newly laid out Tydcombe Road. The Jarvis family remained in the farmhouse until 1904 when 'Tydcombe Villas' on the corner of Chapel Road and Leas Road were built. In 1902 a 16th century spoon was found near the old farmhouse. Ridley Road dates from 1904, and Tandridge Road was the old track to the farmhouse. A large expanse of woodland was cleared in 1919 when Beechwood Lane was made. More houses were built as time passed, but quite a large area of the former Titcombes farmland, with frontage to Leas (Bug Hill) Road, remained fields until developed from the mid 1970s. Squeezed between the Westhall and Titcombe lands, with a narrow side on to Westhall Road, were two Glebe fields, Little and Great Nine Acres, These were sold to the East Surrey Water Company in 1912 and 1925 respectively, and a reservoir constructed. The houses on the road frontage date from the early 1980s. The field opposite, just over 12½ acres, was part of the Cottenhams original freehold land, and building started here in 1904.

SOURCES

Abstract of Title – Property in Tydcombe and Redvers Roads.

Directories.

Enclosure Award 1866.

Tithe Assessment 1842.

Wills – Leonino I & Tuzo Mrs L.

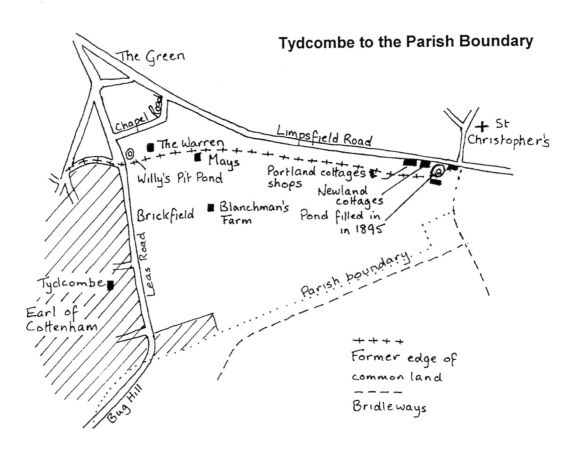

Tydcombe to the Parish Boundary

The Green
Chapel
Limpsfield Road
St Christopher's
The Warren
Mays
Willy's Pit Pond
Portland cottages
shops
Newland
cottages
Brickfield
Blanchman's
Farm
Pond filled in
in 1895
Leas Road
Tydcombe
Parish boundary
Earl of
Cottenham
+ + + +
Former edge of
common land
- - - -
Bridleways
Bug Hill

A short way down Chelsham Road, and set back on the right, is St Christopher's Church, which in a few years' time will celebrate its centenary. This view was taken in 1998.

Chapter 6

Beyond Tydcombe to the Parish Boundary

In the 1840s the enclosed land east of the lane to Bug Hill and south of the open common was held by the Beynons, except for the eight acres now belonging to Sir William Weller Pepys, and the adjacent Thrift Fields held of the Manor by Richard Ward.

The Revd Edmund Turner Batley (1777–1837) rector of Carshalton had married an heiress, Martha Beynon. As required he assumed her surname and invested in land and property. He held a considerable amount of land locally, mostly in Chelsham, but some was in this part of Warlingham parish. The Beynons lived in 'Slines Oak House' which had been built in about 1805, and were there until 1874. In 1844 the eldest son, Edmund Batley Beynon, held 41 acres, which included the farmhouse remembered as Blanchman's. When he died in 1861 this land passed to his brother, the Revd Edward Francis Beynon, whose own holding of just under 12 acres included properties later known as Mayes Place and Birch Cottage, a row of other cottages, and the woodland and Fir Plantation by the top of Bug Hill.

At the time of the Enclosure Award of 1866 the Revd E F Beynon held the land, and he was granted two narrow strips to give access from the road to his land behind. He then purchased the intervening plot of just under two acres for £260, and so acquired a length of frontage to the road. He also bought land off Farleigh Road for £275. Eglise Road lies along the side of this narrow two and a half acre plot.

When the Revd. E F Beynon died in 1874 his will included many charitable bequests, one of which was to Chelsham Parish. To adopt the name and arms of Beynon was a condition of inheritance detailed in his will, and subsequent landowners had the name Crowther-Beynon. It was the Revd Samuel Bryan Crowther-Beynon who, in 1905, donated an acre of land by Chelsham Road for a church. St Christopher's, originally a mission building, was designed by J C King and erected on the plot by the local builder, John Quittenton. The money needed to cover the cost was raised by the local community. In 1997 St Christopher's achieved parish church status, covering an area including all the nearby roads and a large part of Halliloo Valley.

Edward Hannam (or Hannan) of Godalming bought the strip of newly enclosed common between that purchased by Beynon and the parish boundary. He paid £180 for just over one and threequarter acres. One of the five ponds mentioned in the Award was nearby and by 1895 the pond had become foul, and so was filled in. A row of cottages had been built by the pond on the side furthest from Limpsfield Road.

Newland Cottages were built by 1869, and still stand though renamed. Portland Terrace, nicknamed Sheepshead Row because reputedly the women there were always gossiping, was built further along, and in between shops were erected with living accommodation. These premises, named 'Southdown House', 'Peatmoor', and 'Ceylon House', were for many years butchers, bakers and grocers respectively. The Mayes Laundry, on land at the rear of these buildings, was established in 1875. Rutherford Cottages were built on the road frontage, adjacent to the old wall which marked the parish boundary. The end premises became Walter Field's general store, and Nellie Field kept this shop into the 1960s. This corner of the parish was redeveloped in 1970 when flats for the elderly, named 'Uplands' were built.

In the 1870s Thomas Twiddy was living in 'Mays Place'. He was active in local affairs, particularly concerning the Wesleyan Chapel and the Board School. After 1900 a new owner changed the spelling to 'Mayes'. By the mid 1930s several houses had been built along the main road frontage. Caterham & Warlingham Urban District Council acquired the open backland, and in the early 1950s several new roads were laid out. Land in the vicinity of the site of Blanchman's farm was reserved for recreational purposes. Later on housing for the elderly, named 'The Court' was erected nearby on land given for that purpose.

A view of about 1920 showing Portland Cottages and the row of shops. The fence beyond borders the gardens of Newland Cottages.

Newland Cottages, built 1867. (Photographed in 1962). Edward Hannam divided the land he bought at the time of the Enclosure into 11 plots. This one was purchased from him by Matthew Tamplin, lawyer, and sold on to John Ward.

Rutherford Cottages and Nellie Field's shop (photographed in 1967), which stood opposite the bus garage. Demolished in 1970. The flint wall, which still stands, marks what was, until a few years ago, the parish boundary with Chelsham.

George Wren came to 'Upper Mays' in the late 1870s. This was land on the Chelsham side of the parish boundary, with a house facing *The Hare and Hounds* public house, across an expanse of what had been common, and is still open land. For most of the 20th century the present house on this site has been known as 'Chelsham Lodge', a name originally belonging to a house by Fairchilds Farm, owned by George R Smith.

According to Arthur Beadell, George Wren had a small brickfield at Upper Mays. Near the house the land abutted the laundry premises. The OS map of 1912 does indicate a small working in the field just above Plantation Lane. In June 1885 land was put up for auction by the Trustees of the Wigsell Arkwright Estate. This included the Thrift Fields, which lay between Mayes Place and the lane to Bug Hill. George Wren paid £2000 for 16 acres, which included an adjacent plot of enclosed common behind Willy's Pit Pond. Here he set up a brick and tilemaking business, and it seems likely that he obtained both equipment and workmen from the brickfield by the road to Hamsey Green which was sold in May 1885. He moved in 1890 to Fernlee Villas in Glebe Road, built 'The Warren' on his own land behind the pond, and moved there in 1893.

The brickfield would seem to have closed down in the early 1900s. In 1906 George Wren was living at 'The Brambles', probably the first house to be built on the lane frontage. In 1922 the owners of 'Mayes Place' bought a triangular corner plot adjacent to their property, and with legal access to it from Warren Park.

The remaining part of the Thrift Fields, just under nine and a half acres, was offered for sale by auction in October 1935. Surrey County Council acquired the area adjacent to the boundary of Warren Park. The Home Guard practised manoeuvres here in the 1940s, competing for territory with local geese. In 1944 a 'doodlebug' came down here, the blast causing damage to the houses in Warren Park. Caterham and Warlingham Urban District Council acquired the rest of the land in this area, and this, with the adjoining land, constitutes the Blanchman's Farm Community Wildlife Area established in 1991.

The land between 'Mayes Place' and the main road was developed in the early 1950s. During the next 40 years various reports regarding the County Council's intentions came to nothing. Then the land was sold, also 'Mayes Place', and from 1993 a new development of detached houses was built, greatly extending Mayes Close.

April 1981. Sheep in the paddock between Mayes Place, part
of which can be seen in the background, and Warren Park.

St Ambrose Roman Catholic Church in Warren Park, photographed in 1999

One of the plots allotted to Richard Ward at the time of the 1866 Enclosure Award was just over five acres between the land bought by George Wren in 1885 and the main road, with what became Chapel Road on the west side. Richard Ward bought the freehold when it became available, and the land remained in farming use. By the time he died, in 1878, his business as a builder predominated over the farming side, but his sons, John and Joel, continued both activities. In 1891 they sold this five acres to George Wren. Some he utilised to provide a much larger plot for the house 'The Warren' he was about to build. He sold the main road frontage, and the first houses built there were Perrysfield Cottages. Warren Park was laid out in about 1905, and by 1912 there were 18 houses, some built by Messrs Kenworthy of Winchester House, Caterham Valley. Houses had also been built on the Chapel Road frontage by 1912. In the 1930s there was a growing need for a place of worship for the local Catholic residents. In 1936 the diocese bought 'Dunelm', one of a pair of houses in Chapel Road built by George Wren in the 1890s. The garden lay alongside the first stretch of Warren Park, and included on the plot was a building with a corrugated iron roof. This became known, affectionately, as the 'tin church'. It was in use until St Ambrose was completed in 1958, then continued in use as a hall until 1969. Father Tritschler, who came to Warlingham in 1955 when the 'tin church' was still in use, remained until 1981 when he moved on to take up an appointment in Sussex. The site of the original pair of houses is now the car park.

SOURCES

Tithe Assessment 1842.

Enclosure Award 1866.

Croydon Advertiser.

Document on Property in Warren Park.

Local Directories.

STEWART, R L (1979) *The Catholic Church in Caterham 1879-1979*.

Warlingham & Chelsham Parish magazine.

Will of E F Beynon.

Advertisements from the 1950s.

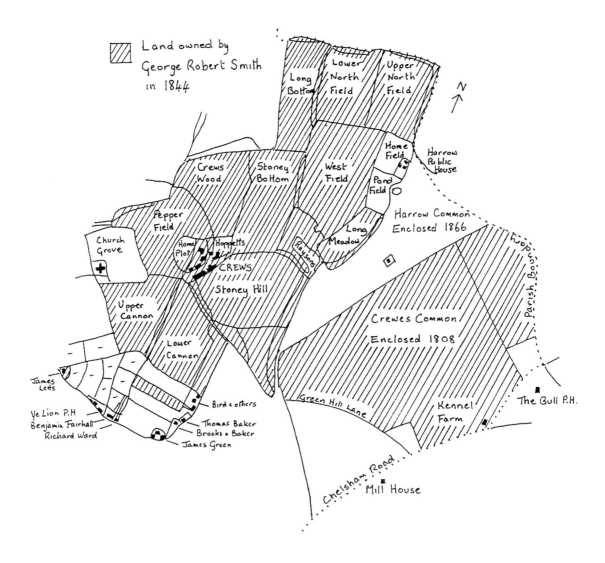

Land owned by George Robert Smith in 1844

Scale approx. 1 cm = 6 chains

Extract from the Tithe Apportionment Map — 23rd April 1844
Land in the vicinity of Crewes Farm owned by George Robert Smith in 1844

Chapter 7

Crewes

CREWES COMMON

Warlingham Manor was given to Bermondsey Abbey in 1144, and Crewes Farm, now known as Crewes Place, would seem to have been the principal residential site in this sparsely populated area throughout the following centuries until Bermondsey surrendered to King Henry VIII in 1537. Frequently a church is built quite near the principal house, but in Warlingham it is situated two fields away on higher ground where it could be seen, and was accessible from all directions.

Members of the Saunders family of Sanderstead and the Carews of Beddington were associated with the land during the early period. In the 1590s the land was conveyed to Edward Weston, possibly related to the Sutton family of that name. By the mid-17th century Crewes formed part of the estate of Richard Rochdale, a London brewer. Early in the 18th century it was sold to John Heathfield, a Croydon brewer, and that family held it for many years.

The Enclosure Award for Crewes Common is dated 30th August 1808, and Charles Pieschell is recorded as lord of the manor. In 1810 there was an auction of property held by William Coles, which included Crewes but was mainly in Selsdon and Sanderstead. George Smith, banker, was the purchaser, and made the recently-built 'Selsdon House' his residence. The Crewes Estate was leasehold, and 12 years later it was offered in seven lots as freehold property. By an Indenture dated 1st November 1822 lots 1 to 5 were conveyed from Augustus Frederick Pieschell to George Smith. Lot 2 included three fields and some woodland in Chelsham parish to the east of the recently enclosed common. Lots 6 and 7 on the west side of the Limpsfield Road were purchased by Giles Long, and most of this land passed to Sir William Weller Pepys, of Tandridge Court, Tandridge, in 1838.

The Smith's banking house was destined to become one of the original roots of today's National Westminster Bank. George Smith died in 1837, and his son, George Robert inherited. Besides the Surrey and Kent properties there was an estate in Scotland, and when the opportunity arose George Robert added to his holding. When he died in 1869 he left two sons, Ernald Mosley, who had an infant daughter, and Walter Caradoc, a bachelor. His will contains some interesting detail, and apart from bequests to family members, some of whom seem a little remote, he left varying amounts of money to all in his employ, from the senior staff at the estate in Scotland and the clerks in the banking house down to the undergardeners, farm labourers and other outdoor servants. Unfortunately, within a few years both his sons had died, Ernald in 1872, and Walter in 1876. There were, however, plenty of other family members to act as Trustees until Mabel Elizabeth Georgiana came of age. In 1888 she married the Hon Alwyne Henry Foulke Greville, and her name features in subsequent sales of Crewes land.

At the beginning of the 19th century the open common extended eastwards, to the far parish boundary with Chelsham. In 1808 that part known as Crewes Common was enclosed. Using modern names the boundary of this enclosure can be defined as Daniels Lane and Green Lane on the north-west, Sunny Bank on the south-west, Chelsham Road, which is on the parish boundary, on the east, and the continuation of this boundary on the east side, which before recent changes included part of Warlingham Park Hospital grounds east of Harrow Road. Two new roads 30 feet wide, were made, both on well used routes. One became Harrow Road. The other, along what was known as Mill Bottom, has remained rural. Once called Green Lane, it is now known as Green Hill Lane. The windmill, a wooden post-mill, stood on the hillside just within Chelsham parish. It burnt down around 1840, but Mill House still stands near the site. Just under 70 of the 132 acres were allotted to Charles Pieschell, and he also acquired the 22 acres sold to cover the costs of enclosure. The area between, in modern terms,

The front of Kennel Farm. Many of the windows in the block on the right, added by Robert G Quinn, contain decorative coloured glass typical of the period.

March 1977. Miss Kathleen Quinn in her living room. The door behind her led through to the hall of the later part of the house.

Part of the rear living room, left much as it was when Kathleen Quinn's parents were alive. Photographed in March 1977.

Sunny Bank and Green Hill Lane, was divided up into a number of small plots, ranging from about half an acre to just over two acres, and allotted to those with a claim, copyhold or small freeholders. Other plots were allotted along the boundary with Chelsham parish, one of nearly three acres being allotted to Thomas Matthew, who held the tenancy of the farm best remembered as Titcombes, or Tydcombes. The new tenants were instructed to 'fence and ditch in a proper effectual manner 'and' to keep the water channels open so that water runs freely'.

KENNEL FARM

In 1808 there was only one house within a small enclosure on the edge of the common, in which lived John Beadel. This became the site of Kennel Farm. Across the way, in Chelsham parish, was Muns Pit pond, and the Award document shows *The Bull* public house on Chelsham Common. The earlier part of Kennel Farm probably dates from the late 1830s when George Robert Smith inherited the Crewes estate. It acquired that name because hounds for the local hunt were accommodated there overnight from time to time, as required. The use of flints, readily available from nearby fields, can be seen at the rear. The house has a large cellar, and there were two wells not far from the house, now sealed over.

Robert George Quinn took up the tenancy in the early 1890s. His son, Edward George, had a business as a sawdust contractor with premises near the Old Kent Road in south east London. In 1904 Edward bought Kennel Farm and just over 89 acres of land from the Hon Mrs Greville for £3,400. He added a large house in a modern style of the time, and a doorway was made to give access between the two buildings. In course of time his son, Ernest George, died, and his daughter, Kathleen, was left sole owner of the property. The land was let out to the Fullers of Halliloo Farm. Kathleen preferred to live in the old house, and the later building remained as it had been when her parents had been alive. In her later years, unable to manage stairs, Kathleen lived in the ground floor rooms. She died in 1986, aged 82. The two parts of the house, never compatible, were easily divided by closing the access made between them. The much older part is now known as 'Kennel Farm Cottage', and the Quinn addition, Kennel Farm House. Three residential properties were created from farm buildings. The land comes within the category of Green Belt and Great Landscape Value.

After the rest of the common land was enclosed in 1866 one of the newly designated roads, Sunny Bank, was along the west side of the former Crewes Common. By the 1890s several cottages had been built and in the early 1900s Albert Road, Alexandra Road and Avenue, were laid out behind. Some of this plot, bounded by Green Hill Lane, became allotment gardens to rent. Land on the east of Harrow Road was sold for the site of Croydon Mental Hospital. It totalled about 68 acres. The building of this Hospital, almost the last to be constructed in this part of Surrey, provided work for local men, but the parish council had to contend with the way the contractors' carts damaged the roads and tracks, and also an argument over a proposed footpath closure. The Asylum, as it was known locally, was officially opened in 1903, and over the years has provided work for many local people. The name was changed to Warlingham Park in 1937. Closure is now imminent, and a housing development is planned for the site.

HARROW COMMON

Harrow Common, triangular in shape, lay between the cultivated land of Crewes Farm and what had been, until 1808, Crewes Common. George Robert Smith held the copyhold, and when it was enclosed in 1866 he was allotted 15½ acres, and also various small strips of wayside totalling about four and a half acres. In 1867 he was able to buy the freehold of his remaining copyhold land. Harrow Road was made official from the edge of the old Crewes Common to the junction opposite *The Harrow* with the route along the edge of the common from Crewes Corner, by then also a recognised road. The route between the two commons was designated a 'Public bridle road'. It became known as Blind Lane, or School Lane, and is now called Green Lane.

When opened in 1903, Warlingham Park Hospital was called Croydon Mental Hospital. This view was taken about 1908.

An early view of E & S Murrell's shop, established in Harrow Road in 1903. It included a sub-post office, and no other shops were ever built in the road.

Looking along Harrow Road beyond Murrell's shop in 1907. *The Harrow Inn* is just visible in the distance on the left.

CREWES

In 1834 the Chelsham curate, the Revd Richard Fell, started a small school for Chelsham and Farleigh children. George Robert Smith became Patron of the school. A small enclosure which existed towards the upper boundary of Harrow Common was enlarged, and he had a building erected there which became Chelsham Parsonage and premises for the school. Footpaths gave access from both sides, and the surrounding land became known as School Fields. By marriage between Smith and Daniell, the Daniells became landowners in Chelsham, and Patrons of the school which, by the 1890s, had outgrown its premises. J H Daniell had a new building erected, and in 1905 the school moved to the new site in Chelsham parish by the approach road to the Mental Hospital. During the next 50 years the school grew and flourished. In 1957 Col R H A Daniell gave the school into the care of the Southwark Diocesan Board of Education. After a further 25 years the future of this school became uncertain, and in July 1984, after 150 years of providing education for local children, Chelsham St Leonard's Church of England School was closed.

With the building of the hospital, a few houses were soon erected in Harrow Road. There was one shop, owned for some years by Edward and Sydney Murrell. Development along Farleigh Road dates from the 1920s, and one small part of the common remains, used as a sports field. When a new parsonage was completed by St Christopher's Church in 1955 the old building and land were sold.

The Harrow Inn was originally a copyhold property called 'Aynescombes', and the holding included two adjacent fields, Home Field and Pond Field. It is situated on the edge of the Crewes estate, to which the land originally belonged, opposite the northernmost corner of the former common. It was certainly an ale house by the late 18th century, and well positioned to receive travellers entering Warlingham from Great Farleigh Green. At the beginning of the 19th century *The Harrow* was held by Anthony Harman, who in 1798 had bought the Croydon Brewery (est.1586). In the 1808 Enclosure Award Harman was allotted a plot on the further side of Crewes Common opposite *The Bull* public house, which he also owned. In 1849 the partnership of Howard Nalder & Bristow Collyer leased the brewery from the Harmans, and in 1866 they were allotted the piece of land between *The Harrow* and the road. *The Leather Bottle* public house, by Warlingham Green, also passed through the ownership of Harman/Nalder and Collyer. The brewery existed until 1936. *The Harrow* Inn has undergone extensive improvement and enlargement in recent years. The roadside pond nearby, originally nearly a quarter of an acre in size and one of the five handed over to the care of the parish officers in 1866, no longer exists.

The *Harrow* Inn, pictured in 1908.

The single-storey extension at the front would have been a late-19th century addition.

CREWES FARM

A view of Crewes Lane which – beyond the house – crosses the valley to emerge on Farleigh Road. This photograph dates from the 1960s. The lane remains unsurfaced.

The woodland and farmland which comprised Crewes Estate was assessed in 1842 as nearly 169 acres, and this had probably remained unchanged since the 16th century. John Hassell's watercolour of 'Crew's Farm' in the 1820s shows the house as it was when the Smiths first acquired the land. The outer door, approached by a few steps, is set in a porch, the shape of which is echoed by the pointed gable in the roof above. The asymmetrical façade has casement windows. There are three dormer windows on one side of the gable, and one on the other. The house is built where the ground begins to fall away into the valley, and Hassell's picture shows a second lower door which probably gave direct access to cellar and kitchen area. Chimney stacks rise at one end of the building, and to the rear at the other end.

Photographs of front and rear dating from about 1905 show that changes have taken place during the intervening years. The house now has sash windows, and flat skylights have replaced the dormers. The end chimneys have gone and there is now a central stack. A bailiff's cottage has been added at the rear. Unfortunately no record exists of the interior of the house in the earlier period, but one is available for 1911.

The freehold estate was put up for sale by direction of the Hon Mabel Elizabeth Georgiana Greville, of Danbury Park, Chelmsford, on 10th August 1911. George Robert Smith had acquired more land, and there was now 189 acres. The house is described as built of brick and stuccoed, with tiled roof. On the ground floor was a hall, a drawing room and a dining room, both about 15 feet square, a tiled lobby, off which was a bathroom, leading to the kitchen, scullery and larder, and large cellar. On the first floor were four bedrooms, one with a dressing room, and above were three attic bedrooms. There were two staircases, both giving access from ground floor to attic.

A view of the front of Crewes Farmhouse as it was about 1910.

This view of Crewes, taken in the 1930s, shows that the building has been enlarged, and the dormer windows reinstated.

'Crewes Place', as it is now known, photographed in 1967. Creeper covers the walls, and two front doors are visible, indicating that the property has been divided.

The outbuildings near the house included coal shed and wash house, poultry and incubator houses, cow house for four and calf pen, timber and iron pig pens, cart sheds, harness room and coach house, stabling for the working horses, to detail just some of them. The property had been used as a high class stud farm, and there was a stallion box and a large number of loose boxes. The pair of brick-built cottages at the Farleigh Road end of Crewes Lane, built during George Robert Smith's time, were also included in the sale.

The 1911 sale document included a list of fields and woodland by their contemporary names, which vary slightly from those in use 70 years earlier. Upper North Field, on the Farleigh side of *The Harrow* Inn and with the parish boundary along two sides, the adjacent Lower North Field and Long Bottom in the valley, are unchanged. So is Crew(e)s Wood, but the continuation of the valley, previously Stoney Bottom, is now called Under Crewes Wood. It is on the eastern side of this valley that the two cottages were built on the edge of woodland by the lane. The stretch of 26 acres lying behind the land attached to *The Harrow* has changed from West Field to Chalk Pit Field, perhaps more correctly Marlpit Field. On the southern side of the lane, the field, which, if one looks across it today, provides a glimpse of the rear of houses in Farleigh Road, has changed its name from Stoney Hill to Park. As with several other fields it had been arable, but was now pasture. On the western side of the farmhouse and adjacent paddocks Pepper Field is now Pond Meadow, the pond being on the edge of that side of Crewes Wood. To the south are Upper and Lower Cannon. Most of the former is now Warlingham Sports Club land. Beyond is Little Cannons, land bought by George Robert Smith from Richard Ward.

Later years brought change. A view of the façade of the house in the 1930s shows both sides have been extended. Dormer windows, three in number, light the attic once more, and there is a room over the porch. In June 1954 the house and a total of just under 62 acres were offered in auction. 37 of these acres were adjacent to the house, which was now called 'Crewes Place'. Recent farming, as the outbuildings indicate, included a herd of cows, and a considerable number of pigs. The description of the interior of the house includes an entrance vestibule, with small cloakroom, leading into the lounge hall, from which the principal staircase rises. Dining room and drawing room are much increased in size. The kitchen premises to the rear include, as before, the secondary staircase used by the domestic staff. There is no mention of the cellar. The principal suite on the first floor includes bedroom, dressing room and bathroom. There are five other bedrooms and a bathroom, and above, three attic bedrooms and a box room.

For some years now the house has been in multiple occupation, and this division will have meant further alterations. The land is preserved within the Green Belt, and is a fine expanse of open countryside.

SOURCES

CREWES ESTATE – Sale documents 1911 and 1954.

Enclosure Awards 1808 and 1866.

Kennel Farm – various documents.

MANNING & BRAY (1809) *History & Antiquities of the County of Surrey*.

QUINN, KATHLEEN – Tape recording.

SHAW H (1989) *A Croydon Brewery* Croydon Natural History & Scientific Society, Vol **17**:10.

TUTT D C (1971) *Chelsham School* Bourne Society Local History Records **10**.

Warlingham & Chelsham Parish Magazine.

Wills – Quinn R G   Smith G R.

Chapter 8

All Saints' Church

Over 100 years have passed since the enlargement of the church, so how it looked, and the condition of the building prior to 1893, is beyond living memory. However, the church architect, P M Johnston, wrote at length about his work at All Saints', and a new resident of that time, C H Goodman, took a great interest in the enlargement. He took some photographs, those before the work commenced being of special interest. 1893 proved to be a very important year for the church.

It seems probable that a church existed on the site in the later 11th century, but it may not have looked much different from the best structure in the nearby farm settlement. There was certainly a church in the 12th century, as the Wattevilles followed their gift of the manor to the Prior and monks of Bermondsey in 1144 with the gift in 1158 of the church and advowson. By around 1250 a new building was completed.

It was a simple rectangular structure, similar to Farleigh church, measuring internally 57 feet by 19 feet, with walls from 30 to 34 inches thick. The chancel was constructed first, then the nave, and both north and south chancel walls show blocks of reused stone at the junction of the work. These, and other pieces of stone found within the rubble-filled walls in 1893, may have been from an earlier building or provided from elsewhere by Bermondsey Abbey. The construction was largely of flint, readily available locally, with dressings of green firestone. Centuries later the architectural style was given the name 'Early English'.

North and south walls were pierced by single lancet windows, the west wall being blank. The east wall probably had a group of three lancets, which were replaced about 1340 by the 'Decorated' style tracery seen today. The two-traceried windows at the east end of the nave date from the 15th century. The priest's door and low-side window are contemporary with the main structure, as is also the stonework of the south and north doors, the latter having a groove for an internal bar to secure it.

By the mid-15th century the church was over 200 years old. Besides the new nave windows, the font dates from this time, and also the wall painting of St Christopher. This is in tempera, that is, colour applied to the wall after the plaster was dry. This would be seen immediately on entering the church by the south door. The 'Great Pillage' of church goods took place during the brief reign of Edward V1 (1547–1553). The Commissioners who came to Warlingham, or whose names appear in the records regarding Warlingham, were men with Surrey connections – Lord William Howard, Sir Thomas Saunder and James Skynner. The churchwardens were John Comport and Richard Woddyn, and in May 1553 John Comport and Hary Haiwod (Henry Haywood). Compared to All Saints', Sanderstead, whose list of church goods included vestments of blue and green embroidered satin, Warlingham's possessions were very ordinary, but the church did own two silver chalices. In May 1553 the items left in the care of the churchwardens were one silver chalice of just over nine ounces, a cope to make a cloth for the communion table, and 'two belles in the steple'. The bells in towers or steeples were not easily accessible, so were noted but not removed. Probably the intention was to return later for them. The larger silver chalice, of 11 ounces, was taken 'for the Kinges use' and all other items were sold.

Features in the church relevant to the Roman Catholic faith were removed, or filled in and plastered over. During the Commonwealth period in the mid-17th century the St Christopher painting was covered with whitewash. Some restoration work was done when Olive, sister of Harman Atwood, held the manor. The exterior of the church was covered with rough-cast, including the blocked priest's door, and nearby on the south chancel wall a small plaque of stucco gives the date 1678 and the initials 'O A'.

In 1764 a gallery was erected at the west end of the church. Drawings made by Edward Hassell in the 1820s show the interior to west and east. Both views show the 18th century box pews, and the pulpit, said to be of

A view of All Saints' Church taken from the field in July 1893 before the start of enlargement.

This photograph shows the south side of All Saints' Church in 1893.

The Hayward tomb, enclosed by railings, fills the space west of the porch.

July 1893. All Saints' Church prior to enlargement.

This view shows the vestry added in 1857.

carved oak, with sounding board above. The gallery fills the west end, and a small round-headed window has been made in the west wall. The font stands in a central position below the gallery. To the east, supported on an arched beam, is a plaster screen extending to the ceiling which marks the division between nave and chancel. The floor is shown to be the same level throughout. What these pictures do not show is the apathy and neglect which seem to have existed over some years.

The situation started to improve a little in the early 1840s when some repairs were carried out. The Religious Census of 30th March 1851 gives the attendance at the morning service as 23, and 27 in the afternoon. Average attendances were given as 30 and 40 respectively, but were dependent on the weather. The church did have a very exposed situation amongst the fields, and was approached by footpaths. Sunday school scholars were given as numbering 28.

The only surviving vestry minute book starts in the 1840s. In March 1856 a suggestion was made that a vestry be built and a wall erected around the churchyard. Some concern must have been expressed about the condition of the church, as on 5th June there is an architect's report—

> 'I find the timbers more or less decayed, a great many timbers of the original roof placed on apparently as far back as the beginning of the 14th century still remain, and other parts are patched with common English fir poles, etc. I should strongly advise as a precautionary measure that the whole of the roof be taken off, and such of the old timbers, if any, which are sound may be reused as well as the old tiling. It would be very impolitic to think of renovating the interior whilst the covering is so bad, and it is only a question of one or two years when it must be renewed or it will become dangerous. I consider the roof over the nave may be replaced by a good substantial new one for the sum of £122.10s.'

A second opinion also said that the nave roof should be replaced, but a third called in by Dr Epps was less pessimistic. On 7th August it was agreed to postpone any improvements, but the churchwardens were authorized to spend not more than £7 to insert beams to support the belfry, and make the bell turret watertight. In October it was decided to go ahead with the building of the vestry against the north door, it having no exterior access. Two of the music books used by the local people who contributed to the best of their ability by singing or playing instruments in the church gallery have survived, and the names include Henry Allen, William, John and George Saker, and Henry Leppard. In 1857 a barrel organ, which was used to play hymn tunes, was purchased, and the live musicians were then no longer required. This barrel organ was later replaced by a small chamber organ, probably secondhand. Also in 1857 the box pews and the decayed and worm-eaten pulpit were removed, being replaced by benches and a pulpit of deal. A stove was introduced, but it probably made little effect on the damp and cold.

It was at about this time, 1857, that the tracery of the east window was restored, being an exact copy of the original. The work was by John Oldrid Scott, a relative of Sir Gilbert Scott. The stained glass was later inserted in memory of Lady Hodgkinson, who died in 1864. In 1867 the gallery was taken down, and a new door placed in the west wall. In 1868 the Act was passed that made Church rates voluntary, which meant even less money would be available for any repairs.

The wall painting of St Christopher was uncovered in 1875, and since that time has been variously 'restored', the first attempt at preservation being by P M Johnston who covered it with varnish in 1897. When he visited All Saints' in 1881 he made a sketch of the traces of scroll work depicting vines and grapes faintly visible on a small section of wall plaster and on the lath and plaster screen which divided nave from chancel. The decoration included heads of angels, and he thought was of similar date to St Christopher. Later that year it is noted in the vestry minute book that the lath and plaster work was unsafe, and should be removed at once.

In August 1886 a booklet was produced by P M Johnston giving a brief history and description of the architecture of All Saints' church, and appealing for funds in aid of the restoration. Some extracts are of interest—

'Warlingham Church, dedicated to All Saints, is very prettily situated, surrounded by open fields, at some distance from the village or any road. It stands on the brow of a small hill, and is partially hidden on the east, south and west sides by thick trees, amongst them being three large yews, one of which, especially fine, is thought to be about seven centuries old.

.... It is thoroughly in harmony with its surroundings and has a most picturesque appearance. The roof, of red tiles, is surmounted at the west end by a tiled bell turret, with a short, red painted, boarded spire, which carries a vane dated 1820. The chancel roof is somewhat lower than that of the nave. The walls, built of flint and rubble, are rough cast outside with a sort of pebble concrete. The worked stone, where seen, is a soft calcareous sandstone, probably from the Reigate or Godstone quarries. It does not weather well, and has perished very much in places. The slopes of the buttresses are tiled ....

We now enter the church through the porch and south doorway.... The rude framework that supports the bell turret at the west end is noticeable on account of its massiveness.... The roof is at present ceiled. It is most likely coeval with the erection of the main structure. The tie beams attract attention from their irregularity; they are, in fact, only hewn tree trunks in their native crookedness. These, and the wall plate, appear to be of chestnut. The rafters, braces, and collar form together a heptagonal shape. There is a raised platform at the west end for the choir, on which stands the organ, closing the western entrance. The font, a very perfect and good example of the 15th century, is octagonal, and has a quatrefoil traceried panel in each face of the bowl, in one of which is a grotesque head. The whole font has been painted white, and is very dirty. It stands on a stone step, now level with the platform, in the south-west angle of the nave. .... The stained deal reredos, curtains and carpets, which at present adorn the Sacrarium are tasteless, as are also the ponderous choir seats. The low deal pulpit, and what does duty for a lectern, propped up on a rough box, are both very poor pieces of furniture for the sacred building. The nave seats of simple design (though very uncomfortable) are more in keeping....'

Mention is made of the piscina and sedile in the south wall of the chancel, and that the height of the latter from the floor indicated that the floor must have originally been some 10 inches lower than at present.

From the 1880s onwards house building mainly – but not entirely – in the Westhall area, brought more church-going residents to the village. It was soon found that the church, which seated only 110, was no longer adequate. A public meeting was held on 9th July 1891 to discuss the matter of possible enlargement and, very importantly, how to meet the cost. It was agreed to proceed, and a committee was appointed which approached the architect, P M Johnston FSA FRIBA asking him to submit plans for enlargement and restoration. The plans he put forward were agreed, after some modification, and in January 1893 a start was made to raise the money required, which at that time was estimated at around £2000. The first subscribers included F W Arkwright, owner of the manor and advowson, who gave £300; Mrs L Tuzo who gave £300; the vicar, Revd F R Marriott, £200, and H Gamman, £100.

Of the six tenders for the work, that of John Marsland of Walworth was accepted, being the lowest, and work commenced on 24th July 1893. The extension would provide space for about 180 additional seats, and the work included a new porch, bell turret, heating apparatus, new wooden flooring and temporary seats. It was decided to defer the building of a new vestry, the provision of oak seating, and some of the work needed on the external walls in order to keep down the cost.

The first thing that had to be done was to move the interments which came within the area of the proposed extension and transfer the remains to new graves. Then the south porch was taken down. It included some quite old timbers but little that could be reused. Inside the church the first work done was to remove plaster from the walls. This brought to light several ancient features which had been filled in and whitewashed over. These included square holes in north and south walls in which the ends of the rood beam had rested, a semi-circular recess in the cill of the low-side window, and in the south nave wall, beneath the 15th century two-light window, a piscina and sedile. Another piscina was uncovered in a similar position below the corresponding window in the north wall. All these features were dated to the 13th century, and their discovery created considerable interest. On 1st August the Archbishop of Canterbury rode over from Addington Palace to see for himself what had been uncovered. Archbishop Benson was particularly interested in the evidence that subsidiary altars had existed in the nave, and was of the opinion that the chancel floor should definitely be lowered to the earlier level, as indicated by the sedile in the south chancel wall.

The plans were modified, being extended further to the west which provided more space for seating. The length of the old south wall with the recently uncovered piscina and sedile was left intact. The low-side window was given a wooden shutter. Opinions vary as to the use of these small apertures which occur in some churches dating from about the mid-13th century until about 1470. It may have been for confessions. The south door was rebuilt, stone for stone, in the new position within the wall of the south aisle, and the lancet window that had been just west of the door was reused in the extended north wall. The chancel floor was lowered seven inches, some evidence of burial within the chancel being uncovered.

The north side of All Saints' Church, photographed in June 1959. The old stones in the chancel wall are clearly visible. The modern vestry now obscures much of this side of the church.

The put-log holes of the original 13th century scaffolding were left exposed as a feature, mainly on the north wall. The chancel roof was found to be well constructed, but that over the nave had to be completely renewed. The tie-beams were sound, but the architect described the roof, which had been hidden by the ceiling, as 'a mere collection of pea-sticks', which rather confirmed the opinions given about the roof back in 1856! Thatching pins found indicated that thatch had preceded tiles. In the 1890s a few thatched buildings still existed locally, and in the past the villagers, who had a responsibility for the upkeep of the nave, would naturally have used thatch. No date is known, but it is possible the roof was not tiled until the repairs put in hand by Olive Atwood in 1678.

Inside All Saints' Church, looking west, as depicted by Edward Hassell in 1829.

In September 1893 it was decided to demolish the small vestry to facilitate the setting of foundations for the future new vestry. Three months later it was decided to proceed with the work on the new vestry. Good quality, well seasoned Godstone stone was obtained from the recently demolished Croydon Old Town Hall. Flints for facing new walls would have been readily available. Local farmers, such as Solomon Windross at Beech Farm, Chelsham, were selling them by the cartload to the Highways Board for road-making.

The interior, looking west, as it was about 1930. Electric lighting was installed in 1934. The gallery was removed in 1957.

The font had been thickly coated with whitewash, and this was carefully removed, 'pickled' being the term used by the architect. It would seem from his description that everything that could be whitewashed had received a coat, but in a way this had helped to preserve the stonework. The articles he wrote cover the work done in some detail.

Eventually the work was completed, and the first service held in the enlarged church was on Sunday 23rd April 1894. The formal reopening, on Monday 21st May, was marked by the visit of the Bishop of Winchester, in whose diocese Warlingham had been until 1877. A further change in 1910 caused Warlingham to be transferred from Rochester to Southwark Diocese. Since the 17th century the owner of the manor had held the advowson, the right to present clergy to the living. In 1925 this gift of patronage was purchased and handed over to the Bishop of Southwark.

In January 1895 there was still a debt of about £1000 outstanding. An oak gallery was constructed at the west end of the church, and a new organ, by Samuels and Twyford, was installed there in June. The debt for this was cleared by August 1896, and the loan for restoration and enlargement was paid off in July 1899.

Gas had come to the village, followed later by electricity for those who could afford it, in place of or as well as gas. Candles and oil lamps continued to provide light in the church. Church Road was made in 1907, replacing the footpath across the field which for many years had been the direct route from the village. Church Lane also developed from a footpath along the edge of the fields. The length to the northwest, connecting with Crewes Lane, was renamed Ward Lane when houses were built there after World War II. All Saints' was eventually wired for electricity in 1934. The church roof was retiled in 1954, and the spirelet given new shingles in 1975.

Many of the items given for use and to beautify All Saints' church are in memory of close relatives of parishioners. Some gifts form permanent furnishings. In 1907 the Revd G R Macaulay, vicar 1900–1925, donated oak pews for the nave. These were designed by P M Johnston, and made by local craftsman Frederick W Honour, who also made the oak door to the vestry. The oak pews in the side aisle date from 1928, made by Arthur E Sabey and William Clenston, and incorporate some wood from an old oak in the churchyard. The oak panelling at the west end, also made by F W Honour, was originally in the chancel but was moved in 1957. It was part of a gift made by G L Hodgkinson in 1907. The altar frontal chest at the east end of the south aisle dates from 1909. The font stood for many years at the west end of the south aisle, and was moved to the east end in 1969. The oak font cover was made and donated by C J Redmond in 1939. The vicars' board was given in 1948, and the ordinands' board in 1965.

Several stained-glass windows incorporate names and other details. During World War II the windows were covered with protective boarding against blast, and also as blackout. Today they are covered with polycarbon sheeting against vandalism, as several have suffered damage. In his articles about the enlargement P M Johnston mentions the location and resiting of a few pieces of older glass, but probably the only fragments now existing are those placed in the four small lights at the top of the east window. There are wall plaques in memory of Charles Langton Lockton, vicar's warden for 30 years, and Charles Cheston of Crewes, who was remembered by the local men whom he trained in the 1st Volunteer Battalion, Royal West Surrey Regiment, during World War I. In the chancel there is a mural tablet recording members of the Tyler family who died between 1751 and 1833. There is a memorial and a roll of honour listing the names of men of the 17th Battalion, Royal Fusiliers, who gave their lives in World War I, and also a memorial to the local men. The flag of the disbanded 17th Battalion was laid up in the church in 1920. Banners belonging to the Mothers' Union and the Women's branch of the Royal British Legion are also displayed.

The first English Prayer Book was compiled by a committee of churchmen headed by Archbishop Thomas Cranmer. It was authorised by Act of Parliament in January 1549, and published on 7th March. There followed three months during which clergy and the people could become acquainted with the content before Whit Sunday, 9th June, the date from which it was to replace previous service books. The two-light window in the south wall depicts Archbishop Cranmer presenting the Prayer Book to the King, Edward VI. The surround was copied from the design used in the old glass then in the opposite window. On 5th August 1875 members of the Surrey Archaeological Society visited the churches at Sanderstead and Warlingham. They were told by Mr Granville Leveson-Gower that it was said Cranmer came himself to Warlingham on the occasion of the new Prayer Book being first used for a service here. The cost of providing the window was met by Dr Edwin Freshfield in 1876, who thought this 'tradition' should be commemorated. It must be said that as far as is known no earlier reference has come to light recounting such an event.

As mentioned before, an unknown amount of documentation was lost or thrown away in the 19th century, but parish registers have survived. Those for Sanderstead commence in the 1560s, but for Warlingham appear to date from the appointment of William King as vicar in 1660. He was certainly related to King Atwood, rector of Sanderstead, and Harman Atwood who held the manor, possibly their uncle (their mother had been Joan King).

The earliest register includes entries for Chelsham until 1680. It is thought that the baptisms of the first four children of Christopher and Elizabeth Hayward were entered all at the same time, thereafter other children of this couple appear under the appropriate date, the last being in 1678. All the completed registers – baptisms to 1985, marriages to 1974, and burials to 1973 – have been deposited in the archives held at the Surrey History Centre in Woking. Other records deposited there include the only surviving vestry minute book, and the parish council minute books.

Not only the ancient bells but also the silver chalice, nine ounces in weight, has long gone from All Saints' church. Humble but long-lasting pewter was in use until 1911, by which time gifts of church plate had been received from several residents. Two items of pewter, dated to the 1690s, are now in East Surrey Museum. A third, which had the appearance of a tankard, has disappeared, but a photograph of it survives.

The 16th century cup, and paten dated 1569, returned to All Saints' from Coulsdon in 1893. The height is 4.6 inches.

In 1893 a small Elizabethan cup, weighing 3oz.12dwt. and a paten with the date 1569 were – by means of a faculty – returned to Warlingham from St John's Church, Coulsdon. From the information in the Coulsdon vestry minutes it appears that John Russell, churchwarden at Warlingham in 1817, had 'become possessed of the chalice by giving in exchange for it when it was out of repair, a new chalice.' He had moved to Coulsdon, and the gift to St. John's Church had been made by his now elderly daughter, Mrs Nevill, as a Jubilee offering in 1887. The small bowl is inscribed to this effect. Some fact, and a little conjecture, can provide a suggested earlier history for this little silver chalice, only four and three-fifths inches in height.

In All Saints' Church, Sanderstead, are memorials to members of the Cockshutt family – Elizabeth who died in 1643, her husband John, died 1649, and their son, also John, who died in 1669, aged 30. On this young man's memorial Harman Atwood is mentioned as being *amicis fidelis* – faithful to his friends. It seems probable he took over the guidance and care of this ten year-old orphan. One sentence in Harman Atwood's will is very relevant. He wrote—

'I do hereby declare that I have already given unto my said sister the Cup and its cover given me by Mr John Cockshutt and I hereby confirm the same.'

January 1907. Standing by the church porch are Revd H M Scott, curate; G R Macaulay MA, Vicar; C L Lockton, Churchwarden, and J Davis, Parish Clerk.

Neither Harman nor his sister Olive had married, so the nearest relatives were the children of their brother King Atwood. Joan, the eldest, was the first wife of the Revd John Sheppard, rector of Caterham, and later of Sanderstead. Susan, the other daughter, married the Revd Joseph Till, who in due course became vicar of Warlingham, and it was to him that Olive gave the Cup and Paten. After his death in 1689 these remained in the parish until removed by John Russell. The indication is that the Cup and Paten had always belonged within a household. Harman Atwood was a lawyer, of Cliffords Inn, and John Cockshutt trusted him to keep them securely.

A memorable event of the 20th century at All Saints' church was the televising of Harvest Festival on Sunday 24th September 1950. The vicar, the Revd J D Underwood, conducted the service, the first ever to be televised from a parish church. Outside broadcasts required a large amount of equipment and there were 11 BBC vehicles parked near the church and 40 technicians were on hand. A 60ft fire escape carried the transmitting aerial. Harry Leppard played the organ, and the verger, Henry Bangs, had to use the hand pump to provide air, as it was found that the electric blower, installed in 1948, made a hum which was picked up by the microphones. In Wallington the service was recorded, and was later available on 78 rpm gramophone records. The vicar reported in the parish magazine that the BBC had been very pleased with the viewer response which indicated that there certainly was a demand for televised church services. The parish received donations totalling £210 towards the almshouses and church restoration.

Proposals made in 1953 were – after prolonged discussions – mostly accepted and effected in 1957. The gallery, and the organ which was beyond repair, were removed. Panelling and choir stalls were moved from the chancel to the west end of the nave. An electronic organ, made by A E Davies & Sons Ltd of Northampton was purchased. This, in its turn, was replaced by the present electric-powered pipe organ. This was built by James Mitchell of Bideford, and dedicated on Sunday, 16th September 1984. Intensive fund-raising over several years had been needed to collect the money required, around £9000.

30th June, 1970. The bell is returned to All Saints' Church.

Following a growing interest in handbell ringing, a set of 16 bells cast at the Whitechapel Foundry was purchased. This cost about £3500, met by donations, and was dedicated in May 1994. The church bell is heard but seldom seen. Arthur Beadell recalled seeing it in the churchyard in 1893. The next time it was out of the belfry was in 1969. When it was returned from the bell foundry of John Taylor of Loughborough, on 30th June 1970, there was an opportunity to measure and photograph it. The weight is estimated as being between 2½ and 3 cwt. Diameter across the lip is 26½ inches, height 23 inches, or 27 including the fitting for the headstock. There is decoration of parallel lines around it but no inscription. It is not the right shape to be one of the bells mentioned in 1553. On this occasion in 1970 a new headstock and clapper were fitted. In the past it was the custom to space the tolling of a bell for a funeral, giving groups of three strokes for a man, two for a woman, and a single stroke for a child. During World War II the church bells were silent; their use being designated as an alarm signal in the event of invasion.

Originally the churchyard was only just over half an acre in extent. To the south was a small wood named Church Croft, and on the east and north sides a large field called Church Grove. The trustees of the Arkwright Estate donated part of Church Croft in 1889, and the remainder in 1900, so extending the churchyard to its present limit on the south side. In 1906 they gave land on the north and east of the church, this being part of Church Grove. This new ground was fenced off but not taken in and consecrated as part of the churchyard until 1916. The remainder of Church Grove, with the exception of the frontage sold for the housing on Ward Lane, was also given to the church. About two acres on the east side, reaching down to Crewes Lane, was given by E H Hodgkinson in 1926, and consecrated in 1927. The remaining part of Church Grove was given by A C Reynard in 1938, and it has not yet been necessary to extend the churchyard to include this land. The oldest yew, south east of the chancel was estimated as being about 870 years old in 1881, so is around 1000 years now. The age of the yew planted in 1919 to commemorate the Peace Treaty is known as when it was brought to the churchyard from Westhall it was six years old. It is on the east side of the church in the extension dating from 1916.

5th June 1927. Consecration of a further extension to the
churchyard. The Bishop of Woolwich is preceded by the
Churchwardens C L Lockton and A C Jones.

SOURCES

BLUNT R H (1872) *The Annotation of the Book of Common Prayer.*

Coulsdon Vestry Minute Book.

DANIEL-TYSSEN J R, FSA (1869) *Inventories of the Goods and Ornaments in the Churches of Surrey in the reign of King Edward the Sixth.*

GOODMAN C H *Parish Notes.*

JOHNSTON P M, FSA FRIBA (1886, 1893, 1902) Pamphlets and articles concerning All Saints' Church.

SURREY RECORD SOCIETY Vol 35 (1997) *The 1851 Religious Census.*

TUTT D C (1991) 'Growth of God's Half-acre'. Bourne Society *Local History Records* Vol 30.

Warlingham & Chelsham Parish Magazine.

Warlingham Vestry Minute Book.

Chapter 9

The Atwoods and Wigsells

THE ATWOODS

Following the surrender of Bermondsey Abbey to King Henry VIII in 1537 Warlingham was included amongst lands acquired by Sir John Gresham, who made Titsey the site of a country residence. The Greshams also established Warlingham Court, and although it probably has no bearing on the choice of site it is of interest to note that the three principal farm sites, Westhall, Crewes and Warlingham Court, form a triangle which, on a map, appears almost equilateral. Batts Farm, which took its name from a family who lived there for many years, was probably already established, attached to Crewes.

When Sir John died in 1557, Warlingham and other local land passed to his son, Edmund, who lived in Norfolk. In 1587 Edmund's son Richard inherited, and in the early 1590s sold the land to John Ownsted of Addington. It was probably at this time that Crewes passed to a separate owner, who continued to lease the nearby common land from Warlingham Manor. After the death of John Ownsted, and his wife Margaret, the estate was split, half to Ownsted's near relative, Harman Atwood, and the other half divided between Ownsted's two married sisters. In due course Harman Atwood was able to reunite the estate in his ownership. Often the mother's surname was given to the eldest son as a first name, and the original spelling of Harman was Herman. As 'Harman' occurs several times a few details may help to separate them.

A large part of the Warlingham land which passed to the Atwoods was unenclosed common, but there was arable, mainly towards the north. Land in Chelsham also came into their ownership. Harman Atwood[1] (1570–1653) had married Elizabeth Lawrence, and they had a son, John. Further children Ownsted and Olive died in infancy, and in 1604 Elizabeth herself died, a week after daughter Anna was baptised. Harman[1] soon remarried, to Joan King from Beckenham, and they had six children, all of whom survived to adulthood. King, the eldest son of this family, became rector of Sanderstead, while the second son, Harman[2] (1608–1676) followed his father and became a lawyer of Clifford's Inn. A deed was drawn up settling the estates on this Harman[2] after his half-brother John relinquished his rights as eldest son. During his time as lord of the manor (1653–1676), Harman[2] had a new vicarage built in Warlingham and established the almshouses. Both were built of brick.

The matter of who would succeed to the estates was of great concern to Harman[2]. The next male in line, after sister Olive, who by deed would hold the estate in her lifetime, was brother King's only son, Harman[3] (1641–1702). Unfortunately Harman[3] did not, in his uncle's opinion, meet the required standard. Harman's[2] will, proved in London 1676, is long, and repays study. As head of the family he expected to be consulted about important matters. Two of his late half-brother's children married without his consent. Of George he says—

> '...his marriage without my consent I have forgiven him, the others having done so.'

and Susan received initially only £20 instead of £100. Although not actually stated the indication is that this third generation Harman was losing money gambling. To have the current debts cleared, estimated at about £600, he was – by legal document – to give up all claim to the estates. Moreover, the conditions by which he would receive an annuity of £20 included to—

> 'keep himself in some good way of employment, tending a livelihood, and be no trouble or disturbance to them enjoying my said lands by his presence or abode with them further than by civil visits not exceeding fourteen days time in any one year which, if he observe not, then the intended and desired allowance aforesaid to cease'.

However, Harman[3] had married, and had a son, born in 1663. It was to this child that the estates were left, but he could not inherit until he was 24 years old. Unfortunately, he died in 1683 when only 20, and great-aunt Olive having died in 1681, the inheritance passed to George, mentioned above.

George and Elizabeth had eight children, two of whom died in infancy. George lived until 1722, and was succeeded by his son, John. In 1765, after the deaths of John Atwood and his wife, Elizabeth, who had no children, the estates passed to the Wigsells via Mary, George's eldest daughter. Mary had married Nicholas Wigsell, and they had two sons, Atwood and Thomas. These took up the accepted professions of church and law, the elder, Atwood Wigsell, becoming rector of Sanderstead and vicar of Warlingham, while Thomas became a lawyer of New Inn.

Atwood livery button, probably early 19th century. Made by Firmin & Sons, of 15 Conduit Street, London.

THE WIGSELLS

Atwood Wigsell and his wife Susannah lived at Sanderstead Rectory, and they had seven children. There is a note in one of the Warlingham parish registers which says—

> 'The Curate's House at Warlingham was rebuilt in the year 1738 at the expense of John Atwood Esq.
> 'This refers to the vicarage, now known as "The Old Vicarage"'.

It was Thomas Wigsell, the lawyer, who inherited, his elder brother Atwood having died in 1757. Thomas died, unmarried, in 1778, and was succeeded by his nephew, another Atwood Wigsell. He died in 1795 following a blow on the head. He had not married but had an illegitimate son born in 1795. His younger brother, the Revd Thomas Wigsell then became lord of the manor, as well as rector of Sanderstead and vicar of Warlingham. All these changes probably made little difference to the ordinary people working in the fields, but having an absentee vicar during two long periods in the 18th century cannot have been good for Warlingham parish.

The Revd Thomas Wigsell had married Jacobina Mary Ann Maria Henderson in 1792, but they had no children. He died in 1805, and she later remarried, becoming the wife of Richard Curran of Kings Road, Chelsea. Trustees managed the estates until Atwood Wigsell Taylor was of age, and took the name Wigsell. His life was short, but he did marry and had a daughter, Sophia Julia and a son Atwood Dalton Wigsell. This son was born in 1821, the year his father died, so again there was a long spell of management by guardians and trustees.

The assessment for payment of Tithes in Warlingham and Chelsham, made in 1842, was confirmed and implemented from 1844. This was the change from payment in kind to a rent charge. The map, and document which accompanies it, provides much useful information. Jacobina Curran received benefit from Warlingham Court Farm lands until her death in 1850. Juliana, widow of Atwood Wigsell Wigsell, remarried, and as Juliana Grieg received an annuity for life of £400.

Atwood Dalton Wigsell followed an army career, attaining the rank of Captain in the 2nd Dragoon Guards, and Colonel of the 2nd Regiment Surrey Volunteers. He did marry, but had no children. He borrowed money in various ways, some being by a mortgage on Batts Farm lands. This seems to have been done with the cooperation of Henry Spence Fairfoot and associates, lawyers of Clements Inn, who were involved in the management of the estate. When Atwood Dalton died in 1878, having lived latterly at Cliff House, Dartmouth, the outstanding debt was in the region of £30,000.

His wife, Mary Anne Wigsell, Robert Wigram Arkwright (who had married Sophia Julia) and Henry Spence Fairfoot were the executors and trustees of his will. This allowed for land and property to be sold to—

'discharge incumbrances affecting the real estate'.

This was done gradually over the following years in respect of holdings in Titsey, Oxted, Croydon, Coulsdon, Chelsham and Warlingham which lay outside the entailed part of the estate, eventually clearing the debt. Mary Anne Wigsell remarried in 1886, and thereby lost any right to inheritance. Frederick Wigsell Wigram Arkwright succeeded his father as tenant for life in 1888. When he died in 1893 his son, Esme, was 11 years old, so once again trustees managed the affairs. On 7th May 1903 Esme Francis Wigsell Arkwright, of Stoneley Grange, St Neots, Huntingdon, came of age and disentailed the remaining estate. The part of Warlingham concerned in the final break-up of the estate was Hamsey Green and the land attached to Batts Farm and Court Farm.

SOURCES

Abstract of Title – Land at Batts Farm and Hamsey Green Farm.

PERCY, F H G *Extensive notes arising from research re Atwoods and Wigsells.*

Sanderstead Parish Registers.

Will – Atwood, Harman (1608-1676).

Chapter 10

Warlingham Court Farm and Batts Farm

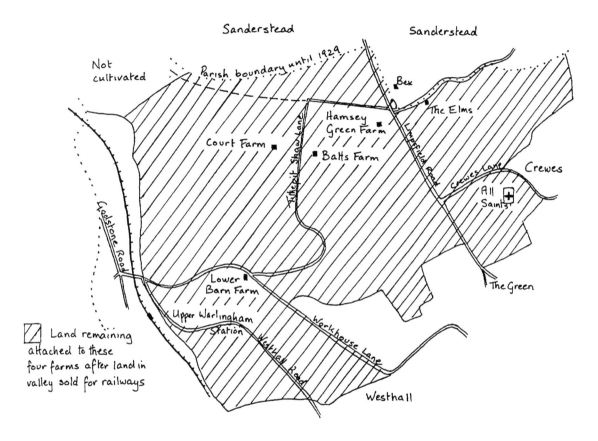

During the 18th century the total acreage of the land attached to Court Farm was increased, partly by acquisition of enclosed land, previously part of Warlingham Bottom, and also by inclusion of one or two fields that had been attached to other nearby holdings. When the Revd Thomas Wigsell died in 1805 he left Court Farm lands to his wife for life, and although she remarried she received the benefit until her death in 1850. In 1844 the tenant, Nathaniel Glover, had 346 acres. The land abutted Crewes Estate on the east, and stretched down to the lowest field, Bourne Croft, below Godstone Road, interrupted only by the width of a few fields attached to Batts Farm. Nathaniel Glover, and his neighbour at Batts Farm, William Williams, both took an active part in the work of the vestry which administered the parish.

Batts Farm had 138 acres. The name Batt, known to be in the parish in the 17th century, has persisted right through to the present day with respect to land in this area. The farm had some fields at quite a distance from the main holding. One was Longlands, a field in the valley south of Bourne Croft, and there were two small fields to the east which touched the northern parish boundary. When the Caterham branch railway line was built in 1855/56, it cut into Longlands and along the full length of Bourne Croft before crossing the parish boundary again opposite Rose Cottage on Godstone Road. This house was originally called 'Maples' and was the home of James Atkins, tenant farmer for part of Sir William Clayton's land. Atkins held a 99 year lease from 1820, but surrendered it in the early 1860s. Another two fields attached to Batts Farm were in this area, Maples Field, adjacent to the house, and Little Yew, part of the upper hillside behind.

A view of Batts Farm, *c.*1905. The house was demolished 1916.
In the distance there is a glimpse of the Court farmhouse.

More land was sold for the railway line through to Oxted, which was commenced in the 1860s. This entered Warlingham parish just north of Riddlesdown chalk pit, which was started in about 1805, and left the parish at the Mumbles Viaduct over Woldingham Road. This stretch of line involved both long embankments and cuttings through the side of the hills to create a reasonably level track.

With the opening of the Oxted line in 1884 it was potentially profitable to put land in the valley on the market. The Trustees of what was now the Arkwright Estate put land up for sale through the auctioneers, Blake, Haddock and Carpenter. A sale held on 24th June, 1885, which also included the land bought by George Wren for his brickfield, offered the following—

> '16 plots of desirable FREEHOLD BUILDING LAND in the main Godstone and Whyteleafe Road, four being opposite Roke and Little Roke Farms, and about half a mile from Caterham Junction Railway Station. The plots have frontages of about 80 feet and a depth of 300 feet, and form capital sites for the erection of private houses. The remaining 12 lots are situate in the Godstone and Whyteleafe Roads in the parish of Warlingham. They have frontages varying from 50 to 245 feet, and are suitable for large or small houses being close to the Upper Warlingham Station on the Croydon, Oxted and East Grinstead Railway, and also near the Whyteleafe Hotel. The gas and water mains are laid in the Godstone Road, and the building restrictions are very slight.'

The new station was named Upper Warlingham to distinguish it from Warlingham station, which is now called Whyteleafe South, on the Caterham line which had already existed for nearly 30 years. It is located on slightly higher ground, and at the time was in Warlingham parish, but is now in Whyteleafe.

WARLINGHAM COURT FARM AND BATTS FARM

Tithepit Shaw Lane, just beyond Court Cottage, as it was in the early 1950s before widening.

The name of the road may be a corruption of 'To the pit in the shaw'.

Until the Enclosure Award of 1866 the farms of Batts and Warlingham Court faced the open Hamsey Green Common. Just beyond Batts Farm was a large pond in front of a cottage with land called 'Mays'. Batts Farm Cottages, dated 1897, now stand on the site of this house. Fortunately two pictures exist of Batts farmhouse, which was demolished in 1916. There was a large main block, and a lower cross-wing. It was stuccoed, with tiled roof, and had windows of varying size and type. It gave the impression of age, and possibly some part dated back to the 16th century. In 1905 a new house was built facing the nearby lane just outside the farmyard.

Tithepit Shaw Lane, now a busy road, should more correctly be called Chalkpit Shaw Lane, as the wood above the bend where the pit is located was called Chalk Pit Shaw, and the road on its modern route crosses the top of Chalk Pit Field. When Workhouse Lane, now Hillbury Road, was extended down the valley it joined the older lane from Court Farm at Lower Barn, or Bottom Barn Farm. Later this became known as King's Farm, the name of the long-standing tenant.

Returning to the hilltop, on the left-hand side is Court Cottage, a listed building. It dates from about 1800, and the only other building in the area with this distinctive flint and stone chequerwork, which is not a local style, is a barn at Chelsham Court Farm, which was also owned by the Wigsells. Could this indicate travelling craftsmen from north Kent, or East Anglia? The next pair of early 19th century cottages are of flint and brick, and the block of three brick-built cottages beyond date from 1898.

Warlingham Court farmhouse consisted of a main block, with a substantial wing of equal height at the rear. Built of brick it gave the appearance of being largely 18th century. The fine large cellars may have been of earlier date. Set well back from the lane, a passer-by would see at once that it was an important farm.

In 1894 George Taylor, farmer and refreshment contractor, came to Court Farm. He established the Tea Gardens and Pleasure Grounds which became a popular venue for groups such as Sunday School outings. There was a small roundabout, and swings similar to those at Gardners on Riddlesdown, but here the ground was level. Sports were organised, races, tug-of-war, quoits and other activities.

In 1902 John Henry Hinton replaced George Taylor. The Taylors, Hintons and Hemsleys were connected by marriage. Alfred Hemsley was a nurseryman at 'The Elms' in Kingswood Lane. His daughter, Edith, married

1904. The approach to Warlingham Court Farm. The Pleasure Grounds were at the rear.

The garden front of Warlingham Court Farm, *c.*1904. The tenant at this time was John Henry Hinton.

Wedding photograph of Edith Hemsley and Albert Taylor outside the main door of Warlingham Court Farm.

A typical crowd of visitors intent on obtaining their tea from the refreshment room.

Autumn 1914. The men on a route march pass a board advertising Court Farm Pleasure Grounds as they turn into Tithepit Shaw Lane.

The facilities available in the various permanent buildings at the Pleasure Grounds were put to good use by the trainees.

Albert Taylor, who was a butcher. For a few years they lived at Aberdeen House in Warlingham, and their daughter, Enid, was born in the room over the shop in 1905. Albert's sister was married to John Hinton, and Enid had very happy memories of the marvellous Christmas parties her aunt used to give in the stone-flagged kitchen at Court Farm. She had some recollection of the ground-floor rooms, in particular her aunt's own special room where small cupboards were concealed behind the panelling. When they moved to Croydon, Enid, with her mother and brother, used to walk up to White House Farm in Sanderstead where another relative lived, and then on across the fields to Court Farm.

In 1914 Court Farm was commandeered as training quarters for army volunteers. On 12th September a large body of men arrived by train at Upper Warlingham station, and preceded by the local band, made its way up to Court Farm. The men lived under canvas, and for some time had no uniforms or equipment. The officers were billeted in the farmhouse, and Albert had to ask permission to take a seat at his sister's table. A few huts were built later on, and some men were billeted with families in the village. Entertainments were arranged by joint efforts of the men and local residents. It was an unpleasant winter. December was the wettest for 60 years. On 22nd January 1915, 12 inches of snow fell in a few hours. The battalion, originally the 7th, was renumbered the 17th Empire Battalion, Royal Fusiliers, and in June it moved on to Clipstone in Nottinghamshire. Some army presence remained in the area, though not in such great numbers. From October 1916 until the end of March, 1919, the Church Hall was used as a Soldiers' Club for convalescents. Between 1919 and the mid-1950s the 17th Battalion held an annual reunion in Warlingham, which included a special service at All Saints' Church.

John Hinton had a further lease of Court Farm for seven years from 1916. The land was then only 268 acres. The pleasure grounds were not revived. In the 1930s the farmer was William Heffer, and during World War II crops were grown in every suitable field. This included the Rugby Football ground to the rear of Hamsey Green Gardens. Land Army girls were billeted locally. A 'doodlebug' which came down at Court Farm on 3rd July 1944 killed several horses. In 1949, when housing was scarce, a caravan park was started on land adjacent to the farm, and 50 years later this park home site still exists. Surrey County Council acquired land in the area, including the farmhouse, which stood empty and became derelict. It was demolished in 1968.

SOURCES

Abstract of Title – Land at Batts Farm and Court Farm.

Croydon Advertiser.

Directories.

Enclosure Award 1866.

TAYLOR, ENID – Tape recording.

Tithe Assessment 1842.

Warlingham & Chelsham Parish Magazine.

WYRALL, E   *17th (S) Battalion, Royal Fusiliers 1914-1919.*

**A souvenir from the Warlingham Court
Farm Pleasure Grounds.**
(Courtesy of Bob Davidson)

Chapter 11

Hamsey Green

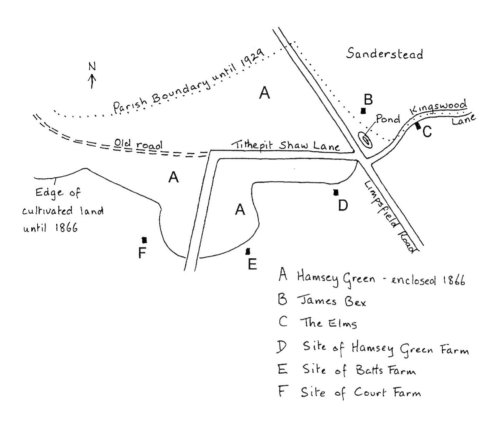

A Hamsey Green - enclosed 1866
B James Bex
C The Elms
D Site of Hamsey Green Farm
E Site of Batts Farm
F Site of Court Farm

The northern side of the parish consisted of an extensive common. It can be defined as all the land from Tithepit Shaw Lane to Clyde Avenue on the west side of the main road, with a narrow return strip on the east side widening out towards Kingswood Lane to include the pond and land behind it. With Court and Batts farms on the southern edge, the common land within Warlingham parish turned along the hilltop in a long tapering tongue of land to end at a point where it met with the boundaries of Sanderstead and Coulsdon. It covered 258 acres, that part near the main road being known as Hamsey Green. The pond, one of the five mentioned in the 1866 Enclosure Award, covered more than a quarter of an acre. The first stretch of Tithepit Shaw Lane is on the route of the old coach road, which, after the newer road turns sharply south towards the farms, continues out onto the hillside. Two principal footpaths crossed Hamsey Green from Sanderstead creating a meeting of five ways. The extension of Wentworth Way to Tithepit Shaw Lane after World War II emerges a few yards to the east of this spot.

After enclosure in 1866 Hamsey Green became pasture or cultivated land. Hamsey Green farmhouse was a building of quality, perhaps erected as a home for a member of the landowning family. In a photograph, dated 1901, the façade of flint and brick is clearly visible. 19th century additions included the porch, very necessary

This view, taken about 1910, shows Hamsey Green Farm at the top of Tithepit Shaw Lane. The view today, with houses and shops, is very different.

for a house facing north, and a probable retiling of the roof adding decorative ridge tiles. At the rear was a centrally placed wing of equal height to the main block. It is recorded that the main stair divided into two branches as it descended from a half landing to the hall, but nothing else is known about the interior. In the early 18th century there were 88 acres attached to Hamsey Green Farm, this being mainly arable. The tenant farmer in 1844 was Thomas Wright, who lived in Kingswood Lane near some of the fields in his tenancy. 'The Elms', built in 1892, stands on his home plot. The tenant in 1866 was John Tillett. The 1869 OS map marks the disused tollhouse and turnpike on the main road a short distance south of Kingswood Lane.

Some years before enclosure James Bex established his premises near the pond facing the common, but on the Sanderstead side of the parish boundary. It was a good position, near the farms and the road by which local people and their animals would travel to Croydon market. James and his wife, Eliza Sophia, had 13 children. By 1900 their third son, Walter, had been running the business for some years. At that time the work included that of builder and decorator, cabinet maker, shopfitter, wheelwright and undertaker. They also had a tea garden, providing welcome refreshments to passers-by. James Bex died in 1903, but Eliza lived until 1927, dying two months after her 91st birthday.

June 1901. This substantial building is Hamsey Green Farm. It had a rear wing of equal height at right angles to the main block.

HAMSEY GREEN

At the time James Bex started his business here the house was built just over the boundary in Sanderstead parish, and the foreground was the edge of the - as yet - unenclosed Hamsey Green Common. This photograph, *c.*1905, shows the third son, Walter, as owner. The Bex family also had a tea garden here. The cottage still stands.

World War I delayed the breaking up and sale of the Arkwright estate. It was not until 1919 that the Hamsey Green area and other nearby land was affected. It was included in Indentures, all dated 27th March 1919, drawn up between Captain Esme F W Arkwright, of Sharnbrook House, Bedford, and John Gutzmer Hossack, of 42 Old Bond Street, London. The purchase price for all the land under offer was £100,000. Hossack borrowed £70,000 from Barclays Bank at Grays, Essex, using all the relevant deeds and documents as security. The other £30,000 was put up by Frank Spurr, draper, and Charles Asplin, solicitor, both also of Grays, Essex. For their contribution these two men each received an interest in one quarter share, while Hossack held the remaining half. In November 1920 Hossack borrowed a further £36,300 from Leonard Nathaniel Goldsmid Montefiore, to be repaid with interest in May 1921. However, on 14th April 1921 John Gutzmer Hossack died. Once again there was a situation which would take years to resolve. The estate documents eventually ended up in the Solicitor's office in Grays, Essex, where they remain.

On 25th June 1929, on receipt of £30,500, Frank Spurr and Charles Asplin conveyed Hamsey Green Farm and 198 acres of land, 19 of which were in Sanderstead parish, to Arthur Edward Cresswell, of Coney Hall Farm, West Wickham, Kent. Cresswell moved to live at Chelsham Place Farm. In early 1932 he sold land with

A view of Hamsey Green pond in the early 1960s.

Boundary changes in the 1990s mean that this Warlingham pond is now on the Sanderstead side of the boundary with the London Borough of Croydon.

frontage to Limpsfield Road to developers Wood McClelland. They built the houses of Hamsey Green Gardens, the first estate road in Warlingham to have gas, electricity, water and main drainage all laid on when built. Trenham Drive and Verdayne Gardens were also in hand in the early 1930s.

In February 1934 Messrs Watney, Combe, Reid & Co, having acquired the corner site at the top of Tithepit Shaw Lane, applied to the Oxted Licensing Sessions for a licence for a new hotel premises, to be called *The Good Companions*. As a number of houses had been built and many more were planned for nearby land in Sanderstead it was thought there would be a demand for premises with high-class catering. There was a restriction which prevented the building of a licensed premises within Sanderstead parish, but this site was in Warlingham. In 1929 an alteration had been made to the boundary in the Hamsey Green area which meant that all but the top shop in the parade under construction were in Sanderstead, then the boundary crossed the road and continued much as before. There was considerable opposition to the application, not only from the Warlingham licensees who were represented by a solicitor, H P Mason, but from all the local clergy, the branch of the Temperance Association, and from more than 50 residents living within a half mile radius. Mr. Bex, who lived across the road from the proposed site, had collected 118 signatures of people in favour. After deliberation the justices decided against granting a provisional licence.

In due time, and no doubt delayed by the war, the proposal was put forward again, granted, and in 1955 *The Good Companions* was built. The most recent boundary change at Hamsey Green means that it now stands just within the Sanderstead area of the London Borough of Croydon.

The first shops in Hamsey Green Parade opened in April and May 1934. The top shop was taken by F H Barratt, newsagent, tobacconist and confectioner who had the sub-post office. Next to him was the estate agent, Moore, and then R H Ferris, chemist. E Challis Baily was the first butcher, and next was the baker, Stafford's. No.13 must have been lucky for Leslie G Robinson, hairdresser, as he remained in business there until retirement in 1978. The next three shops were Dolbert's, draper, Sanderstead Supply Co, builders merchants, and the Empire

This view towards Hamsey Green Parade was taken in 1950, when the streets were gas-lit and this crossroads still looked quite rural.

Stores. The sub-post office is now located at No.9, which started as a wireless and electrical supplies shop. Redmond's, stationers and fancy goods, had a subscription library containing 3000 volumes. Beyond, others of long standing included Worcester's shoe shop, Mitchell's, the greengrocer, Price's household stores, and Ernest Roger, dairyman, who was eventually taken over by Express Dairy. Across the road by the pond, Mr Selby established a garage for petrol and car repairs. By the 1930s Walter Bex was predominately an undertaker, and sold out to E E Morgan in 1939. A few houses were built on the Sanderstead side of Kingswood Lane, but the lane, except for the short length to Meadway, was to remain in its original state, narrow and unsurfaced, until late 1970. Except for a few trees on the further side, most of the former rural aspect of the pond had gone by 1930, due to road improvements. Over the years the amount of water has shrunk so much it is now little more than a large puddle. The maintenance is now the responsibility of the London Borough of Croydon.

In the later 1930s some houses and bungalows were built on the first stretch of Tithepit Shaw Lane. From 1934 onwards Robert James Clarke, builder, of 87 Whyteleafe Hill, had his men employed building the 'Sunnyside Estate', the main development along the lower section of Hillbury Road. The site of Lower Barn Farm, opposite the junction with Tithepit Shaw Lane, was left until last. More houses were built in Oakley and Searchwood Roads, and on the lowest stretch of Westhall Road opposite the railway.

Lower Barn Farm at the junction of Tithepit Shaw Lane with Hillbury Road. Many of the houses in this area were built in the 1930s.

During World War II the bombs which fell in fields and woodland did comparatively little damage, but there were houses destroyed in the Hamsey Green area. Princes Avenue, Clyde Avenue and Tithepit Shaw Lane were hit, and in Tudor Close a 'doodlebug' flying bomb came down on 28th July 1944. The field between the Hamsey Green farm buildings and the main road was used as allotments. In June 1941 a small boy was killed when an aeroplane made a forced landing at Hamsey Green.

The local Residents' Association, based on Hamsey Green Gardens, had been very active in the 1930s, and it was revived at once when war ended. On 8th May 1945, a bonfire, one of many all over the country, was lit on the open area at the front of Hamsey Green Gardens, and from somewhere a few fireworks were produced, and set off. The Hamsey Green and District Residents' Association continued for a further seven years.

In May 1949, 78 children were transferred from the Warlingham Primary School, which had become very overcrowded, to new premises at Hamsey Green. This was the beginning of the schools complex which was built over the next few years on land off Tithepit Shaw Lane, originally open common. Over the years rebuilding has taken place, and further buildings added. Currently, the three schools, Hamsey Green Infants, Junior, and Warlingham School, provide a full range of education on one site.

In the early 1950s the trees and fields on both sides of the Limpsfield Road, just south of the pond, were replaced by houses and a new parade of shops. As time passed more shops were built on the Sanderstead side, opposite the original parade, and houses erected in any space in the area which became available. Amongst all these changes the house where the Bex family lived still stands, set well back and hardly visible from the main road.

SOURCES

Abstract of Title – Batts Farm and Hamsey Green Farm.

Croydon Advertiser.

Directories.

Enclosure Award 1866.

SAMSON, C Information regarding the Bex family.

School Log Book – Warlingham Primary School.

Tithe Assessment 1842.

Advertisements
from the 1930s

Chapter 12

From Hamsey Green to *The Leather Bottle*

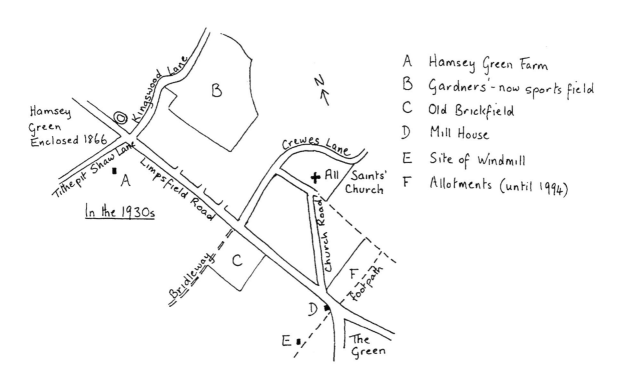

A   Hamsey Green Farm
B   Gardners' - now sports field
C   Old Brickfield
D   Mill House
E   Site of Windmill
F   Allotments (until 1994)

It was decided in the 1920s that the main road from Sanderstead, through Hamsey Green and Warlingham, which had been known variously as Sanderstead, Croydon, Limpsfield or Westerham Road, should be known as 'Limpsfield Road'. When numbering was introduced gaps were left to allow for further housing. Fortunately a good stretch of the road from Hamsey Green to Warlingham village has, to an extent, escaped this advancing tide. In the past many fields had names. Meadway and Trenham Drive were built on Lower Court, and Verdayne Gardens on Middle Court Field. The large field beyond, not visible from the main road, was created by removal of several hedges. For some years this has been a sports field, and includes a children's play area. In 1933 Richard E Gardner acquired this land for use as a private airfield. He was managing director of Yardley's Cosmetics Company, and a keen pilot. His son, Charles, became well known as a successful air race pilot, winning the King's Cup Air Race in 1936 and 1937. World War II put an end to private flying for the time being. Later on the field was used for air cadet glider training. The hangar existed until 1975 when it was wrecked by fire.

The dug-out used by the local Civil Defence volunteers during World War II can still be located in the bank at the front of Hamsey Green Gardens. The next field beyond the access to the sports field behind Hamsey Green Gardens was occupied by the East Surrey Poultry Farm in the 1920s and 1930s. The owner, G F Allen, lived in 'The Flint Bungalow', which stood opposite Verdayne Gardens. James Cornford lived in a house on this site in the 1840s, and some part of the flint and brick walls may have dated to his time. Crewes Avenue was laid out across Upper Court Field and Mead Plot, and beyond Crewes Lane was Lower Church Field.

Kingswood Lane in July 1970, a few months before work started to widen and surface the road beyond Meadway.

July 1970. Looking along the track towards the former hangar at Gardner's aerodrome, off Kingswood Lane. It was destroyed by fire in 1975.

A view across the front of Hamsey Green Gardens in 1934. Some of the pre-war houses nearby, being built about that time, have been completed.

'The Flint Bungalow', photographed in 1958. This stood opposite Verdayne Gardens. A house is shown on this site in the 1842 Tithe Assessment map.

Across the road the field is one of four in the area which had the name Sheeplands. This is the site of the earliest brickfield. The first piped water was pumped up to this field in 1868. There was some living accommodation nearby, as in 1873 Mark Payne and James Stacey, who received outdoor poor relief, gave their address as 'Brickfields'.

In the brickfield the 'temperer' mixed the clay to make 'pug', and it was moved by barrow to the 'moulder' and 'flattie' who created the bricks using the 'pug mill'. The 'page-boy' loaded the bricks onto a special long barrow, and they were unloaded and laid out on boards in the field by the 'bearer off'. When partly dry the bricks were spaced out for further drying. The final main process was the burning of the 'greens', using a kiln or the older process of clamps. This brickfield by the main road closed in 1885, and the items offered at the auction held in May included—

    a six horse-power portable engine by Reynolds & Co.,
    all driving gear,
    clay, chalk, and pug mills,
    engine and moulding sheds,
    about 1500 feet run of double bank boards,
    2000 feet run back covers and lee boards,
    50 kiln boards,
    50 sheets of corrugated iron,
    300 feet run wheeling plates and planks,
    crowding, off-bearing and other barrows,
    moulding tables,
    pallet boards,
    screws,
    sieves,
    clay and
    water troughs etc.
    5000 two-inch drainpipes.

All were sold without reserve and as George Wren probably bought from here for his new brickfield on the further side of the village, he may well have paid a bargain price. Wren's brickfield caused the tenant of nearby Mayes Place to complain that smoke and fumes were damaging his fruit trees. Following an injunction to abate the nuisance George Wren had to set his clamps at the furthest side of the field near the wood. After Wren's brickmaking ceased James and William Tappenden re-opened the old brickfield abandoned in 1885. They had a kiln, and the work there lasted about 12 years, closing in 1914. In the 1930s pigs were kept in the field, and in the years just after World War II it was the regular pitch for the travelling fair.

The Noble Lowndes sports ground, on a field which had the name Pond Sheeplands, is one of several sportsfields on this side of Warlingham. The next plot, of just under 11 acres and having a frontage to Limpsfield Road of 530 feet, had been attached to the Crewes estate, but was part of a Lot which George Smith did not buy. In 1840 it came into the possession of Francis Tummons. 'Mill House' was built on the corner site nearest to *The Leather Bottle*, and a windmill erected, set back near the edge of the field. It is described as a brickbuilt smock mill of five storeys, with sails on a revolving cap. It replaced the much earlier wooden post mill, sited just over the parish boundary in Chelsham, which had burnt down in *c.*1840. The location of the post mill is remembered by 'Mill House' and Mill Common in Chelsham Road.

In the 1840s and 1850s the Warlingham miller was Amos Ashby. He was followed by Aaron David Ashby, and it was during his tenancy that, on 24th April 1865, the mill caught fire. It was badly damaged, and the ruin stood for some years, Tummons having decided against expenditure to restore it to working order. The 'Mill House' and land came under new ownership after his death in 1878. The house was enlarged, an extension on the side became a shop, and a bakehouse was built nearby. In the 1890s William Brown, baker and grocer, also had the sub-post office.

Section of millstone from Ashby's windmill, which until 1865 stood in the field behind 'Mill House'. Now in the grounds of Warlingham Library.

The whole property was put up for sale in 1924. On the ground floor of 'Mill House' was a sitting room, dining room, parlour with access to the shop, kitchen and larder. Above were five bedrooms and a drawing room. It is worthy of note that the principal rooms were wired for electric light. The scullery, dairy, and two WCs were in buildings out in the back yard, and there was a large kitchen garden. The bakehouse had been converted into a four-roomed cottage, with a galvanised iron roof. The farm buildings beyond could accommodate 26 cows and eight horses; also there were two ranges of pigstyes, chicken houses, several cart sheds and other buildings. H Hope rented a plot of land at the rear as a timber yard.

In the 1930s the shop sold bread and cakes and King's 'Mill House Tea Rooms and Summer Gardens' offered refreshments to passers-by. During World War II the Women's Voluntary Service made use of the shop premises; its local branch headquarters were at 'Dunsmore' in Landscape Road. In May 1945 a sub-food office was established there, staffed by WVS members, which saved local people the time-consuming journey to and from Caterham Valley.

A footpath, approached by a stile, led between the grounds of *The Leather Bottle* public house and 'Mill House' and out along the edge of the field past the site of the mill. The further section still exists, starting from the top corner of Shelton Avenue, alongside the Vicarage field and into Mill Walk which emerges into Hillbury Road by Cannon Place cottages.

1906. Looking towards The Green, and (centre) *The Leather Bottle.*
On the right is 'Mill House', in front of which is a water meter. Just
beyond is another of the first gas street lamps.

Until the early 1950s Shelton Avenue consisted of a few bungalows. Then 'Mill House' was demolished and the land developed. H Hope & Sons moved their coal and wood yard to a site off Mint Walk. The new buildings included a library and a police house. The Warlingham branch of the Surrey County Library had been opened in September 1927 in the Village Club. The first honorary librarian was R W Peacock, headmaster of the Council School in Farleigh Road. The library was open one day a week, and after a while the books were housed in the Mission Room where store-cupboards were provided. The library was manned by volunteers, a few of whom gave their time for many years. One of the longest serving of these volunteers was Mrs Alice Tutt, who ran the children's section from 1938 until 1954. The present library was officially opened on Saturday 1st May 1954.

Warlingham was originally in the Metropolitan Police Area, and in the later 19th century came within the area of the Horse Patrol which was based at the cottages in Limpsfield Road, north of Hamsey Green. During World War II there were two Metropolitan Police blue telephone boxes in Warlingham, one by The Green next to the siren, and the other opposite *The Harrow*.   From April 1947 Warlingham came under the Surrey County Police area, and the blue police boxes were removed.

The route from Limpsfield Road alongside the old brickfield and through to Tithepit Shaw Lane is now only a bridleway, but in the past provided an important access to the fields. Crewes Lane was also originally an access track to fields. As now a path went off to the left – this crosses Crewes Avenue – while another, now developed into Ward Lane, passed along the top of Lower Church field to the church. Ahead the track soon reached one of the fields belonging to Crewes Farm, and continued as a path around the edge of the field to the farm. Before the enclosure of the common in 1866 the route from Crewes Farm was along Crewes Farm Lane which is now a bridleway. After enclosure this route was doubled in length, and in the later 19th century the paths from the farm towards Farleigh Road and Limpsfield Road developed into the present Crewes Lane, the latter direction cutting out the need to go through the village centre. Most of this lane remains unsurfaced.

In 1913 Auguste Corner Reynard was granted a 14 year lease of 39 acres in this vicinity which included Lower Church field. Later on he was able to buy some of the land, and sold the Limpsfield Road frontage of Lower Church field to developers in 1930. The remainder was acquired by Caterham and Warlingham Urban District Council, and developed from 1946 onwards.

Upper Church field had a similar long frontage to the road. It had been arable, but when the use changed to pasture or meadow a diagonal route evolved, crossing to the church from the corner nearest to the village. Access was through a 'kissing gate', but there was also a field gate to open for church parades and funerals. In 1907 Church Road was made on the route of this path. The older route to the church, the footpath alongside the adjacent Glebe field and along the top of Upper Church field, now Church Lane, still exists. The sports field, previously part of the Crewes estate, had the name Upper Cannon.

Allotments were established on Glebe field in 1893. The tenancy was on an annual basis, and the opening ceremony took place on 25th March. Nine allotments were lost when land fronting the road was sold for the building of the Post Office sorting office. This stood from 1938 to 1993, and the site is now occupied by the warehouse of Norwood Aquarium Ltd. In 1958 further frontage was sold and the telephone exchange was built. In 1993 the church authorities gave the allotment holders one year's notice, and the allotments were then relocated to the Vicarage field which remains glebe land. In 1998 a small public car park was established behind the warehouse, and building on the remainder of the land started in November of that year.

SOURCES

Abstract of Title – Land by Limpsfield Road.

BEADELL, A *Memories cf Warlingham.*

GOODMAN, C H *Parish Notes.*

Mill House – Sale document 1924.

Tithe Assessment 1842.

Warlingham & Chelsham Parish Magazine.

Chapter 13

Enclosure of the Common on the North-East of Limpsfield Road

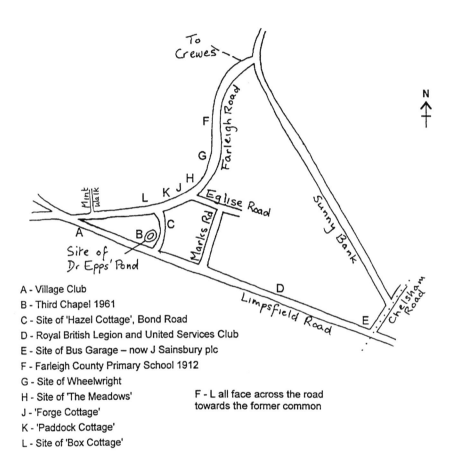

A - Village Club
B - Third Chapel 1961
C - Site of 'Hazel Cottage', Bond Road
D - Royal British Legion and United Services Club
E - Site of Bus Garage – now J Sainsbury plc
F - Farleigh County Primary School 1912
G - Site of Wheelwright
H - Site of 'The Meadows'
J - 'Forge Cottage'
K - 'Paddock Cottage'
L - Site of 'Box Cottage'

F - L all face across the road
towards the former common

Before the Enclosure Award of 1866 the whole area bounded by Farleigh Road, Sunny Bank, a short stretch of Chelsham Road, and Limpsfield Road was open common. Farleigh Road and Sunny Bank, already well established routes along the edge of the common, and Bond Road, a connecting route below the rising ground, were made official roads in 1866. Chelsham Road lies on the parish boundary. Most of the 18 acres of land sold to cover the legal cost of enclosure were in this part of Warlingham.

The Earl of Cottenham was allotted a 15 acre corner plot with a long frontage to Limpsfield Road, and with frontages also to Chelsham Road and Sunny Bank his plot had five sides. Behind this plot a parallel strip of two and a quarter acres, with only a narrow frontage to Sunny Bank, was allotted to Sir William Clayton.

Three adjacent strips, totalling 10 acres, with frontage to the main road and of similar depth to the Earl of Cottenham's plot, were sold to Daniel Church for £800. It was in this area that notable archaeological finds were later discovered. The next section, bounded by three roads, was divided up – Charles Bassett paid £210 for the one and a half acre corner plot facing the main road and Bond Road. Mrs Julia Bassett was allotted the two and a half acres with Bond Road and Farleigh Road frontage. She held the copyhold of two cottages on this land, the only enclosure on the wide expanse of common. Beyond, a half acre strip was allotted to Richard Ward. The next plot was that purchased by the Revd E F Beynon for £275, and then came one and a quarter acres allotted to George Saker. The remainder of this part of the common, down to Crewes Corner and on the further side of the road, some 16 acres, was allotted to Atwood Dalton Wigsell, lord of the manor.

Dr Epps' pond, created in 1847, was by Bond Road. It was a large pond, enclosed by hedge and gate to exclude animals, and was one of the five mentioned in the Enclosure Award. The site, near the main road, was in the corner of a plot held by the Sayers, and the upper part of that field was allotted to Richard Ramsey Bond, the elder.

'Sunney Bank' cottages were built by Richard Ward in 1867, and a few other cottages were soon built nearby on the Crewes Common side of the road. The name, Sunny Bank, spelt correctly, became the road name, and is very apt. After the death of Atwood Dalton Wigsell in 1878, it became possible for several copyholders to buy the freehold of their land. The £496 paid by the Earl of Cottenham included the 15 acre plot he had been allotted. It was to remain undeveloped until after 1920, by which time the current Earl had relinquished any direct interest in the land. Richard Ward and Richard Ramsey Bond also acquired the freehold of land they held. Daniel Church increased his holding to over 12 acres by acquiring Beynon's plot which abutted his land. With the new Oxted railway line about to open it was time to sell. Eglise and Marks Roads were laid out, and on 17th June 1884 the Church Estate was advertised by C & F Rutley to be sold by auction at 6.00 pm. at *The White Lion*. The land was offered as—

'50 plots of valuable building land with frontages of 50 and 25 feet and depth 130 feet.'

The advertisement mentioned good roads, water laid on, productive soil, and the location 600 feet above sea level with extensive views. It would seem the response was poor, probably due to the much larger Westhall Estate being available, nearer the station.

On 7th October 1885 the remaining 30 freehold building plots and a house named 'Oakwood', which had been built on a plot with a 66 foot frontage to the main road, were offered again by C & F Rutley in an auction at *The White Lion*. All the land was eventually sold, and the houses built were well spaced out. 'Marston', built around 1906 for Alexander Hay, stood in extensive grounds. After a span of 90 years this house was demolished, replaced by three detached houses with frontages to Eglise Road. Marston Drive had been built a few years earlier on land here. Manor Close was built off Eglise Road, and this pleasant area is now fully developed.

In documents Richard Ramsey Bond is described as an estate agent, but judging by the amount of land and property which is detailed in his will, it would seem he was acquiring the best for himself. He was living in 'Seymour Cottage' in Godstone Road by the Caterham railway line, when he paid £290 for the freehold of the land and cottages that had been held by Mrs Julia Bassett and the whole of the triangular plot from Bond Road to the Village Club Hall. His name occurs again in connection with 'Box Cottage', nearby in Farleigh Road.

Richard Ramsey Bond died in 1891. His will, drawn up in July of that year, indicates that the land and property in London and Middlesex was to go to his daughters, Mary and Sarah. That in Caterham and Warlingham was bequeathed to his son, Richard Ramsey the younger. This Richard, and his family, lived in 'Hazel Cottage'. This was on the site of the much older cottages mentioned previously, but whether any of the earlier structure remained is not known. With Bonds living in 'Hazel Cottage' and owning the nearby land it is not surprising that the road acquired the name of Bond Road.

By a deed dated 13th April 1900, Richard Ramsey Bond the younger conveyed a plot of land to the vicar and trustees to be used for the erection of a club hall for the benefit of the local people. The money to pay for the building was raised locally over the next two years. The local firm of John Quittenton undertook the

The Working Men's Club, now known as the Village Club, in 1904. It was opened on 17th November 1902, built by Quittenton on land given by Richard Ramsey Bond the younger.

The third Methodist Church was completed on this site near Bond Road in 1961, and the Hall in 1971.

'Hazel Cottage', Bond Road, in 1961 – not long before it was demolished. Richard Ramsey Bond the younger lived here. Flats were built on the site.

construction, and the Working Men's Club was opened on 17th November 1902. The membership soon reached about 100. The facilities included bathrooms – a great luxury. It would be nearly 30 years before main drainage was available in the village, so the cess-pit/soakaway provision was an important element of the structure. During World War I the hall was commandeered for army use, and this was to occur again for civil defence purposes in the World War II period. Over the years the building has existed through good and bad periods, but there have been great improvements since the 1970s, and numerous local events take place in what is now called the Village Hall.

During the next few years terraced houses were built along the main road. When Richard Ramsey Bond left Warlingham about 1910 he still retained ownership of some property in the area. 'Hazel Cottage' stood until the early 1960s when it was replaced by 'Hazel Court' flats, and houses were built on the Farleigh Road frontage of what had been known in the past as Mr Bond's field, often used for local events. Dr Epps' pond was filled in a year or two before the advent of main drainage. Surplus soil from the drainage work was used to build up the site, which since 1931 has been a household waste site, currently run by the County Council. Only by looking down into the corner of the Methodist Church car park can one obtain an idea of the original levels in this area.

The first buses came through Warlingham in 1921. Within a year or so, with more vehicles in operation, a garage was deemed necessary to resolve the problem of an overnight location. In 1924 a site was acquired on the corner of Limpsfield Road and Chelsham Road, and the garage was officially opened on 20th January 1925. Consisting mainly of a metal framework and corrugated iron sheeting it was condemned by the local residents as 'very ugly'. Although in Warlingham, the operating company named it 'Chelsham Garage'. In 1931 it was enlarged, increasing capacity from eight to 24 buses. Shop premises were built alongside, with tea rooms behind which became a transport café. Beyond the shop a garage was established to meet the needs of the increasing number of private motorists.

**The Bus Garage in 1962, much enlarged since it was originally built in late 1924.
Next door is the General Store and Pudney & Sims' garage. By September 1994
J Sainsbury plc had opened its store on the site.**

ENCLOSURE OF THE COMMON ON THE NORTH-EAST OF LIMPSFIELD ROAD

It was also 1924 when a strip of land 150 feet deep, and with a frontage of 550 feet from behind the bus garage site into Sunny Bank, was sold for £825 to Francis Crichton Jackson. Houses were built on this land, and also further down Sunny Bank by the early 1930s. A few houses were built on the slope of Farleigh Road, but a large area here, and another with access from the main road, remained undeveloped until the 1950s when Cranmer Gardens and Close, and Crowborough Drive and Close were built.

The local branch of the Royal British Legion acquired a site on the main road in the 1920s. The present Royal British Legion and United Services Club building dates from 1950.

After 65 years the lease held by the bus company expired. The site was cleared in 1990 and the land sold. The redevelopment of the site became a very controversial matter which took a full three years to resolve. The site on which J Sainsbury plc eventually built its store, which opened on 13th September 1994, was considerably larger than that previously occupied by the bus company.

At the time of the 1866 enclosure there were a few buildings alongside the track which became Farleigh Road. Here the blacksmith and wheelwright lived and worked. Members of the Baker family followed this trade over many years, and the slope from the school to Crewes Corner is still known as Baker's Hill. In the 1920s the old cottages near the footpath to Mint Walk and the remaining buildings where the wheelwright had worked,were demolished. The Crew Bank Laundry along with Wade & Sons, engineers and machinists, and Jacksons, plumbers, sanitary and heating engineers were in this vicinity for many years

Beyond the entrance to the footpath to Mint Walk were these weatherboarded cottages, and then Baker's, the wheelwright. This view dates from about 1905.

Until 1912 children of all ages were taught in the Council School on the Common. The need for a new school for the older children was agreed, and a site found in Farleigh Road. The design used was similar to that at Roke, built a few years earlier, having a central hall with classrooms leading off both sides. The official opening of the new Council School was held on Saturday 14th September 1912. The headmaster was Melville W R Perry, who had replaced J D Clarke in 1910. J Bushby continued as chairman of the school managers, with H T E Jarrett the clerk, as before. Probably the greatest change to affect the school was in the 1950s when those in Tithepit Shaw Lane opened. This school is now called Farleigh County Primary School and there is no lack of demand for places. In 2012 there will be a centenary to celebrate, and it is hoped that the school will continue far beyond that special occasion.

Farleigh Road School in 1999. The word 'Road' does not appear in the present name - Farleigh County Primary School' - but the only connection the school has with Farleigh is that it is in a road that eventually crosses into that parish.

Beyond the access to the footpath to Mint Walk was a two and a half acre plot, mainly meadow, which gave the name to the cottage built in the corner by the road. Dr Epps, who practised homoeopathy, came to 'Meadow Cottage' in 1845, and remained for some years. The first medical doctors to reside in the village came here. Dr Ross Todd had the house rebuilt, and renamed 'The Meadows'. The house was demolished in 1986, and 'The Meadows' was the name given to the new development on the land.

The next building is 'Forge Cottage'. Today this is one cottage, but was originally two. The older cottage dates possibly from the late 17th century, and the brick built cottage probably from the later 18th century. The long established forge site was on the land now occupied by a modern house. Blanchard took over from Baker, and in the 1880s it was William Blanchard and his family who lived in the cottage by the forge. In 1891, when Dorcas Ward, owner of the whole site, died, William Blanchard was able to buy the two cottages, forge and land for £380. For some years he and his son were at this forge, and Arthur Baker, dealing much more with the wheelwright's work, was at the other premises along the road.

By 1910 a larger forge building, set end on to the road, had replaced the older buildings which had abutted the cottage. Many a child loitered on the way to or from school to watch the blacksmith at work. The forge eventually closed in about 1950, and the new owner of the property had the changes made which, along with modern improvements, have combined to make 'Forge Cottage' a most attractive residence.

Built on a site previously a corner of the land attached to the forge, 'Paddock Cottage' dates from 1859. Originally two up and two down, with a central stair, it was enlarged at the rear – about 100 years ago and at the side c.1960. The original walls are very thick. Dorcas Ward must have been in poor health, and she was only 49

Blanchard's Forge
in Farleigh Road,
and 'Forge Cottage'
in about 1905.

The final resting
place of the bellows
from Blanchard's
Forge – in 1966 in
the garden of 'Forge
Cottage'.

Farleigh Road about
1912. On the left is
'Forge Cottage', and
beyond is a glimpse
of 'The Meadows'.

when she died in 1891. She bequeathed 'Paddock Cottage' and garden, her silver plate, the greater part of her furniture, books, pictures, glass, ornaments and other household goods to her companion, Mary Ann Jane Brooke, who had cared for her.

Next to 'Paddock Cottage' stood 'Box Cottage', also known as 'Webb's Cottage' from the family of that name who lived there many years.

SOURCES

Croydon Advertiser.

East Surrey by 'Bell Street'.

Enclosure Award 1866.

Indenture – Forge Cottage.

Wills – Bond, R R (Elder), Ward D.

Advertisements from the 1930s

Chapter 14

North of The Green and Farleigh Road

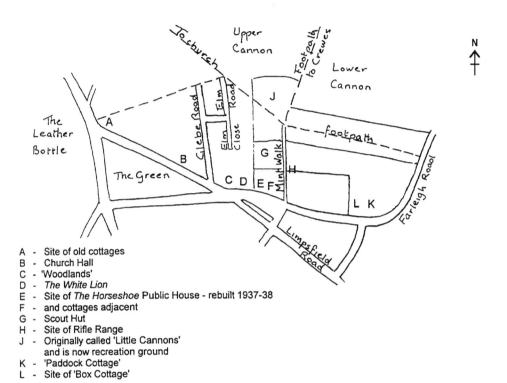

A - Site of old cottages
B - Church Hall
C - 'Woodlands'
D - *The White Lion*
E - Site of *The Horseshoe* Public House - rebuilt 1937-38
F - and cottages adjacent
G - Scout Hut
H - Site of Rifle Range
J - Originally called 'Little Cannons'
     and is now recreation ground
K - 'Paddock Cottage'
L - Site of 'Box Cottage'

When George Smith bought the Crewes estate in the 1820s he also bought two detached lots, both on the east side of the open common. One was a strip of one and a half acres, which had a narrow access from the edge of the common, and through this land the footpath from Farleigh Road to Mint Walk still passes. The second consisted of two cottages on a small plot opposite *The Leather Bottle*.

His son, George Robert, could not obtain more land to the west as that was all part of the Wigsell estate but he did buy Richard Ward's land to the south which abutted his, except for the house in Mint Walk and a good size plot behind it. He also bought two plots which in 1844 had been owned by James Izzard. One was the large field bordered by Farleigh Road which stretched up the slope to Mint Walk, with 'Box Cottage' in one corner. The other was the land abutting the cottages opposite *The Leather Bottle* which he already owned, and this gave him a frontage to The Green when the common was enclosed in 1866. He also bought the greater part of the meadow which had given 'Meadow Cottage' its name, and so held all the back land behind the forge and other cottages on Farleigh Road. He died in 1869.

Richard Ward was about two years old when his parents came to Warlingham in 1805, and 40 years later he and his wife Elizabeth were living in a house facing the open common on the corner of Mint Walk. They had five children, Alfred, John, Joel, Ann Sarah and Dorcas, and were very active supporters of the Wesleyan Methodist chapel. Behind his house Richard Ward owned a long narrow strip of land extending back to the modern Boxwood Way. Nearby he had fields called Little Cannons on the west side of the footpath to Crewes, and a field on the east side which was between fields owned by George Robert Smith. It is possible that peppermint was grown somewhere in this area, which gave Mint Walk its name. On the further side of the common land Richard Ward held the Thrift fields, by Bug Hill road, leased from the manor. He also held about half of an enclosure on the common, part meadow and part land where 'Fir Cottage', known since 1915 as 'Manor Cottage', and 'Roselea' stand. Apart from farming Richard Ward set up as a builder, and was also an undertaker.

The remaining land, which after enclosure had frontage to The Green, was owned by Charles Edmonds, who lived at Bishopstone, near Shrivenham, Berkshire. In 1866 he paid £30 for a strip of newly enclosed common, some 30 perches, which was in front of a barn and a pair of cottages on the edge of his land. In the next year or so these buildings were demolished. The Wards bought land next to *The White Lion*, and built 'Woodlands' which became the home of Joel and his wife Annie. This is the only Ward family home still existing at the present time, though used as office premises. The land at the side, previously garden, has been for many years now a car park for *The White Lion*. On 24th April 1883 three and a half acres of land were sold to The House Property Trust Ltd. Glebe Road and the further stretch of Elm Road were laid out. The first houses built were 'Fernlee Villas', dated 1883. Others were built, a gradual process over some years, and many are named and carry a date. About an acre, behind *The White Lion*, was not used for housing until the later 1930s when Elm Close was built.

The old cottages that stood opposite *The Leather Bottle,* not long before they were demolished in 1957. Beyond is the Post Office Sorting Office.

The Hon Mrs Mabel E G Greville, granddaughter of George Robert Smith, inherited his Warlingham land, some of which she put into an auction held on 15th July 1890. One piece fronted The Green, and the houses there were erected by the local builder, Quitterton. The Smiths had renovated and altered the pair of cottages some years previously, the dormer windows added to the upper floor having altered their appearance considerably since the watercolour by John Hassell in the 1820s. The cottages stood until 1957, and were replaced by a block of shops. An odd triangular piece of land at the rear has for many years been the location of small business premises.

Ebenezer Wilson established a draper and grocer's shop in premises by The Green near Glebe Road, and this was soon doing well. About 10 years later, in 1898, Richard Joseph Ringer took over the Warlingham and

The Green, 1904. On the far side is the first Wesleyan Chapel, to the front of which a substantial porch was added. The large barn is visible beyond the window of *The Leather Bottle* on the right.

Mrs G Reed and her pupils of Blenheim House School, 1928. This was a 'Dame' school held in one of the pair of houses named 'Blenheim Villas', which faced The Green.

The recently completed Church Hall, in 1915 taken over for use as a temporary military hospital. From 1916 to 1919 the Hall was used as a soldiers' club.

Chelsham Stores. He and his wife Mary had come from a similar business in Handcroft Road, Croydon, where they had been for about 20 years. Their daughters, Winifred and Maud, worked in the Warlingham shop. Another premises over on *The Leather Bottle* side of The Green became a hardware shop, run by their son, Stanley. Their sons, Walter and Horace, emigrated to New Zealand, one in 1912 and the other in 1914. Son Herbert married Kate Hollamby, and they had three daughters. For a few years they lived across the road at 'Homewood', another former Ward family home, where there were tea gardens. When Walter emigrated in 1912, having run a shop at Tatsfield for several years, Herbert and his family moved there. Later on the family lived in Brighton, and in 1923, while travelling to Surrey, Herbert was killed in a railway accident. His wife took two of the girls, Muriel and Patricia, to New Zealand to be brought up with their cousins.

The building to the side of Ringer's stores contained living accommodation. On the ground floor the front room was used by a branch of the Union of London & Smith's Bank Ltd. Before World War I this was open on Monday and Friday from 11.00 a.m. to 2.00 p.m. After the war the name changed to the National Provincial & Union Bank of England, and the opening hours were Monday to Friday, 11.00 a.m. to 2.00 p.m. In 1927 the new National Provincial Bank building, designed by local architect, Briant A. Poulter ARIBA, opened on the corner of Glebe Road. Hours were then extended to 9.30 a.m to 3.00 p.m. Monday to Friday, and 9.00 a.m. to 12 noon on Saturday.

Ringer's Stores in 1914. The Bank used the front room of the living accommodation.

Richard Joseph Ringer died in 1924, and the shop was taken over by Robert E Coatman. Stanley Ringer continued with his hardware business until retirement. In 1938 Cullens Stores Ltd took over from W E Coatman, and the premises were subsequently rebuilt, with flats above, approached from the rear. As a family grocer, with a hardware section, it remained very much part of the village scene for the next 50 years. After a short time as a delicatessen, the shop closed in December 1992 and reopened in December 1993 as a branch of the wine merchants 'Bottoms Up'. One of the pair of houses built on the frontage by Glebe Road became a tobacconist's and confectioner's in the 1920s. In 1984 the adjoining house, used by an estate agent, was demolished, and the site redeveloped.

Small private schools, often known as 'Dame' schools, still existed until the early 1940s. In the 1930s there was one, run by the Misses Simmons and Quittenton, in a room in the Village Club. Another, of slightly earlier date, was at 'Blenheim Villas' by The Green, run by Mrs G Reed. Other private schools in the 1930s included

'Amandus', in Westhall Road, and 'Gracedieu' School in Chelsham Road. As the population grew the School hall and the Mission Room by the Almshouses became inadequate for local meetings. It was decided that a parish hall would fulfil the needs of all the organisations which required an indoor venue. Fund raising started in 1911, and by January 1914 the building fund had reached £1150. A site was found near Ringer's Stores, and J C King, architect, was appointed. The estimate of £1427 basic cost from the local builder Quittenton was accepted, and work started in June 1914. Early in 1915 the Hall was in use, then in March it was commandeered by the military authorities for hospital accommodation. The staff were nurses from the Voluntary Aid Detachment of the British Red Cross Society. From October 1916 to March 1919 the hall was used as a soldiers' club. Costs for heating and other fitments not included in the estimate had to be met, and fund raising continued until the debt was extinguished in 1922.

In 1925 Charles Langton Lockton, churchwarden at All Saints', set up a small museum in the upper room of the Hall. A wide range of items of local interest were brought together in a display case. These included archaeological finds, descriptions of which appeared at the time of discovery in the parish magazine – a churchwarden's wand, pewter, and manuscript music used in the 19th century in All Saints' church, a 16th century spoon found at Tydcombe Farm, cow and sheep bells, horseshoes, etc. Paintings by Charles L Lockton of local scenes and buildings which existed during his earlier years in the village were displayed on the walls. These paintings are now housed in the library. Other items were added to the museum in later years, such as the plaque from the gun which stood on The Green between the wars. In 1980, when the East Surrey Museum was established in Caterham, the items in the Warlingham Museum were transferred there.

Many events have taken place in the Church Hall over the years – music and amateur dramatic performances, bazaars, jumble sales, markets, film shows, dancing, badminton, whist drives and meetings. In 1939 the Hall was again commandeered, but was handed back to parish use at the end of 1942. In 1953 a clock was put in the bullseye window in the façade to commemorate the coronation of Queen Elizabeth II. In the later 1980s and into the 1990s locally raised funds and a grant from Tandridge District Council were used for necessary repairs and refurbishment. Since 1990 the Hall has been managed by a charitable company composed of representatives from local organisations, under the name of Warlingham Church Hall Ltd.

The Church Activities Club in the Church Hall on 6th December 1938. The social evening was arranged by the Cricket Club, and many members of the Sports Club were present.

The Vicar, Revd F R Dickinson, can be seen towards the rear of the group.

C L Lockton constructed this scene from a sketch and information provided by Ann Sarah Windross.

Before the Common was enclosed the barn and cottage stood near *The White Lion*, the former about where Glebe Road is now.

In the 1840s Richard Shallcross owned *The White Lion*, sometimes just called *The Lion*, which faced the open common, but was set back behind a pond and a row of trees. Nine trees survived well into the 20th century, the last being removed in 1978. The pond was filled in around 1885, as was another pond nearby where the fine turkey oak stands today. *The White Lion* is listed as Grade II, 17th century, and as is to be expected includes work done later. Internally there is some indication of a building earlier than the general date given. The earliest photograph available shows the building before the rebuilding phase of the later 19th century. Fortunately only the weatherboarded section – which may well have needed replacement anyway – was lost. Over the years alterations have been done to this later wing, the mock tudor effect being added in the 1920s.

Licensees known to be of long standing include the Sayers from 1799 to 1825, followed by Stephen and Samuel Davey, the Churchills from 1868 to 1940, and G W Adams from 1940 to 1970.

Beyond, by Mint Walk, was a row of old cottages. Older residents will remember them, as they were not demolished until 1937. Such information as can be gained from photographs would indicate a possible late 17th century date, similar to 'Forge Cottage'. The vestry minute book has an entry for 13th October 1847 – 'New licensed beer house, prop. G. Brooks'. This was the start of *The Horseshoe*. The 1869 OS map shows the building which, with additions at the rear and alteration of detail to the façade, stood until 1937. In a directory of 1855 George Brooks is given as grocer, beer retailer and postmaster. A family by the name of Lee were licensees for many years, certainly from the early 1870s onwards, and in 1899 there was 'Emma Lee & Sons, Beer retailers and Bakers'.

The cottages lost any earlier name they may have had, and became Horseshoe, or Lee's, Cottages. All were demolished when the present *Horseshoe* public house was built in 1937/38.

Another piece of land which the Hon Mrs Greville put into the 1890 auction was that bordering Farleigh Road which included 'Box Cottage'. Richard Ramsey Bond the elder bought this for £600. The sale included an agreement to realign the upper boundary to make Mint Walk 12 feet wide. 'Ivy Cottages', on the corner of Mint Walk and Farleigh Road, replaced Richard Ward's house, probably in the 1870s. Richard Ramsey Bond the younger, who inherited his father's property in Caterham and Warlingham in 1891, provided a strip of land along Mint Walk for the erection of premises for the Miniature Rifle Club. The building cost £175, and was opened on 9th January 1909.

The White Lion as it looked about 1890 before the weatherboard addition was replaced by a more substantial wing.

This view, taken in 1910, shows the great difference between the old building and the addition remains distinct, despite the creeper which has been allowed to cover it.

This view, *c.*1930, shows the mock Tudor work added to the façade, and new windows and door.

The Horseshoe Beer House was first licensed in 1847. This flint and brick building was probably constructed that year, as it did not exist at the time of the 1842 Tithe Assessment.

Demolished 1937/38.

The Horseshoe Public House in 1999.

The cottages, pictured in 1902, were known latterly as Lee's or Horseshoe Cottages. They dated – in part – possibly from the later 17th century.

Demolished 1937/38.

On 4th October 1929 Bond conveyed a small plot adjacent to 'Ivy Cottages', to the Urban Electricity Supply Co. Ltd. After his death in 1935 his widow put land into auction. On 24th August 1936 Charles Tuckfield, of White Knobs Farm, Caterham, paid £2165 for 'Box Cottage' and land, and the land across the road still vacant, in the corner of which was the waste site – called officially the 'Civic Amenity Site'. In September 1936 Tuckfield conveyed a plot with frontage to Farleigh Road to Henry Lee, of 'Nyddcombe', Chapel Road, and houses were soon built there. The Webbs, who were long standing tenants of 'Box Cottage', remained there during the changes of ownership. In 1938 Tuckfield sold 'Box Cottage' and the remaining land to Harold Thomas for £1050. The rifle range was demolished, and Boxwood Way was built. 'Box Cottage', on its own small plot, remained until after World War II, then was replaced by a modern house. Other houses were built, leaving one vacant area, and this was bought by the Methodist Church Trustees in 1951 for £150.

'Box Cottage' was probably built in the 18th century. In 1842 James Green was the tenant here. This photograph dates from the early 1900s.

The land, bordered on the east by Mint Walk and on the west by the rear gardens of Elm Road, was known in the past as Little Cannons, and it was included in the land purchased in the early 1920s by the Warlingham Sports Club. Quite soon the Scouts took over the southernmost part, while the rest remained a field across which the footpaths were in regular use. In 1934 Caterham and Warlingham Urban District Council purchased this open space for an official recreation ground and a playground for children. The formal opening was performed by the Chairman of the Council, Cllr H Foulds on Saturday 2nd June 1934. Those present included boys and girls from Warlingham school, with headmaster H Myatt, and representatives from the Scouts, British Legion, St John Ambulance and Fire Brigade. The original playground equipment was set up along the length of the ground, a paddling pool, swings, a see-saw and an ocean wave, also known as a witch's hat, the site of which is still visible. The modern equipment includes swings, a slide and a climbing frame, and is on an enclosed corner site.

In the autumn of 1909 a proposal was made that a group be started for local boys, 11 to 13 years of age, who were too young to join the Church Lads Brigade. The 1st Warlingham Scout Troop was officially registered in 1912, and the Cubs were established in 1916. Soon after the end of World War I Major C A Boraston became Scoutmaster, and the troop flourished under his leadership, and that of Fred E Wade. The land by Mint Walk was initially rented, then purchased, and an ex-army hut erected there for headquarters. In August 1924 work commenced on the making of a swimming pool. This took three years, and was officially opened on 6th June 1927. It was well used in the 1930s, but after World War II the cost of repairs and general upkeep became increasingly prohibitive. In July 1955 new gates erected at the entrance to the pool were dedicated, in a ceremony led by a past vicar, the Revd F R Dickinson, to the memory of the late Major C A Boraston who had done so much for the troop between 1921 and 1931. Eventually the decision was made to sell the land on which the old headquarters stood, fill in the swimming pool, and build a new headquarters on that site. This was opened in November 1969, and the then vicar, Canon F R Longworth-Dames rededicated the gates. Currently the Cub Scouts meet on Monday evenings, and the 1st Warlingham Scout Troop on Friday evenings.

The Fife and Drum Band was formed in June 1934 under the direction of Drum Major Etches of the Whitgift Cadet Corps. It closed down during the war as many members were in the services, but was revived postwar. In 1951 it amalgamated with Purley 285 Squadron ATC Old Cadets' Band, and assumed the title 'The Flute Band of the Warlingham B-P Scout Guild'. The bandmaster since 1952 has been M Harewood, and for 46 years Warlingham Church Hall has been the venue for an annual concert. The Warlingham Branch of the B-P Scout Guild holds an annual reunion in the Warlingham headquarters in Mint Walk.

SOURCES

Box Cottage – document.

Croydon Advertiser.

Directories.

Enclosure Award 1866.

GOODMAN, C H *Parish Notes.*

HAREWOOD, M.

RINGER – Correspondence with descendants in New Zealand.

Tithe Assessment 1842.

Vestry Minute Book.

Warlingham & Chelsham Parish Magazine.

Advertisements from the 1920s.

Chapter 15

Warlingham Green

In the 1866 Enclosure award just over half an acre of the common, situated at the point where the road from Hamsey Green divided, was designated as an area for public enjoyment and became the village green. The stone, now so embedded within the traffic island that its full size cannot be seen, marked the dividing of the ways long before *The Leather Bottle* was established. Thereafter it has lain at the foot of the inn sign. The road on one side of The Green, sometimes called Warlingham Lane, continued on through the parish and across the heathland, to descend eventually to Limpsfield in the Weald. The other branch passed westwards along the edge of the common towards Westhall Farm. Beyond the farm a narrow lane led between the fields followed by a steep descent to the valley.

There was no official road on the south-west side of The Green where 'Yew Tree Cottage' and the first Wesleyan Chapel stood. Not surprisingly many did take this short cut, and it was proposed, initially in 1885, that a road be made. Eventually, in 1889, the vestry agreed that an official road be made 'from Mr Bond's barn to Mr Ward's garden', and so the triangle was completed. Over the years the central area has shrunk a little due to road improvements. The one-way system was introduced soon after World War II ended.

The stone marking the division of the ways outside *The Leather Bottle*.

The children enjoyed playing on The Green, which was a area of rough grass crossed by paths worn bare by constant use. By the late 1880s there were only two trees, one on the corner near *The Leather Bottle* which stood until around 1970, and another opposite 'Yew Tree Cottage'. This old ash tree had a girth of 11ft 6 ins, and was blown down in November 1902. Lime trees were planted around the edge of The Green as a commemoration of Queen Victoria's 1887 Jubilee, but in course of time some were destroyed. The parish magazine of February 1893 does not use the word 'vandalism' but it was implied in a gentle way—

> '...Those which have been broken will be taken up and others planted. The difficulty arises from the carelessness (we trust it is nothing more) which causes the destruction of the trees. We are loth to believe that it is anything more than carelessness, and we trust that all who have any desire to see the appearance of the village improved will co-operate in preserving the trees, which in the future may become so pleasant a feature.'

These trees still stand, with one or two of later planting. Lopping, or pollarding, used to be carried out at intervals, but it is some years since the last occasion.

4th August 1916.

A service on The Green on the second anniversary of the outbreak of war.

4th December 1921.

The unveiling and dedication of the War Memorial.

R A Price, Vice-Chairman of the War Memorial Committee, is about to start his speech.

Major-General Sir G Ellison stands nearby.

The Howitzer was given by the 17th Battalion, Royal Fusiliers in January 1920.

It was given up for salvage in World War II, but the plaque was preserved.

WARLINGHAM GREEN

The Green was an assembly point for church parades and other events. Open air services were held there during World War I. In January 1919 a War Memorial Committee was elected, which included representatives from the trading and farming sections of the community as well as from the churches and parish council. Having given lengthy consideration to the various proposals, a public meeting was held in June at which the committee stated the outcome of its deliberations. It recommended that the surface of The Green be drained and levelled, the grass cut and trees lopped, paths laid out, the ditch on the north side filled in, and a railing placed to prevent cattle straying onto the grass. A number of people had favoured a memorial in the shape of a clock tower, but the committee had decided that a choice be made between three designs, models of which were on display in the hall, along with a suggested lay-out for The Green. If there was enough money a clock might be placed in the bull's eye window of the church hall. Eventually this was done, but not until 1953, to commemorate the Coronation.

When a vote was taken, the sculptured statuary entitled 'Shielding the Defenceless' put forward by J E Taylerson, received 33 votes, a clear majority over the other two designs which received 12 and 14 respectively. As with the building of the village club hall and the Church Hall, the necessary finance had to be raised locally. By November £250 had been donated. On Saturday 10th January 1920 nearly 200 of the now disbanded 17th Battalion Royal Fusiliers came to Warlingham, and during a service their colour was laid up in All Saints' Church. A Howitzer, which they had captured at Cambrai, was placed on The Green, positioned on a concrete platform. Tea, provided in the church hall, was followed by singing and dancing.

By October 1920 the War Memorial Fund had reached £457, well on the way to the total required which eventually worked out at just over £500. The ceremony of unveiling and dedication was held on Sunday afternoon, 4th December 1921, a bitterly cold day. The Warlingham Brass Band played while the people assembled and to accompany the hymns, which were led by the combined choirs of All Saints' and the Wesleyan Church. Two buglers were present from the Guards' Depot, Caterham, to sound the 'Last Post' and 'Reveille'. Before the Service of Dedication there were two quite long speeches, one by R A Price, vice-chairman of the War Memorial Committee, and the other by Major General Sir G Ellison, KCMG, CB who performed the actual unveiling. Judging by the lengthy report the proceedings must have taken at least three-quarters of an hour – time enough for everyone, however warmly wrapped, to become rather cold! The Guides and Scouts were present, under the command of Miss Sandy and Mr Boraston respectively. The paths were laid out, and the central seat provided, in the spring of 1923.

The Warlingham Brass Band was founded on 5th July 1894. Over the years it performed at many local events. In 1924 it is recorded that the band moved its headquarters to the recently built sports pavilion where they were less likely to disturb the neighbours. This move may not have pleased all the players, as previously they had met at *The Leather Bottle*. In 1926 they bought new uniforms, and in 1928 new instruments, these latter to be paid for in quarterly instalments. It then became the Warlingham Silver Band. Membership dropped in the early 1930s, and in 1933 the band was dissolved, the instruments being stored at *The Horseshoe* public house. In October 1935 the band was reformed, with bandmaster W Boswell, and from that time on was linked to the Royal British Legion, taking part in the Armistice Day parades.

When scrap metal was needed at the beginning of World War II the Howitzer was given up for salvage. The plaque from it was preserved in the museum. A public air raid shelter was dug on The Green. There was no likelihood of not hearing the siren sound an 'alert' as it was situated on the pavement in front of 'Yew Tree Cottage', along with the blue police box. After the war it remained there, being tested occasionally to check that it still worked. It became just another item of street furniture, and was eventually removed some 45 years after the war ended. The air raid shelter also remained, and in 1955 was the subject of correspondence with the Home Office via the local MP Charles Doughty QC. At the time Government policy decreed that it must remain, and it was the 1960s before it was filled in and the ground levelled.

This aerial photograph of the centre of the village dates from the early 1930s and shows several buildings that have been demolished or rebuilt. The allotments make an attractive patchwork.

WARLINGHAM GREEN

6th November 1949.

The vicar, Canon W H Roseveare, leads the Remembrance Day Service.

The war memorial, which is of Portland stone, is listed Grade II. A stone plaque was added at the foot of the pedestal in remembrance of those who gave their lives in World War II. In 1971 the worn paving stones of the paths were replaced, using concrete.

Since the start in 1949 the annual crowning of the May Queen has taken place on The Green. Another annual event is the singing of carols on Christmas Eve, and, of course, the Remembrance Day Service. The Silver Band continued into the 1960s, eventually being disbanded through lack of support. The instruments were loaned to the Surbiton Royal British Legion, and there is now no trace of them.

Today, with cars parked on every side and a continuous stream of traffic passing through the village, The Green is a far from peaceful place.

SOURCES

Enclosure Award 1866.

Vestry Minute Book.

Warlingham & Chelsham Parish Magazine.

A view across The Green in 1963.

The building of shops with flats above has started on the far side. The Green looks neat and well cared for.

The Leather Bottle, probably in 1887. On the left is the butcher's shop, with a passageway through to the abattoir behind.

These cottages stood on the ground attached to *The Leather Bottle,* and were demolished in March 1906. The footpath to the field behind 'Mill House' is visible to the right.

Chapter 16

The West side of The Green

The house building which started in the early 1880s brought a steady increase in the population, and consequently an increase in the demand for locally available goods and services. There was a need for more shops, and it was along this side of The Green that front rooms were converted, and one or two gaps filled with a building constructed to include shop premises. A view of 1912 shows 10 shops on this side. The land on which these buildings stand backs onto the last remaining glebe field.

Pine wood, generally known as deal, was brought into the south coast ports in the second half of the 18th century, and the use of it for construction spread across the southeast of England and into Essex. As cladding it was called 'weatherboard', no doubt because nailed to a timber frame it created a substantial and lasting wall. In Warlingham it was sometimes preserved by applying tar, making it black. However, the earliest available picture of *The Leather Bottle,* dated about 1887, shows the front to be whitened, probably to make the building visible from a distance. The earliest known licensee was William Sampson in the 1780s. At that time the building probably consisted of just the main front block. As with *The Harrow* this public house was owned by Anthony Harman, and then the brewers, Nalder and Collyer. In the 1850s Nathaniel Wilmshurst was the licensee. He was a churchwarden, and several entries in the vestry minute book indicate that meetings started at All Saints' then removed to *The Leather Bottle*, no doubt a more pleasant location on a winter's night. Stephen Dean, whose name is on the inn sign in the old photograph, was licensee in the 1870s and 1880s. This photograph also shows the cottages by the footpath to the Mill field, and in the 1880s their gardens came right down to the road. On the other side is the butcher's shop, and access to the yard behind where the local abattoir was situated. The characters by the door are dressed for a Comic Cricket Match.

The Nalder & Collyer boundary marker that used to be visible set into the ground at the edge of *The Leather Bottle* yard.

In 1861 a new club room was built at the rear of *The Leather Bottle*. In the 1890s a number of public houses were rebuilt. Here the façade was updated, with new window frames and door, signboards, what is either small tilehanging or metalwork on the upper wall, and a fancy metal frieze. A single storey extension at the side provided a saloon bar with entrance from the yard. Above the weatherboarding can still be seen. The yard was created by cutting the cottage gardens back. A tall arch type sign advertised the stabling available at the rear. The cottages were demolished in 1906. A view in the 1920s shows a further change to groundfloor frontage, and in the early 1930s there was a major rebuilding.

The old butcher's shop next door was replaced by a building which provided two shops and living accommodation above and behind. The abattoir remained in use into the 1930s. It was a licensed premises, which indicates more control and better hygienic conditions than those operating at the turn of the century. In the 1920s the two shops were occupied by W Stratton, who sold and repaired boots and shoes, and The Cosy Cafe, proprietor R Brett. Around 1930 Strattons took over the premises next door, and alterations included a

Leather Bottle, Warlingham

The updating of *The Leather Bottle* in the early 1890s included a side extension and façade.

new shop front. The business was carried on for some years after the war by Peggy Stratton, who many will remember. In 1987 this shop was divided again into two units.

The building next door has features which indicate some part of it may date back to the building shown on the 1842 Tithe Map. In the 1920s there were three shops here, A E Frampton, confectioner and tobacconist, H Billingshurst, barber, and G Marriott, fishmonger and poulterer. When Billingshurst moved to his new premises further along in 1928, Frampton's took over his shop and also put in a new shop front. The end shop remained a fishmonger's for some years, a later owner being E Pillings. For some while now it has been a veterinary surgery.

Ye Olde Leather Bottle photographed in about 1936.

In the early 1930s there was a major rebuilding with added mock Tudor effect popular at the time.

A view dating from the early 1900s shows that the next building was a block of three cottages, set back a little, and still retaining their small front gardens. The end cottage had a single storey front extension added to provide shop premises. Using the modern numbering this is No.14, the Tandoori restaurant.

Looking across The Green in the early 1900s.

Ringer's hardware shop is on the extreme left, and the
adjacent cottages had not yet become shops.

A view across The Green in 1986.

There have been a number of changes, and there is a lot more traffic passing through.

In the days before the adjacent cottage became a newsagent and delivery rounds were established locally, the papers were brought up from W H Smith at Upper Warlingham Station by boys who attended Maple Road school in Whyteleafe. In 1902 the headmaster, Mr Honey, reported to the school board that several boys arrived late due to delivering newspapers. He asked that a ruling be made that all pupils in Standards 1, 2 and 3 should be in school by 9.00 a.m. and the register closed at 9.40 a.m. The clerk to the board wrote to W H Smith to say children were delivering papers in school hours, and that the firm was liable to a fine of 40 shillings for each offence. The reply was that the clerk at the station was unaware that regulations were not complied with, and that boys left the station in time to be at school by 9.45 a.m. which was the time he understood to be correct. Some 10 or more years later the situation still existed. Fred Coppard, who did a paper round, recalled that boys who did milk or paper rounds were often caned for arriving late at school. His longest delivery round, with papers loaded on his bicycle, started at *The Hare and Hounds*. Then he cycled to *The Bull*, 'Ledgers', the Hospital, and on to *The Harrow*, where he was often given cocoa or ginger beer – then across into Farleigh Court Road and back via the footpath to Kingswood Lane and Tithepit Shaw Lane to Whyteleafe.

The Hare and Hounds **in 1998.**   *Photo courtesy of Paul Sandford.*

In 1935 W L Coe took over the Warlingham newsagents, and his son, Bill, carried on the business until his retirement in 1987. During his later years a front extension was added to the shop. No.16 may also date in part back to a building on the site in 1844. Previously No.9 it was Stanley Ringer's hardware shop, a double-fronted premises. It seems possible that No.18 started as a single storey side extension, with the upper floor added later. The Village Stores occupied these two premises for some years, then Sykes & Co., who had the modern shop front put in. The end shop, No.20, was a draper's for 40 years, under the name E K Woods. It was taken over in 1975 by 'Maggie' Sheridan, and became a quality dress shop. Beyond the next alleyway is a block of three flint and brick cottages which still retain their tiny front gardens. The double-fronted 'Rose Cottage' is dated 1865. The end building was Billingshurst's new premises, dating from 1928. Under various owners it has remained a hairdresser's and/or barber's ever since. It was common knowledge in the village that Billingshurst took bets, and when betting shops became legal he had a licensed betting office in a front room of 'Rose Cottage'. Tucked away behind is another pair of cottages, dating from the later 19th century.

ROBINSON & HEATH

Telephone:
UPPER WARLINGHAM
10.

ABERDEEN HOUSE, WARLINGHAM

LICENSED ABATTOIR
1 THE GREEN,
WARLINGHAM.

20 Years' Reputation for Quality.

Highest Grade meat only selected by experts and offered at lowest current market prices.

R. K. JACKSON,

Plumber, Glazier, Hot Water & Gas Fitter

" Shenden," Meadway, Warlingham.

Telephone: Upp. Warlingham 278

P. E. GOOD

Builder, Contractor & Decorator

Experienced Workmen.	Personal Supervision.
General Repairs.	Decorating.

Garages, Briquette Fireplaces, Etc.
(*Plans and designs submitted*).

Outwood, 34 Church Road, Warlingham.

Telephone—Upper Warlingham 339

W. L. COE,

Newsagent, Stationer, Bookseller & Tobacconist

Fancy Goods and Library.

The Green, Warlingham

W. STRATTON,

1, THE GREEN, WARLINGHAM,

Practical Boot & Shoe Maker

All kinds of REPAIRS neatly and quickly executed.

Socks, Laces, Polishes, &c, kept in stock.

Work called for and sent home.

Charges strictly moderate.

Balch Bros.

Whyteleafe Branch.
'Phone Upper Warlingham 89.

Warlingham Branch.
'Phone Upper Warl'm 316.

DAIRY FARMERS

Whyteleafe & Warlingham.

New Milk Delivered daily to Kenley, Purley, Caterham, Whyteleafe, Upper Warlingham.

WREATHS, CROSSES
BOUQUETS
and
All Floral Designs
made to order.

♦♦♦

CUT FLOWERS.

THE GLEBE

Fruit & Vegetable Stores,

❧❀❧

'Phone Upper Warlingham 288

SALADS IN
SEASON.

♦♦♦

High-Class Fruit.

♦♦♦

POT PLANTS, etc.

OUR MOTTO IS QUALITY AT LOWEST MARKET PRICES

FAMILIES WAITED ON DAILY.

Proprietor: A. J. OSMOND

Advertisements from the 1930s

Beyond, at the start of Westhall Road, the plot is now fully occupied by Manor Park Garage. In the past 'Harvey Cottage', built in the 1820s, stood here, with garden at the front. When built this house had a flint and brick façade, but it was updated in the 1890s, the bay windows making it look like a more recent building. For some years Cooper's builder's yard was alongside. On the other side of 'Harvey Cottage', built against the vicarage fence so that it had no rear door, was the flint and brick built 'Vicarage Cottage'. Tom Sales extended this in the early 1870s to provide more room for his growing family. On the road frontage he had a butcher's shop. This was closed in 1909 when he died. 'Vicarage Cottage' was demolished in 1959, and 'Harvey Cottage' in December 1971.

Tom Sales in his garden at 'Vicarage Cottage' in about 1904.
A very small part of 'Harvey Cottage' is just visible on the right.

SOURCES

COPPARD, FRED – tape recording.

School Board – Clerk's paperwork.

Tithe Assessment 1842.

Vestry Minute Book.

Chapter 17

South and East of The Green –
The Wards and the Methodist Church

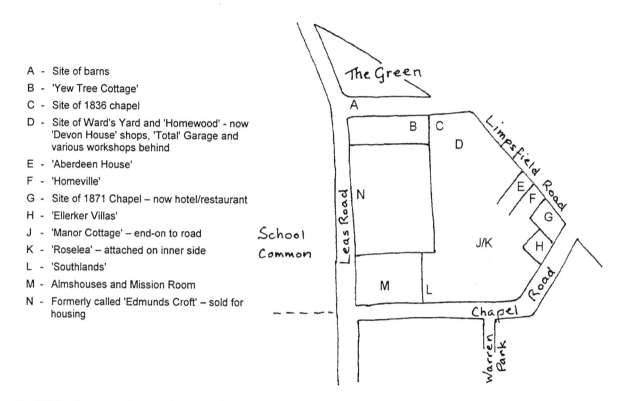

A - Site of barns

B - 'Yew Tree Cottage'

C - Site of 1836 chapel

D - Site of Ward's Yard and 'Homewood' - now 'Devon House' shops, 'Total' Garage and various workshops behind

E - 'Aberdeen House'

F - 'Homeville'

G - Site of 1871 Chapel – now hotel/restaurant

H - 'Ellerker Villas'

J - 'Manor Cottage' – end-on to road

K - 'Roselea' – attached on inner side

L - 'Southlands'

M - Almshouses and Mission Room

N - Formerly called 'Edmunds Croft' – sold for housing

In 1866 a large enclosure already existed on the common land which, due to its size and location, was instrumental in shaping the village when the common was fully enclosed. The almshouses were in the south-west corner. North of them was a field called Edmunds Croft, then plots on which stood barns, two cottages and the first Wesleyan Methodist Chapel. On the east side of the enclosure the land was held by Richard Ward, and this included 'Fir Cottage', 'Roselea' and another field. 'Fir Cottage' was renamed 'Manor Cottage' in 1915. At Enclosure Richard Ward was allotted a further amount of land adjacent to that which he already held. Two newly designated roads which bordered much of this large area were, in due course, named Leas Road and Chapel Road. The cottages and Chapel faced the land of just over half an acre which became The Green.

The almshouses feature in the chapter concerned with charities. 'Manor Cottage' has, of course, been updated over the years, but its structure would appear to be in part 18th century. When some alterations were carried out in 1910 a tombstone was discovered set in a wall. It measured 35½ inches by 23 inches, and was 2½ inches thick. The outer side was faced with flints, and the inner side had an inscription, still as fresh as if it had been just cut. It read—

> 'In memory of Mrs Mary Ovett whife of Mr Chripr Ovett of London who departed this life June the 14th 1765 aged 23 years'

There is an entry in the parish register for 1765 which was obviously written later as it comes in between 4th and 25th October. It says 'August Mary Ovet'. If Mr Ovett had the body of his late wife removed elsewhere for burial it could explain why the tombstone was not used. When it was used for walling is not known, nor does the report of the discovery say what happened to it afterwards.

Richard Ward obtained the freehold of the land he held in this part of the village soon after enclosure. It is said he started his building business around 1835, and as his sons grew older they took their part in this and the farming. The 1869 OS map shows Ward's builder's yard in the northern corner of his land, close by The Green, and also the house 'Homewood' where son John and wife Maria lived, which was adjacent to the yard. 'Woodlands', which still stands across the road by *The White Lion*, was built a few years later. Joel Ward and Annie Louisa lived there. 1870 saw the establishment of Quittenton's building business, Ward's first major competitor for local work.

Richard Ward was very much involved in the firm establishment of the Methodist Church in Warlingham. There had been applications to the Bishop of Winchester in 1797, and again 10 years later, for a license to use a local dwelling house for meetings of 'Protestant Dissenters from the Church of England'. 20 years later an application made by Thomas Edwards, dated 4th November 1828, is also signed by Richard Ward. When Thomas Edwards' cottage near *The White Lion* became too small to accommodate the gathering a move was made to an old stable building in the grounds of 'Fir Cottage'. This became known as 'The Chapel House' and was used until 1839.

From 1806 to 1825 Sarah Sayers was licensee of *The White Lion*. She owned a small plot of land adjacent to that owned by Richard Ward, and she gave part of it for the erection of a chapel. This first Methodist Chapel carried the date 1839, and was licensed for worship early in 1840. The 1851 Religious Census provides the information that the capacity was 108, and 50 standing. On the census day, 30th March 1851, 56 attended the morning service and 100 in the evening. 20 children attended the Sunday School, of which Richard Ward was the superintendent, a position he held for many years. After Enclosure this chapel faced The Green.

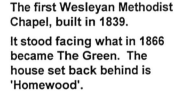

The first Wesleyan Methodist Chapel, built in 1839.

It stood facing what in 1866 became The Green. The house set back behind is 'Homewood'.

In 1870 it was decided to build a larger chapel. Richard Ward gave a site in the corner of his land, and the architect, George Marshall, made no charge for the plans. Built by Ward's workmen, this chapel on the corner site gave Chapel Road its name. The memorial stone, now incorporated in the east wall of the present building, was laid on 21st June, and the chapel opened on 27th September 1871. As a result of all the many generous contributions, which included flints picked from the fields frequently sold by local farmers to the Highways

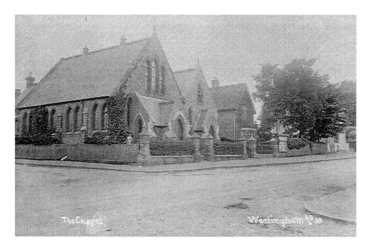

Above – This view, taken about 1920, shows the second Chapel, opened in 1871, and the side aisle added in 1908. Beyond is ' Homeville', incorporated within the hotel and restaurant now on this corner site.

Right – Ann Sarah Windross (née Ward) 1839 - 1925.   A studio portrait, dating from about 1900.

Below – 1921.   An extract from household accounts kept by Ann Sarah Windross. Her income was rent from the cottages that she owned.

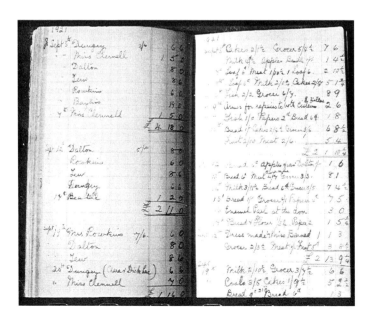

Board for roadmending, the cost was only just over £741, and all debts were cleared by 1874. Latterly Richard Ward and his wife Elizabeth lived at 'Homeville' which was built alongside the chapel. Richard died in December 1878, and Elizabeth in 1883.

The business was left to John and Joel, and all other assets were divided between the five children, Alfred, John, Joel, Ann Sarah and Dorcas. On their land in Chapel Road the Wards built 'Southlands' in 1885, and 'Ellerker Villas' in 1894. The Villas were commissioned by Solomon Windross of Beech Farm, Chelsham. Solomon and his family had come south from Ellerker, near Hull, in the 1870s. Sadly his wife died, and in 1882 he married Ann Sarah Ward. Also living at Beech Farm, with his daughters Hannah and Emma, was Solomon's niece Annie Elizabeth Windross.

By the 1890s John and Joel were both into their 60s and there was no younger family member in the trade to carry on the business. The following advertisement appeared in August 1896—

'Warlingham Village, Surrey Hills–

Valuable Freehold Properties, Residences, Cottages and Building Plots, being the estate of Messrs J & J Ward.
Two detached Residences, rent £30 and £18, the Builder's Yard, Workshop and Residence.
Six Building Plots and 1¼ acres of Building Land in the centre of the village.
Eleven Cottages and gardens, and 1¼ acres of Building Land, with three good frontages.
Also at Caterham, two detached Residences, Greenfield, rent £30, and The Poplars, rent £25.'

The auction was held on Thursday 6th August 1896, at *The Greyhound Hotel,* Croydon, the auctioneers being the firm local to Warlingham, C & F Rutley. Solomon Windross bought three of the cottages, and the vicar, the Revd Frank R Marriott, bought two plots adjacent to 'Homeville'. In due course the butcher's shop, Aberdeen House, was built alongside 'Homeville', and he sold the other plot to Quittentons. Trading continued under the name of J & J Ward for some time, the brothers still involved to an extent in the business, but eventually the owner became Frederick William Honour. Joel died in 1905 and John in 1910.

When Solomon Windross died in 1898 his wife Ann Sarah had to leave Beech Farm. With Annie Elizabeth Windross she returned to Warlingham, and they lived in property she owned in Chapel Road, or in nearby Warren Park in a rented house. Her income was the rents from her properties, and when Ann Sarah died in 1925 she still owned 3, 4, 5 & 6 Sunny Bank Cottages, 1 & 2 Cannon Place, 'Southlands', and 'Ellerker Villas'. The latter villas she bequeathed to Annie Elizabeth Windross, who lived at 4 Chapel Road until her death in 1966, aged 91.

Work started in 1908 to enlarge the chapel on one side. The work was carried out by Frederick W Honour, and the enlarged building was opened on 23rd June 1909. In 1939 the centenary of the building of the first chapel was celebrated, starting with a special service on Sunday 7th May. Various other events followed during May and June. As mentioned elsewhere a site was acquired further along Limpsfield Road in 1951. In 1954 a wooden building was erected there which provided much needed extra space. When it was discovered that the Chapel Road building was structurally unsound plans were made to build a third chapel. The last service held in the 1871 building was on Sunday 11th December 1960. The premises were sold for £3500, and the building was soon demolished. 'The Hut' – the name by which the wooden ex-pavilion was known – did duty as chapel for the greater part of 1961. The foundation stone of the new chapel was laid on 25th March, and the opening ceremony took place on 25th November 1961. A new hall was constructed in 1971, and opened on 4th December.

When the Rumballs came to live in 'Homeville' they changed the name to 'Archdale'. Edith Rumball bred English Setters, and she travelled all over the country showing and judging this breed of dog. At the house she had boarding kennels. She remained in the house into old age, and died in 1982. The premises were sold to

Fabio and Sonia Filipponi who, incorporating a good part of the original fabric, created their restaurant 'La Villa di Sonia' which opened in 1985. The adjacent former chapel site had remained empty since December 1960. The owner of the land did not submit an acceptable plan for redevelopment, and the plot attracted litter, weeds, and eventually a thicket with small trees. Fabio Filipponi negotiated a purchase of this waste land, and in 1990 the present hotel was built.

For over 20 years the butcher in Aberdeen House was a tenant of the Revd Frank R Marriott. Henry Chandler and Albert Taylor were two of the earliest. In 1923 the Revd Marriott, then living at Woodstock in Oxfordshire, sold the premises to the current tenants, Arthur Robinson and Arthur Seymour Heath, for £1100. In the later 1930s the property was bought by E Challis Baily, 'Homewood' was sold quite separately from the building business, and in the early 1900s tea gardens were established there. Alfred J Elmes was the owner for a number of years and in the early 1920s there were still refreshment rooms there. The house was still standing until the later 1930s when the corner site was redeveloped and the present block of three shops, Devon House, built. The petrol station at the side, currently *Total*, also dates from the 1930s. When it was enlarged in more recent years one of the two properties built on the land alongside Aberdeen House was demolished.

In 1871 Richard Ward paid £50 for the original chapel building and incorporated the property into his adjacent holding. The former chapel was subsequently used as a carpenter's shop and by the Salvation Army. On 9th November 1901 the vicar of All Saints', the Revd G R Macaulay, took out a lease at £16 per annum. It was then used as a parish meeting room, and by the time this tenancy ended in 1913 funds were being raised towards the cost of building the church hall. In May 1914 the first garage in the village was started here. This has been Parker's Motors Ltd for many years now, and all traces of the original building have long gone.

Aberdeen House in 1905. Albert Taylor, butcher, stands at the door.

Christmas time at Aberdeen House in the 1980s. Owen Baily serves Mrs F Clarke of Warren Park. Don Prior, Owen's assistant throughout many years, works nearby.

On 28th November 1881 Richard Ramsey Bond the elder took the tenancy of land previously held by the Sayers. This was the field known as Edmunds Croft, between the almshouses and The Green, and included the two barns on the corner site. There were also two fields, both called Fowlway, which were on the left side of the main road towards Hamsey Green, beyond the brickfield. On 13th July 1885 he bought the freehold.

September 1901.

Cottages stood near the Chapel, facing The Green. The old Ash tree, girth 11 ft 6 ins, was blown down in November 1902.

The barns were demolished in 1905 when the land was sold.

Facing The Green, adjacent to Bond's land, was 'Yew Tree Cottage'. This cottage still stands, but the front is completely obscured by the modern building in what was the front garden. The original cottage was built by William Bridger. Brick was used where necessary, but otherwise flint, and the roof was thatched. In 1832 the tenancy passed to Henry Saker, to his younger brother George in 1853, and to George's son John in 1881. Sometime during the years that the Sakers held the tenancy extensive building work was carried out, giving the house an upper floor, and a tiled roof. On 27th December 1890 John Saker paid £37 for the freehold, and on 14th January 1891 he sold the house to Richard Ramsey Bond.

1963. 'Bradford Buildings' replaced the old barns in 1905. 'Yew Tree Cottage' is now partially obscured, and building is in progress alongside.

In the 1890s John Harrup was using the barns, which were thatched, for livery and bait stables, and a small temperance coffee house. A board outside gave the invitation — 'Weary traveller, step within'.

In 1891, on the death of his father, Richard Ramsey Bond the younger inherited his father's property in Warlingham and Caterham. In 1905 he sold his holding here to Charles Ernest Kenworthy, builder, of Winchester House, Caterham. The date of the sale of barns and 'Yew Tree Cottage' was 28th July, and early in August the barns were demolished. Bradford Buildings, erected on the corner, were set back to line up with the front garden wall of 'Yew Tree Cottage'. Kenworthy had paid Bond £500 for this land and the cottage facing The Green, and in September 1906 he sold 'Yew Tree Cottage' for £350. The field behind was also sold by Bond, and houses built along the road frontage. Bradford Buildings contained four shops with accommodation above. The corner shop was a grocer's for many years, with proprietor G H Griffiths until 1925, then Louis H Emm. In 1968 the Westminster Bank took the premises. After its amalgamation with the National Provincial Bank the building on the corner of Glebe Road ceased to be bank premises. A baker and a chemist occupied two of the four shops over a long period, but since the 1980s bank and chemist have each occupied two spaces. In 1963 a small supermarket was built in the space next to Parker's Garage.

1999. Only the chimney of 'Yew Tree Cottage' is now visible.

The red telephone box has been replaced by a modern Cardphone kiosk.

SOURCES

'Aberdeen House' – documents.

Croydon Advertiser.

Enclosure Award 1866.

GOODMAN, C H Parish notes.

Religious Census 1851 (1997) – Surrey Record Society **35**.

SWIFT, R C (1978) *Praise and Trust.*

Warlingham & Chelsham Parish Magazine.

Wills – Ward - Richard, John, Joel, Ann Sarah.

'Yew Tree Cottage' – document.

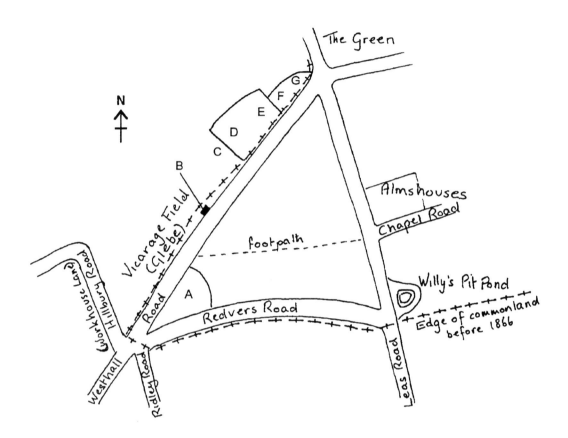

A - Site of School and schoolhouse
B - Site of old cottage – demolished 1898
C - Guide Barn
D - Barns – now converted
E - The (Old) Vicarage
F - Site of Vicarage Cottage
G - Site of Harvey Cottage
    (F & G now Manor Park Garage)

School Common

Chapter 18

School Common and the Vicarage

SCHOOL COMMON

The other area of common land, designated in the 1866 Enclosure Award as set aside for public enjoyment, was just over four acres in extent and officially named The Common Recreation Ground, later called School Common. Sheep were permitted, and Richard Jarvis, of nearby Tydcombe Farm, made use of it for grazing. In 1889 he said he could no longer afford the payment of 30 shillings a year. The vestry was unable to find anyone else interested so reduced the fee, and he continued to pasture his sheep there for only five shillings a year. In 1892 a cinder path was laid down, the origin of the present path across the common. For many years there were three small posts at each end, a remnant of the post and rail fence which was placed around the boundary. As with The Green some replacement trees were planted in 1893, and in 1897 several wooden bench seats were added which lasted many years.

The Parish Council Fire Appliance box can be seen here on the corner of School Common. In this view – *c.*1911 – the end of 'Vicarage Cottage' can be seen on the right.

An established route already passed along one side towards Westhall Farm, and another along the other side by the Almshouses was made official, now known as Leas Road. The third side of this triangle had no official road crossing it until 1900 when Redvers Road was laid out. From 1866 the large pond, nearly a quarter of an acre in extent, which was situated towards the edge of the open common by the lane to Tydcombe Farm, was only accessible from the side nearest to the road. This was one of the five ponds handed over into the care of the parish officials in 1866. A name for this pond has been handed down by word of mouth, and so Arthur Beadell, in his *Nature Notes of Warlingham and Chelsham* uses the spelling 'Willy's Pit', while Louis Emm spells it as 'Willey's Pit' in his *Memories of Warlingham*. A local boy, Frank Churchill, was drowned in this pond in 1883 when thin ice gave way beneath his weight. In 1931, when main drainage was being installed in the village, a large quantity of excess soil was deposited here, filling most of the pond. Work was carried out in the autumn of 1998 to restore it. The central tree was planted there about 45 years ago after doing duty as a Christmas tree on The Green.

The almshouses face the common, and the central house was originally intended to provide accommodation for a curate. In 1824 the Charity Commission inquiry reported that –

> '...the Curate resides in the vicarage house, which he describes as a much more convenient and comfortable residence than the two rooms appropriated for his use by the founder. These rooms since they have ceased to be occupied by the Curate (now upwards of 60 years) have been used for the purpose of a school. The present school, which is conducted by two sisters, is supported by voluntary subscription to which the Vicar largely contributes...'

One of John Hassell's watercolours, dated 1822, is entitled 'Harman Atwood's School'. It depicts the rear of the central house with a small single storey building adjoining it. This was demolished in 1857 when the present building was erected, placed in a central position and covering the rear door of the house. The school bell was housed in a small turret on the roof. This was removed in 1936 when it became unsafe.

In 1857 Mrs Sarah (Sally) Sampson retired after many years as mistress of this National (Church of England) school. Mrs Mary Ann Hunter took her place. After the Education Act of 1870 two years passed before there was a move in Warlingham to set up a school board. This was formed on 30th April 1872, and consisted of the vicar and four leading residents. In the early years these were Thomas Twiddy, Henry Lee, Richard Jarvis and Joel Ward. At the vestry meeting held on 19th September 1873 the assembly was informed that –

> '...the Warlingham School Board requires a quarter of an acre of land from the south west corner of the Parish recreation ground for the purpose of erecting new schools...'

This was agreed, though not without some opposition. It was a sensible choice of site, on land owned by the parish to be put to good use for the benefit of the parish. When authorised by the Education Department in London a loan to finance school building could be obtained from the Public Works Loan Board.

The new building opened in December 1874, with 75 pupils, some of whom came from Whyteleafe. The first headmaster was Henry Lawson. The old school building was used as a laundry for a while, then in 1878 when repairs were needed to All Saints' church, permission was obtained to hold services there. It was used for church and parochial activities, and became known as the 'Mission Room', the name which it still has today. Before the alterations which started in the 1950s, the rear door of the house was still in use. A partition wall divided the Mission Room from the house, creating a passage which, when all doors were closed, was very dark. The room was lit by gas, not available until some years after the school left the premises, and with a good coal fire burning brightly in the grate, was reasonably cosy.

In 1876 J & J Ward built the headmaster's house alongside the school on the common, at a cost of £325. The school was enlarged in 1885, and again in 1894. The school in Maple Road, Whyteleafe, was built in 1892 and was administered by the same school board. In the autumn of 1879 a new headmaster, John David Clarke, was appointed to Warlingham. He and his wife Ellen came from Bath. His starting salary was £110 per annum. The School house was rent free, and coal was provided. Water was laid on, but gas was not then available.

In 1880 school attendance was made compulsory to the age of 10, and by 1899 it was to the age of 12. From April 1900 the infants' school became a separate department, but all remained in the one building. Attendance was often poor due to bad weather, and chicken pox, measles, mumps and whooping cough were prevalent amongst the younger children. In November 1902 Mr. Clarke found it necessary to give a young lad, Thomas Penny, '...a good slapping on the seat of his trousers (but not in front of the other children)...'

This photograph of the School on the Common dates from the 1960s.

In the foreground are the wartime air raid shelters.

He was made to leave school 10 minutes after the others, and Mr Clarke asked the village policeman, Mr Bridge, to call round and speak to his father.

The Education Act of 1902 empowered the local authority, which in the case of Warlingham was Godstone Rural District Council, to provide education. From 1st April 1903 the board school became the council school. The syllabus in the infants' department included reading, writing, arithmetic, needlework for the girls and drawing for the boys, singing, marching and other physical exercise, and lessons based on common objects. In 1904, when John D Clarke completed 25 years as headmaster, he was presented with 40 guineas and an illuminated address. He remained until 1910 when he was promoted to a school in Mitcham. In 1912 his successor, Melville Perry and the older children moved to the newly built school in Farleigh Road.

At some time during further alterations to the school on the common the bell turret was removed. At the start of World War II overground air raid shelters were erected by the edge of the playground which at times suffered from flooding. There were many interruptions to school routine, especially in 1940. When the 'doodlebugs' were threatening the area in 1944 some mothers and children were evacuated to Yeovil.

In December 1939 a YMCA hut was erected on the common for the benefit of soldiers billeted locally. After the war ended this hut was put to use as an extra classroom for the school. By November 1948 there were 295 children on the roll.

The first school in the complex built on the land by Tithepit Shaw Lane was Hamsey Green County Primary School, which opened on 20th May 1949 with 78 children transferred from the school on the common. 30 years later, with a full range of schooling at Hamsey Green and a decline in the number of children needing school places, Surrey County Council, which now controlled education, decided that one of the schools in the village must close. Over the next four years this matter of great local importance was the subject of meetings, a petition, and general discussion amongst parents. Eventually and at quite short notice the school on the common, Warlingham County First School, as it was then called, was closed. This was in July 1982. For the next five years the buildings stood empty, with windows boarded up, while discussions regarding its future made slow progress.

Squatters had to be evicted from the school house. The site was eventually redeveloped into flats by Croudace Construction. 'Redvers Court' was completed in the first few months of 1989. Newcomers may be puzzled when longtime residents refer to the open space here as School Common, but it has been known by that name for over one hundred years, and those who received their early education at the school will not forget it.

THE VICARAGE

On the other side of Westhall Road is the Vicarage field, which is the only glebe land remaining apart from that around All Saints' church. In 1844 a small part was arable and the rest pasture. The allotment holders were successfully relocated to part of this field in 1994, after the drainage had been improved.

The earliest known mention of a residence for clergy in the parish of Warlingham with Chelsham is in the *Valor Ecclesiasticus* of 1535. This is a return of church property and the tithes and emoluments received which provided the clergy with their income. It was required by a law passed in 1534 after the King, Henry VIII, broke away from Rome and declared himself head of the Church in England. The tithe of wool and lambs is given as producing a value of seven pounds a year, far more than the other produce listed which includes calves, milk, pigs, geese, rabbits, eggs, hemp and flax. In 1836 an Act was passed enabling this church 'tax' in kind to be converted into a money payment. The Tithe Assessment Award and the accompanying map provide very useful information about early 19th century Warlingham and Chelsham. 100 years later, in 1936, the last remaining tithe rent charges were abolished.

It is probable that the 16th century vicarage stood on the same site as the present building. It would have been constructed of locally available materials, and thatched in a similar way to the nearby tithe barn. Some of local artist and churchwarden Charles Langton Lockton's paintings show thatched buildings which still existed in the 1890s. In 1667 the Revd Joseph Till married Susan Atwood, daughter of King Atwood, rector of Sanderstead, and niece of Harman Atwood, lord of the manor. Harman Atwood held the advowson – the right to present clergy to the living of Warlingham with Chelsham. When the living fell vacant in 1673 Harman Atwood had a new house built. It seems that though Joseph Till held the living of Warlingham with Chelsham from 1673 he was not formally inducted until 1680. The Warlingham parish registers include entries for Chelsham until 1680 when the Chelsham Registers commence.

The Vicarage and the nearby thatched barns (behind the trees), photographed in the 1890s.

The house ceased to serve as the local vicarage in 1984. Both the house and the principal barn – now converted into a residence – are Grade II listed.

SCHOOL COMMON AND THE VICARAGE

On the inside cover of one of the Warlingham registers is the information that 'The Curate's House at Warlingham was rebuilt in the year 1738 at the Expence of John Atwood Esq.' John Atwood was then lord of the manor. His nephew, Atwood Wigsell, was rector of Sanderstead and Vicar of Warlingham, and would have lived in the Sanderstead Rectory. The curate at Warlingham was Owen Evans.

June 1905. A 'Sale of Work' fund-raising event in the Vicarage garden.

No picture of Harman Atwood's vicarage exists, but it is considered that the present building incorporates some of it. The main block facing the common, which is seen by the passer-by, dates in basic appearance from the 1738 rebuilding. The use of two colours of brick and the brick pilasters is decorative, and the 'tumbling-in' work on the chimney-breasts denotes good craftmanship. The windows on the first floor extend down to floor level, an unusual feature to find in a small country property. The present porch dates from the 1980s, replacing the simple porch of 19th century date. In 1955 the attic was made into a self-contained flat for a curate, with access via an outside staircase. Two new dormer windows were inserted, deemed necessary to provide more light. As may be expected in a house of this age other additions and alterations have been made over the years. It is listed Grade II and ceased to be used as a vicarage in 1984. No.15 Chapel Road became the vicarage, and a new residence for the clergy is included in the development planned for the former glebe allotments.

The Vicarage as it looked in 1925.

In 1992 planning permission was granted to convert the two listed barns by the former vicarage into a residence. One barn has some timber framework of 18th century date. There used to be two ponds in the woodland area between the barns and the road. The larger was filled in during the 1880s but the smaller existed well into the 20th century. This was just to the right of the gate, now long gone, which gave access to the vicarage field. Further along, a house stood within a small enclosure facing the common. It was condemned and demolished in 1898.

This photograph, taken in 1998, shows the new Guide Barn on the left – which replaced the one destroyed by fire – and the conversion of the vicarage barns into a residence and a detached garage.

The Guide barn is situated just within the vicarage field. In 1915 a group of local girls met in Crewes Barn under the enthusiastic leadership of Sheila Sandy and Dora Bunclark, and in 1916 the 1st Warlingham Guide Company was officially formed. Over the years meetings have been held in a variety of places, including the miniature rifle range in Mint Walk, the school on Baker's Hill, Farleigh Road, the Scout hut, the Mission Room, and the vicarage barns. Eventually in 1960 the Guides achieved their own headquarters in the vicarage field.

This house, demolished in 1898, was mainly constructed of brick, flint, weatherboard and thatch. It stood facing the Common, in a tiny enclosure by the edge of Vicarage field.

Over the years the movement grew to include Rangers, Brownie Guides and Rainbow Guides. On the occasion of the 70th anniversary celebrations 17 past and present leaders, which included Muriel Bentley, Margaret Holland, Vera Carr and Mary Stone, came together for a luncheon party in the Guide barn, and later in the year a gathering was held of many past members of the company. In October 1990 fire destroyed the headquarters, when not only equipment but also important historical material was lost. Donations and energetic fund-raising provided the money for a new barn, which was formally opened on 28th November 1992. From the Disaster Fund Committee emerged The Friends of Guiding of 1st Warlingham, which continues the fund-raising aspect. On 25th May 1996, 80th anniversary celebrations were held in the Guide barn. Currently the Brownie Guides meet on Monday evenings and the 1st Warlingham Guides on Friday evenings.

SOURCES

Enclosure Award 1866.

GOODMAN, C H *Parish Notes*.

Parish Registers.

School Board Clerk's paperwork.

School Log Books.

Tithe Assessment 1842.

TUTT, D C 'Warlingham Almshouses' Bourne Society *Local History Records* **14** & **15**.

Vestry Minute Book.

Warlingham & Chelsham Parish Magazine.

GODSTONE UNION WORKHOUSE.

Dietary for Able-bodied Paupers.

MEN.

	Breakfast.		Dinner.						Supper.		
	Bread.	Oatmeal Gruel.	Bread.	Cheese.	Meat Pudding.	Suet Pudding.	Pea Soup.	Vegetables.	Bread.	Cheese.	Mutton Broth.
	ozs.	pints.	ozs.	ozs.	ozs.	ozs.	pints.	ozs.	ozs.	oz.	pints.
Sunday ..	6	1½	—	—	12	—	—	8	6	1	—
Monday .	6	1½	7	1½	—	—	—	—	6	1	1
Tuesday . .	6	1½	5	—	—	—	1½	—	6	1	—
Wednesday	6	1½	—	—	—	12	—	8	6	1	—
Thursday .	6	1½	7	1½	—	—	—	—	6	1	1
Friday ..	6	1½	5	—	—	—	1½	—	6	1	—
Saturday. .	6	1½	—	—	—	12	—	8	6	1	1

WOMEN.

	Breakfast.		Dinner.						Supper.		
	Bread.	Oatmeal Gruel.	Bread.	Cheese.	Meat Pudding.	Suet Pudding.	Pea Soup.	Vegetables.	Bread.	Butter.	Mutton Broth.
	ozs.	pints.	ozs.	ozs.	ozs.	ozs.	pints.	ozs.	ozs.	oz.	pints.
Sunday ..	5	1	—	—	10	—	—	6	5	⅓	—
Monday ..	5	1	6	1¼	—	—	—	—	5	⅓	1
Tuesday . .	5	1	4	—	—	—	1½	—	5	⅓	—
Wednesday	5	1	—	—	—	10	—	6	5	⅓	—
Thursday .	5	1	6	1¼	—	—	—	—	5	⅓	1
Friday ..	5	1	4	—	—	—	1½	—	5	⅓	—
Saturday..	5	1	—	—	—	10	—	6	5	⅓	1

Weekly menu for able-bodied adults in the Godstone
Union Workhouse, Bletchingley, in 1873.

Chapter 19

Charities

THE POORHOUSE

After the Dissolution of the Monasteries in 1536 each parish became responsible for very poor residents, or those unable to work due to illness or old age. In the course of the next 200 years several laws were passed to deal with vagrants and poor relief. The office of overseer of the poor was created in 1572, and in 1598 the parish was empowered to levy a poor rate. The Poor Law Act of 1601 regularised the administration of this rate. The General Workhouse Act of 1723 allowed parishes to obtain property for use as a workhouse or poorhouse. No early records exist for Warlingham, but an entry in the parish burial register dated 9th June 1784 states 'John Buckshier, from the Poor House, aged between 70 and 80 years.' Later on in 1799 there are entries on 16th July – 'Dame Leigh, from ye Poor House', and 26th July – 'Amy Wood, Poor House'. Therefore some local provision had been made but the population was small, only 187 in 1801, so the need for parish help may have also been low.

Following the Poor Law Amendment Act of 1834, parishes combined to form 'Unions'. Warlingham was in Godstone Union which covered 14 parishes, with a workhouse at Bletchingley. A board of guardians was appointed to administer the poor relief, while the Vestry continued to levy the rate. An early entry in the only surviving vestry minute book provides the information that in 1844 the two cottages, formerly the Warlingham poorhouse, were let for two shillings a week each.

May 1901. The present house on this site in Hillbury Road is called 'The Grange', and probably incorporates some of this earlier house called 'The Plantation'. The Workhouse cottages stood to the right, on land now part of the garden.

The farm track on which these cottages stood had over the years become known as Workhouse Lane. The 1842 Tithe map shows that a house had been built on the adjacent plot. This was named 'The Plantation', and it would seem the owner applied to the guardians of the poor to purchase the plot where the former poorhouse stood. In February 1848 a meeting of the Warlingham vestry agreed that the premises be sold, and the offer of £150 was acceptable. For his money the new owner acquired a quarter of an acre of land adjacent to his house which enlarged his garden – the cottages were soon demolished – and half an acre of land to the rear. In 1904 when the land on the corner of Westhall Road and Workhouse Lane was sold for housing, the name of the lane was changed to Hillbury Road. 'The Plantation' was much altered and enlarged and is known today as 'The Grange'. Looking at the house from the road, the poorhouse cottages stood to the right in the garden.

Workhouse Lane was renamed Hillbury Road soon after 1900. This view along the first stretch from Westhall Road, taken in 1967, shows the grass verge and hedgerow removed when widening started in December 1969.

In 1871 the population of Warlingham was 773. The guardian of the poor was Richard Jarvis, of Tydcombe, and he and Stephen Dean from *The Leather Bottle* were the parish overseers of the poor. In the half yearly statement of the Godstone Union accounts to Michaelmas 1873, 27 Warlingham residents are listed as receiving out-door relief in money and kind. Most causes of need were age or illness. One man, Richard Burnell, was blind. There were also confinements, and in other parishes in the Union there was the occasional victim of an accident, cripple or imbecile.

In this view from the hillside near Court Farm, taken in autumn 1914, Hillbury Road can be seen winding down the valley, from the left, past Lower Barn Farm and on towards Whyteleafe.

The accounts only give figures for residents in the workhouse but no detail, so whether anyone from Warlingham was an inmate at that time cannot be ascertained. The food was adequate, but monotonous, the same each week. It included oatmeal gruel, mutton broth, pea soup, meat pudding, suet pudding, cooked meat, vegetables, bread and cheese. Size of portion varied according to whether the recipient was male or female, active or infirm. The children were given milk and an extra luncheon meal of bread and treacle. One may wonder how they measured out accurately half an ounce or threequarters of an ounce of black treacle! All paupers over 60 were allowed half a pint of porter each day. The staff included a nurse, and a schoolmistress for the children. In 1911 the National Insurance Act was the first step towards the modern benefits scheme. In 1913 the workhouse was officially renamed the Poor Law Institution, and in 1929 boards of guardians were abolished and their powers transferred to county or borough councils. For some time past only the very elderly and infirm had been taken into the workhouse, and councils were encouraged to convert the buildings into infirmaries.

Charitable Bequests

In common with most Surrey parishes Warlingham and Chelsham receive a small annuity from Alderman Henry Smith's Charity. Two deeds were drawn up, one in October 1620 and the other in January 1626, and these were confirmed by his will, proved in April 1627. An extract from the deed states

> '...The churchwardens and overseers of the poor of the said several parishes respectively shall give and distribute the said monies given...to the said charitable uses to and for the relief of aged poor or infirm people, married persons having more children born in lawful wedlock than their labours can maintain, poor orphans, such poor people as keep themselves and families to labour and put forth their children as apprentices at the age of fifteen...and not to or for the relief of any persons who are given to excessive drinking...or to any vagrant persons or such as have no constant dwelling...'

The recipients must have been resident in the parish for at least five years and the benefit was to be given in clothing, or in bread and meat or fish.

The money received derives from an estate in Bexhill, Sussex, and it seems that this bequest, which amounted to between £3 and £4, was usually distributed in bread. In January 1895, 224 loaves

Money received from Smith's Charity for the year 1895, less a deduction of fourpence to cover the poundage on the postal orders.

were purchased and these were distributed in quantities from one to three and a half, according to the size of the family.

In the 19th century Chelsham parish received bequests from Alderman Thomas Kelly, and the Revd Edward Francis Beynon of Slines Oak, both of which generate a small annuity. In 1917 Warlingham received a bequest from George Luke Hodgkinson. In 1977 these five bequests were brought together into one scheme approved by the Charity Commissioners with the name 'The Chelsham, Farleigh and Warlingham Relief in Need Charity', which is administered by seven trustees.

HARMAN ATWOOD CHARITIES - THE ALMSHOUSES

When Harman Atwood (1608–1676), who owned the manors of Sanderstead and Warlingham, had put the building of the new vicarage in hand in 1673, he was approached regarding the possibility of providing some housing for the poor of the parish. He gave half an acre of land for the almshouses on the open common, a short distance from the vicarage. These consisted of two single-storey blocks set facing each other and at right angles to a central house, now known as 'Atwood Cottage'. The housing was for two needy people from Warlingham, one from Sanderstead and one from Chelsham. Rooms were provided in the central house for a curate to assist the vicar. The location, which was at a point where tracks passed across the common, has proved to be a good choice, as this corner site where Chapel Road meets Leas Road is well away from the greater part of today's constant traffic flow through the village.

To put his wishes regarding the almshouses into effect Harman Atwood had a lengthy tripartite indenture drawn up. This involved Harman Atwood himself, who was to retain absolute control during his lifetime, seven trustees who would take up their duties at his death, and the vicar, the Revd Joseph Till, who was to live in the parish and carry out his duties diligently and correctly. Providing he did so, he was to receive all the rectorial tithes of grain and corn from the manors of Warlingham and Chelsham which had formerly been going to the rector of Sanderstead – £10 a year from each Manor, and the fees due for interments made within the chancels of the churches of Warlingham and Chelsham. The trustees appointed were Sir Marmaduke Gresham of Titsey and his son Edward, Henry Mellish of Sanderstead, John Holbrook rector of Titsey, John Hawtrey rector of Sanderstead, John Sheppard of Croydon cleric, and John Saxby the elder, yeoman, of Chelsham Court. In 1675 John Sheppard was master of Whitgift and married to Joan, niece of Harman Atwood, and sister of Susan, wife of Joseph Till.

The Almshouses, sometimes known as The College, face the School Common. This view dates from about 1900.

CHARITIES

The almshouses were for—

> 'four poor aged or poor impotent people widowers and widows or single persons of honest lives and conversations and that have been before the time of their placing there laborous and industrious in their respective callings be it husbandry or day labor or what else be honest industry tended to a livelihood....'

However, before the document had been fully completed Harman Atwood found that his good intentions were not proceeding quite as he wished —

> 'the first motive to build the said housing was from the complaint of some of the chief inhabitants of the Parish of Warlingham as wanting housing and forced to hire rooms for several of their poor and thereupon enquiry finding four very aged and impotent persons in that Parish fit to be taken into consideration he did with all convenient speed undertake the work and three of the four died before it was finished and the fourth left the parish as probably not willing to accept the same. And the year has come about since it was built and not one as yet appears either fit or desirous of the same and a chief one of those that formerly complained of the want of housing as aforesaid hath since those were in building complained thereof for that the parish could not find them wood that should be placed therein and that they had rather have had the money it cost building, and the builder finding this in his life doubts what his trustees may find after him...'

The tripartite indenture was signed on 18th November 1675. It stated that the trustees were not obliged to keep all four homes occupied but only when suitable poor people who fulfilled the conditions were in need of housing. The poor were not even considered if they had –

> 'spent their time or estates idly loosely or wickedly specially in drinking petty filching or purloining what belongs not to them...'

One place in the parish was quite exempt—

> '...there be several mean and poor houses in that part of Warlingham called the Kings Hold being held of the Manor of Crewse the inhabitants thereof are oft very burthensome to the Parish marrying and living at their own hand working playing and drinking by fits and some of them receiving other poor people to inhabit with them or in some part of their small tenements hereby multiplying the poor there and finding they set rent free take more liberty than other men until by their idleness or carelessness poverty overtakes them and then sell what they have to a fresh inhabitant and cast themselves on the provision of the Parish...'

Those that were accepted into the almshouses were certain to be turned out if they indulged in—

> 'excessive drinking, frequent swearing, lying, backbiting or evil speaking, begging, pilfering, false dealing, harbouring a visitor overnight without permission, or for any foul disease or evil course of life or behaviour.'

They were obliged to—

> 'live soberly quietly and lovingly and to be aiding helpful assisting to each other but specially in time of sickness or weakness...dutiful and observant to the Vicar ...and his Curate who living so near them are most fit to be intrusted and therefore demised to take the care and oversight of them...'

Each resident was to receive two shillings a week, and in September every year a load of good wood for firing to the value of ten shillings was to be provided for the almshouses. In his will Harman Atwood bequeathed £20 a year, to be derived from the lands of Chelsham Court, which would provide the weekly payment. From 1922 this small income was derived from Purley Downs Golf Club Ltd and has now been commuted.

The tripartite indenture, which is given in full in a report of inquiries into charities, published in January 1825, is a long document of which only short extracts have been quoted here. One matter not included was any ruling regarding the appointment of new Trustees when needed. An indenture, dated 15th January 1716, names the trustees who are not local clergy as being Sir Charles Gresham, Baronet, William Hoskins, Henry St John, Henry Bowyer, and Anthony Saxby. Henry St. John, a lawyer of Inner Temple, was the father of Susannah who married the Revd Atwood Wigsell in 1735. The benefits apportioned to the vicar of Warlingham with Chelsham were granted by a lease, and there was a condition that he must live in the parish. Joseph Till was succeeded in 1689 by William Buckle, who was also rector of Sanderstead parish from 1705 to his death in 1715. The next vicar of Warlingham with Chelsham was Joseph Abell. A note in the parish register gives the information that he was a Fellow of Merton College, Oxford, and at the time of his induction, 28th July 1715, was also rector of Farleigh. The same register has the following note—

> 'September 14th 1715 By the Reverend Mr Joseph Abel Vicar a Donation to the Chaplains house of the Hospital of Warlingham when Mr More duted Imprimis four flag bottomd chairs, and one arm Elbow Chair, a fire Shovel & a pair of Andirons a pr Bellowes & tongs a Brass Candlestick, a Safeall and Snuffers a Large Peuter dish and two peuter plates & four round trenchers & a dish & porringer of Welsh ware a white bason, Chamber pot & porringer Delf ware & a half pint pot earthen a white tea Cup, a pepper and flour box of tin a glass salt, a hat case a Brush a Spoon & a Basket, and a Spigot & tap.'

John More was the curate, and the vicar was providing the basic items he would need.

When Joseph Abell died he was buried in the Chancel of Farleigh Church on 2nd November 1722. Warlingham with Chelsham had three vicars in the course of the next 10 years and then in 1733 the lord of the manor, John Atwood, presented his nephew, the Revd Atwood Wigsell, to the livings of Warlingham and Sanderstead. He and his wife Susannah had seven children, and as they appear in the Sanderstead baptisms one may assume that Sanderstead rectory was their home. Atwood Wigsell predeceased John Atwood, and it was Atwood's brother Thomas who inherited the estates. In 1778 he presented his nephew, another Thomas, to the livings of Sanderstead and Warlingham with Chelsham. In 1795 this second Thomas became, by inheritance, the landowner.

This view, taken in about 1900, shows the Mission Room, which was the schoolroom until 1874. The turret was removed in 1936 because it became unsafe.

CHARITIES

The inquiry found that the Revd Thomas Wigsell had received the benefits due to the vicar of Warlingham although no lease had been granted and he did not reside in the parish. Moreover, as the owner of the manor of Sanderstead had the final word as to what should be done with the benefits in such circumstances, and this was the Revd Thomas Wigsell, little could be done about it 'without the intervention of a court of equity.'

The report stated that—

> 'This foundation, which is now known by the name of "The College" has been for many years under the sole management of the Lords of the Manor of Sanderstead who have filled up the vacancies from time to time as they occurred, and who, being also Lords of the Manor of Chelsham, have made the weekly payment to the poor inmates themselves without the intervention of any trustees.'

It was considered that the appointment of new trustees was a priority, and this was done by an indenture dated 7th February 1831. They were—

> '...William Henry Whitbread of South Hill in the County of Bedford Esquire, Alexander Greig late of Purley in the County of Surrey Esquire, Laurence Keir of Warlingham in the County of Surrey Esquire Thomas Wright of Kingswood Lodge near to Croydon in the said County of Surrey Gentleman, John Brown of Chelsham in the said County of Surrey Yeoman and Henry Rowland of Coulsdon in the said County of Surrey...'

These names are quoted again, except Laurence Keir, in the 1842 Tithe Apportionment document. Alexander Greig married Juliana, widow of the Revd. Atwood Wigsell Wigsell. John Brown was a tenant farmer for the Beynons in Chelsham.

As the 19th century progressed it seems no further trustees were appointed, which meant that eventually the only people responsible were the rector of Sanderstead and the vicar of Warlingham with Chelsham. The weekly payment was made but the premises suffered from lack of maintenance. In 1900 the sanitary authorities threatened to condemn the property, a fate which had overtaken several local cottages. The vicar, the Revd G R Macaulay appealed in the parish magazine for funds to meet the cost of urgently needed repairs. The local people responded generously and the work was done by local men, carried out according to the specification and under the supervision of the architect, Mr J C King. At the time it was recorded that three coins were found in the sand under a brick floor, two Charles II farthings dated 1672, and a William and Mary halfpenny of 1694. It was later reported that 'for the present the inmates of the cottages have nothing to complain of, and make no complaint with regard to their dwellings.'

The next 50 years passed in much the same way, with occasional appeals for funds to pay for urgent repairs. Without Trustees only the Vicar of Warlingham felt any responsibility. Then in 1953 a Charity Commission Scheme was set up. Dated 24th March 1953 it covered the Atwood Charities of the Almshouses and Curate's House, and an Endowment Fund. It was decided that the new body of Trustees should consist of two ex-officio members, the Vicar of Warlingham and the Rector of Sanderstead, and nine representative members. This remains firmly established, the only change being as a result of a Local Government change such as Tandridge District Council appointing two members instead of Caterham & Warlingham UD Council. This did not, however, solve the problem of lack of finance.

Fund-raising continued, and donations were gratefully received. The improvements carried out in 1958 were paid for in part by a grant from the local Council. In 1975 the tercentenary was marked by a week of special events. The installation of a damp course and central heating was very costly but vital. Damp had been the cause of deterioration ever since the almshouses were built.

Planning for the most recent improvement works started at the end of the 1980s. John Rowland, Dip Arch ARIBA prepared plans for the construction of a new wing and for the work to be done on the ancient buildings.

Croydon Churches Housing Association was the development agent for the Trustees, and the contractors were Highlife Construction Co Ltd. Work started in March 1996. The new wing was built on the Chapel Road side of the plot. It contains two homes, each with kitchen, living room, bedroom and bathroom. It is so placed that a small open-sided courtyard has been created, the Mission Room forming one side. As regards the original almshouses, the toilet blocks added in 1958 were demolished and each wing altered and refurbished to provide one home with bathroom and bedroom, kitchen and living room. Work was also carried out on Atwood Cottage.

On Monday, 23 June 1997, a large gathering of representatives from all the organisations involved during the planning, financing and construction of the work came together for a short ceremony during which Cllr Iain R Pavely, Chairman of Tandridge District Council, unveiled a plaque on the new block. Excellent refreshments were provided by Mrs Carol Martin of Atwood Cottage, which included a splendid iced cake. The four residents were present, and also Mrs Warlow, who had donated a garden seat in memory of her late husband, Russell. A second seat was donated by Knight's Garden Centre.

23rd June 1997.

Cllr I R Pavely, Chairman of Tandridge District Council, unveils the plaque commemorating the opening of the newly built and refurbished Almshouses.

Also in the picture are the Clerk to the Trustees, A Soden, Croydon Cllr Eric Shaw, and the Deputy Mayor of Croydon, Cllr Pat Ryan.

This Grade II listed premises now provides good accommodation, with adequate space for each resident. They pay a fair rent, and their gas and electricity costs.

Grants, donations and small legacies helped towards the cost of the work, but a sizeable loan remains, repayment of which will take some years. Donations are always welcome to help defray costs. We are sure Harman Atwood would greatly approve of all that has been done to carry on the good work he initiated.

SOURCES

1842 Tithe Assessment.

Godstone Union Accounts. ½ year to Michaelmas 1873.

GOODMAN, C H Parish Notes.

Harman Atwood (1608-1676) Indenture.

TUTT, D C (1975/76) 'Warlingham Almshouses'. Bourne Society *Local History Records* **14 & 15**.

Vestry Minute Book.

Warlingham and Chelsham Parish Magazine.

Chapter 20

Celebrations, Organisations and Personalities

Queen Victoria's Golden Jubilee was celebrated in 1887. In 1893 everyone in the parish was given a half-day holiday on 6th July for the wedding of Princess May and the Duke of York. From 3.00 p.m. there were races, a comic cricket match – for which the men wore fancy dress – tea, an entertainment which took place in the schoolroom, followed by supper and then fireworks, the day's events ending at 10.30 p.m. For Queen Victoria's Diamond Jubilee the celebrations on 22nd June 1897 included sports and tea for the children, a comic cricket match and dinner for the men, and later in the evening a bonfire and fireworks on The Green.

The **Warlingham Horticultural & Agricultural Society** was established in 1853, and Dr Epps was its first president. The following year it staged a Ploughing Match & Root Show: the former in G R Smith's field near the *Adam and Eve* on the Godstone road, and the latter in an enclosure adjoining Mr Ashby's mill at Warlingham.

It is known that **The Cottage Garden Society** existed in 1887. It put on an annual show in July, which in the 1890s was often held in the field now filled by the houses of Shelton Avenue. There were many prizes, given not only for the wide range of fruit, vegetables and flowers available at that time of year, but also for eggs, poultry, pigs and the best-kept cottage gardens. There were also prizes for needlework and other home industries, for local crafts, for wild flowers and grasses, and for table decorations. After the establishment of the allotments in 1893 these were also included, and there were classes for the professional gardeners who worked in the gardens of the large houses in the Westhall area. **Rose** and **Chrysanthemum Societies** were formed, and in 1901 the Cottage Garden Society became **The Warlingham and District Horticultural Society.**

The annual church service, dinner and fête held by the Friendly Society, **The 'Pride of Warlingham' Lodge,** Manchester Unity Oddfellows, was normally in July. In 1896 the church parade and service was on Sunday 19th July in glorious summer weather...

> 'We were glad to see and hear the Warlingham Brass Band taking part in the march round before and after the Service, and acquitting themselves so creditably. The firemen, who marched in uniform, must have been very hot. Monday, the fête day, was even hotter than the Sunday (85°F in the shade), and the sun powerful .... there was a large attendance, and the attractions in the way of swings, roundabouts and such like, seemed to be more numerous than ever....'

The Warlingham Brass Band had been formed in 1894. Another event of 1894 was 'a novelty in the form of a jumble sale' which raised just over £14. It was to be the first of countless jumble sales which have raised funds in the village.

In the later 1890s enthusiastic residents were putting on entertainments in the schoolroom on winter Friday evenings. Occasionally the older schoolchildren took part under the direction of their schoolmaster, J D Clarke. A **Musical Society** was formed in November 1900, and it gave its first concert in April 1901. This Society was still in existence in the 1920s, and in April 1924 gave a performance of *The Golden Legend* by Arthur Sullivan. Also in that April a small drama group presented three sketches. From this evolved the WADS, **The Warlingham Amateur Dramatic Society**, which was very active throughout the 1930s. After World War II, with the leadership and encouragement of Diana Budd ARCM (1921–1997), **The Pilgrim Players** were formed, and presented their first play *Quiet Weekend* as part of the 1953 Coronation week programme. This company existed into the 1980s. More recently **The Warlingham Players** have carried on the theme of local music and drama.

Chelsham, Warlingham and Whyteleafe.

June 26th, 27th, 1902.

Coronation
Celebrations.

The cover of the 1902 Coronation programme.

Owing to the King's illness the events planned for 27th June were deferred until 9th August.

COMMITTEE:

Chairman—Rev. G. R. MACAULAY.

Treasurer—Mr. C. H. GOODMAN.

Mrs. CHURCH   Mrs. GOODMAN   Miss ROGERS

Revs. J. F. G. GLOSSOP, H. M. SCOTT, G. R. COULTAS, and J. M. MURRAY.

Drs. ETCHES and POLLOCK.

Messrs. F. BUSHBY, H. F. CHANDLER, G. CHEESEMAN, D. H. CHURCH, G. CHURCH, W. GOODWIN, P. W. HEWETT, G. HONEY, C. L. LOCKTON, J. NEWBERRY, A. L. PIKE, E. G. QUINN, W. RINGER, W. WORDLEY, J. D. WOOD.

Hon Secretary—Mr. J. D. CLARKE.

The Warlingham branch of **The Mothers' Union** was founded in July 1901, so will soon celebrate a centenary. In 1902 the Boer War ended, and a note in the parish magazine stated—

> 'News of Peace was not generally known in Warlingham until the morning of 2nd June... the place was soon made gay with flags. The schoolchildren were in an exuberant state all day, and in the evening there were loud demonstrations of rejoicing in which the band took a leading part.'

Queen Victoria had died in 1901, and the dates appointed for the Coronation of King Edward and Queen Alexandra and local celebrations were 26th and 27th June 1902. A nationwide chain of bonfires was planned for the 26th. It seems that the official programme arranged by the Chelsham, Warlingham and Whyteleafe Committee, which was centred in the Court Farm–Hamsey Green area, did not please everyone. Within the village other residents made their own plans for 27th June. During the century the 'them and us' situation has smoothed out a great deal, and has changed, but not fully disappeared.

When the King fell ill with appendicitis it was thought everything would have to be postponed, but then it was decided that the chain of bonfires should be lit on the 26th as planned. The route of the procession was down Westhall Road, through Whyteleafe, School (Maple) Road, and up the hillside track beyond.

> '.... a goodly procession started at 8.30 p.m. headed by the Warlingham Band, the Whyteleafe Band, Warlingham and Chelsham Fire Brigade on their engine, the Church Lads' Brigade with colours, the

Whyteleafe Fire Brigade, some decorated carts, and many torch bearers. It was a most striking and picturesque sight to see the procession approaching, and the wildness of the night made it more so. One moment the flaming torches would seem extinguished in the brightness of the lightning and the band drowned in the thundering; the next the darkness and silence gave full effect to the waving lights and martial strains. But spirits were as inextinguishable as the torches....'

Despite the weather, it seems that when the bonfires were lit, all went well.

Coronation Celebrations 1902. All ready for the Comic Cricket Match on the Common.

The programme for 27th June was eventually carried out on the new Coronation Day, 9th August. Adults, and children from Chelsham, Fairchildes, Warlingham and Whyteleafe Schools, in total nearly 600, assembled at Court Farm. After the opening ceremony there were children's sports and a chance to have fun on the swings. Mr Hinton provided a meat-tea, first for the children and then for the old folk and other adults present. Then there were adult sports, and the day ended with prize-giving and the presentation of Coronation mugs. The Warlingham children returned in time to enjoy the torchlight procession and bonfire arranged by the village committee, whose celebrations had included a comic cricket match and sports on School Common.

The celebration of Empire Day on 24th May, Queen Victoria's birthday, was introduced into the schools in 1905. This was in commemoration of the assistance given by the colonies during the South African Boer War (1899-1902). The children took part in a simple ceremony on School Common, and then were granted a half-day holiday. It was still observed in some British schools as late as the 1930s.

The Coronation of King George V and Queen Mary took place on 22nd June 1911. Unfortunately in Warlingham some of the day was wet, but the only part of the proceedings which had to be postponed was the children's sports. There was a pageant entitled *Britannia and her children*, and a costume cricket match. The children performed a garland and maypole dance, then tea was postponed for half an hour while they went home to get dry clothes. All the children were given a Coronation mug and a new King George V shilling, this latter being the gift of Mr and Mrs H Daniell, of 'The Ledgers', Chelsham. All the people aged 65 and over received tea or tobacco in a Coronation packet. The day ended with a procession of decorated vehicles, accompanied by people carrying flaming torches, and then fireworks. It was in 1911 that fund raising started for the building of the church hall.

During World War I an open-air service was held each year on The Green on the anniversary in August of the declaration of war. In November 1919 a United Service of thanksgiving for peace was held in the village club hall. The following July a service was held on The Green, and later in the month the peace celebrations were held. On School Common in the morning of 19th July the now traditional comic cricket match was played, then in the afternoon the children sang patriotic songs and enjoyed sports. Tea was provided in the church hall, now returned to parish use. Later there was dancing in the hall, a carnival procession, and a bonfire on the common.

In August 1921 **All Saints' Church Choir** had an outing to Brighton, its first trip since 1913. The church parade of the 'Pride of Warlingham' Lodge of the Oddfellows was revived, but not the fête. It was the custom to collect for charity from the bystanders, and in 1925 £6 was donated to the Caterham Cottage Hospital, and £12 to Croydon General Hospital. There was often some event to attend, usually of a fund-raising nature. In 1927 the Church Social, planned to be held in the Vicarage garden, had to be postponed until the evening, and held in the church hall. The day chosen was 29th June when there was a total solar eclipse, and it was also overcast. Also in 1927, on 30th November, the first 'Give and take' fair (now known as 'Bring and buy') was held, and proved a great success. On 24th August 1929 a Baby Show and Fête, with sideshows and races, was held in Mr Webb's field, off Farleigh Road, which raised £75 for the **Warlingham Silver Band.**

Sir Alan Cobham brought his **'Flying Circus'** air display team to the Hamsey Green area more than once in the early 1930s. In 1934 he made use of 'five acre' field which was north of the present Hamsey Way. Owing to boundary changes much of this area, originally part of Hamsey Green common, is now in Sanderstead. A lady, who was one of the new residents at Hamsey Green and is now in her late 80s, enjoyed a trip in the Handley-Page Clive 1000 h.p. airliner which had accommodation for 22 passengers. Her husband, however, kept his feet firmly on the ground! Other aircraft in the display team included the De Havilland Tiger Moth, Lincock, the Avro Cadet, and the Cierva autogiro.

Sir Alan Cobham and his Flying Circus at Hamsey Green.

The first Hospital Gala Week was held in 1934, from 27th July to 5th August. This was to raise funds for the Caterham Cottage Hospital. People from all parts of the Caterham and Warlingham Urban District were invited to join in and ensure the events were successful. Those held in Warlingham included a Drumhead Service on The Green, a dance in the church hall, and a whist drive in the village club hall. On Wednesday afternoon, 1st August, there was a Grand Carnival and Procession. The Warlingham procession, consisting of decorated vehicles, started from Hamsey Green Gardens, then through the village and down Westhall Road to join the Caterham and Whyteleafe procession in The Square. The route was then along the valley road to Caterham where judging took place in the vicinity of Soper Hall. Inside the Hall there was a bazaar, the stalls provided by the various parts of the district. On Saturday 4th August, a grand Gala was held in the Valley sports ground, White Knobs, with sports, a baby show, various displays and sideshows. It proved to be a very successful week.

In 1935 a decision was made to combine the Hospital Gala Week with the local Jubilee celebrations, the dates being 6th to 12th May. Events arranged were similar to the previous year, with the addition of the selection and crowning of Caterham's first Carnival Queen in the Capitol Cinema. As part of the Jubilee celebrations

CELEBRATIONS, ORGANISATIONS AND PERSONALITIES

Warlingham Scouts built a beacon on Nore Hill. There was a torchlight procession from The Green on the evening of 6th May, and the beacon fire was ceremoniously lit at 10.00 p.m. Because the Warlingham committee was not satisfied with the local Jubilee celebrations, a fête was arranged for the children to be held on Whit Monday, and an entertainment for the old folk on 22nd June.

On 28th January 1936, the wireless broadcast a commentary on the funeral procession of King George V, followed by the funeral service at St George's Chapel, Windsor. As All Saints' Church had been wired for electricity in 1934, F & D Robinson, the local electricians, were able to set up a wireless and loudspeakers in the church. As the time for the transmission from Windsor drew near the church filled to overflowing. Due to the great crowds in London the Royal Train was delayed, but eventually the commentary started. It covered the route through Windsor to the Chapel, and then the full service followed. It was a very moving occasion for all present.

For Hospital Week, 14th to 20th June, Warlingham decided to hold its own events. A Drumhead Service was held on School Common on the Sunday. On Monday evening a Comic Cricket Match, Ladies *v.* Gentlemen, was held on Bull Common. Kathleen Quinn bowled the first ball, and the write-up indicates that it was an hilarious evening, the ladies being declared winners by a small margin. On Tuesday the Caterham and Warlingham Fire Brigade and the No.51, Croydon and Streatham, Division of St John Ambulance gave displays. The concert, dance and whist drive were all well supported, and the week ended with a fête and children's sports. £140 was raised for Hospital funds.

It was obvious that 1937 was going to be a busy year for organisers and helpers. Apart from events arranged by individual organizations there would be the local contribution to the nationwide coronation celebrations, and the annual Hospital Gala Week. Special services were held on the Sunday prior to Coronation Day, which was Wednesday 12th May. B S Buss, who owned the cycle and wireless shop, fixed up loudspeakers on The Green. A large congregation assembled on The Green for an open-air service, and listened to the broadcast of the Coronation Service from Westminster Abbey. In the afternoon there was a large carnival procession, organized by the **British Legion**. Starting from Hamsey Green it made its way to School Common via Farleigh Road, Sunny Bank and Limpsfield Road. Events on the common included a fête and costume cricket match. The weather turned wet but an historic pageant went ahead as planned. 14 episodes from British history were represented, involving 140 performers. Amongst the local organizations involved were the **Guides, Rovers, The Village Club, St Christopher's,** and **Warlingham Toc H** which had been formed in 1933. All was under the direction of Pastor F B Hickson, of the Methodist Church.

In the evening there was a dance in the church hall. At 10.00 p.m. the large bonfire, built by the Scouts in one of E G Quinn's fields, was lit and there was a display of fireworks. On Friday 14th May, the infants were given a tea and entertainment. 195 older children, with 16 adults, spent the day at London Zoo, conveyed there and back in four London Transport buses. The Urban District Council gave every schoolchild a copy of a book entitled *The Crowning of the King and Queen.* The final celebration was a party in the church hall on 20th May organised by Toc H for the over 65s. The funds to pay the expenses, including prizes, were raised locally, and because people had been generous it was possible, as a lasting memorial of the Coronation, to place four new teak seats in the village, one on The Green and three on the Common. The Hospital Gala Week was 11th to 17th July, and included many of the usual events, culminating in a Grand Gala Day in the vicarage field on the Saturday.

On the surface was celebration, but beneath loomed the threat of war. A chart, dated 20th March 1937, was issued entitled 'DIAGRAM OF CONTROL & ORGANISATION FOR AIR RAID PRECAUTIONS IN THE CATERHAM & WARLINGHAM URBAN DISTRICT & THE TRAINING OF VOLUNTEERS'. This was drawn up by Ambrose Keevil, District Controller, and covered all aspects of local administration likely to be needed in a wartime situation. The District was divided into six Sub-Areas, Warlingham being Sub-Area A. The training of volunteers in First Aid was to be the responsibility of the members of the British Red Cross and St John Ambulance Brigade.

A HISTORY OF WARLINGHAM

The official inauguration of the Warlingham section of No.51 (Croydon and Streatham) Division, No.1 District of the St John Ambulance Brigade, was on 23rd October 1936. 18 local men had passed the examination in First Aid, and 10 of them were enrolled on the first Warlingham register of the Brigade, along with L W Allder, who had previously qualified. Soon there were ladies who passed the First Aid examination, and nursing was added to the available skills. Funds were raised to obtain the first Warlingham ambulance, and this, which cost £100, was dedicated on Sunday 10th April 1938.

The 1938 Hospital Gala Week was held in June, as usual. Besides the regular events there was a baby show, a flitch contest, a tattoo, and a display by the **Warlingham St John Ambulance** members. 1939 brought a special celebration for the Methodists, being the centenary of the opening of the first chapel. That year's Hospital Gala Week was the last. In the autumn of 1938 Ambrose Keevil had been moved on to a higher administrative position, in time becoming Commander of the London Sector of the Home Guard. His deputy, Major R J N Milner, took over local control.

Everyone who was in Warlingham during World War II will have his or her own memories and experiences to relate. The Red Cross and St John members combined under the official name 'War Organisation of the British Red Cross Society and Order of St John of Jerusalem'. **The Women's Voluntary Service** was formed in 1938, and the local group with Organiser Mrs Rowland, who lived at 'Dunsmore' in Landscape Road, made use of 'Mill House' near The Green. This original group ended its work on 31st August 1945, but the Women's Royal Voluntary Service still continues its good work in the district, delivering Meals on Wheels, providing a weekly Luncheon Club in Warlingham and a Library Service.

During the war there were special weeks to raise money and encourage people to buy War Bonds, Savings certificates and Savings stamps. In 1941 it was 'War Weapons Week' in February, and later in the year the WVS had a Salvage Drive. In February 1942 it was 'Warship Week', and money was being raised for the Spitfire Fund. 'Wings for Victory Week' was held in June 1943, and events raised money for the RAF Benevolent Fund. In July 1944 came 'Salute the Soldier Week' which included many of the favourite events, a dance, concert, whist drive, sports and fun fair for the children. There was also a display of Pre-Service Glider Training by the 162 Gliding School at Gardner's Aerodrome, Hamsey Green.

The VE Day celebrations in 1945 which marked the end of war in Europe, were both localised and of an organised nature. On 9th May there was an open-air service on School Common, followed later in the day by children's sports, a bonfire and dancing. Everyone was in high spirits, despite the light rain. On 21st July there was a very successful Children's Victory Gala, attended by more than 1400 people. The VJ Days, 8th and 9th August, were marked by an United Thanksgiving Service, bonfire and dancing, sports and street tea parties.

Members of St John became No.111 Warlingham Ambulance and Nursing Division, London (Prince of Wales) District, and a Cadet Division was successfully established. The first ambulance had soon been replaced by a more comfortable and up-to-date model. Over the next 30 years there were further replacements, and many varied duties were successfully accomplished. In the later 1970s Warlingham joined with Sanderstead to form 364 Sanderstead and Warlingham Combined Division. The Ambulance Station, near the British legion Club on Limpsfield Road dates from 1971.

The Afternoon **Women's Institute** was established in 1946. The Evening W.I. dates from 1970. In 1949 the first Warlingham May Queen, Valerie Elliott, was crowned. The 1950 May Queen, Margaret Lake, with her attendants, took part in the Carnival Procession held on 17th June, part of the Seventh Centenary Celebrations of All Saints' and St. Leonard's Churches. The week of celebrations, 11th to 18th June, started and ended with Sunday services where the visiting preachers included the Bishops of Southwark, Woolwich and Kingston, and former vicars Revd F R Dickinson and Canon W H Roseveare. During the week there were several entertainments in the church hall, a Drumhead service on The Green, and children's sports on School Common. On the Saturday, as well as the Carnival Procession, there was a dog show, stalls and sideshows in the vicarage field, and country dancing by the Women's Institute on School Common. Television came to All Saints' Church in September 1950.

FESTIVAL OF BRITAIN

Pageant

OF

WARLINGHAM & CHELSHAM

SATURDAY, 23rd JUNE, 1951

Parade leaves Tithe Pit Shaw Lane, Hamsey Green, 6 p.m., arriving Warlingham Common approx. **7** p.m.

Route

HAMSEY GREEN, TITHE PIT SHAW LANE — LIMPSFIELD ROAD — BAKERS HILL — CREWES CORNER — SUNNY BANK — CHELSHAM ROAD — LIMPSFIELD ROAD — VILLAGE GREEN — LEAS ROAD — REDVERS ROAD — SCHOOL COMMON

N° **155**

PROGRAMME PRICE 6d.

Every local organisation was invited to take part in the Pageant, and most did so. The May Queen on this occasion was Ann Golden.

A few of the performers in the 1951 Festival of Britain Pageant held on 23rd June.

In the foreground are Saxons, and behind a glimpse of the Ancient Britons.

1951 was Festival of Britain year when the Festival Exhibition was staged on London's South Bank, and towns and villages everywhere celebrated with a wide variety of local events. Caterham & Warlingham Urban District Council produced a booklet which had a centre page spread listing the principal local events. The official opening was a fête on Whit Monday 14th May, in White Knobs Sports Ground, Caterham. Events in Warlingham were mainly in the week 16th to 23th June, culminating in an historical pageant of Warlingham and Chelsham. A report in the parish magazine, now renamed Parish News, is worth quoting—

'The Parish News would like to be allowed to offer to all concerned with the arrangements for Warlingham and Chelsham's Festival Celebrations most sincere congratulations. The whole week was a very great success. Every event went well. The Cricket Club beat Sanderstead, the old folks enjoyed their tea, the Baby Show glowed with health and beauty; the Gymkhana was a treat of high spirits and horsemanship, the Fancy Dress dance was enjoyable. The Village Club ran a Whist Drive, the Methodists gave a really first-class piece of amateur drama in *Painted Sparrows*.

The children's sports entertained hundreds of youngsters and their friends. The Guards' Band beat a most impressive Retreat on the School Common, and the St.John Ambulance display which followed was a striking representation of the Good Samaritan and its modern counterpart. The Women's Institute exhibition and folk dancing were excellent, *Youth Entertains* skilled and humorous. But the Pageant of Warlingham through the ages on the final Saturday was beyond all praise. Those who took part were public benefactors, and those who conceived and organised it deserve our heartfelt thanks. From the cheerful courage of the naked – well nearly – Ancient Britons, to the breathtaking dignity of the Cavaliers, and the happy inspiration of St.George on his white charger, it was all a joy, and an education. Well done Warlingham and Chelsham.!'

**Festival of Britain Week.   Entrants for the Baby Show
held in the Village Hall on 16th June, 1951.**

CELEBRATIONS, ORGANISATIONS AND PERSONALITIES

The prime mover behind the pageant was W L Morgan, who was pageant master, and a great deal of work went into producing it. Authentic period costumes were hired for principal characters, and every organization in the village was encouraged to take part. The parade was led by the **Warlingham British Legion** (formerly Warlingham Silver) **Band**, and the Caterham Silver Band, then the tableaux followed in sequence from '55BC Ancient Britons' through to 'Warlingham today', this latter group including organizations such as the **Pony Club** not represented elsewhere. The **Warlingham & District Horse Club**, which had been founded in 1950, added greatly to the parade. When all had arrived at School Common, six short scenes were enacted. After the judging the winners in each class were presented with their prizes by Mrs A T Gannon and Colonel Ambrose Keevil. There were also 40 lucky programme prizes donated by local traders. These included items such as shoe repairs, laundry and drycleaning, a permanent wave, nylon stockings (as yet difficult to obtain), a cake, fruit and vegetables, unrationed meat (possibly offal), cigarettes and various bottles of drink. When the accounts for the week's festivities had been finalised, the profit, amounting to £290, was donated to the Almshouses Endowment Fund.

Warlingham produced its own souvenir programme for Coronation Week, Saturday 30th May to Saturday 6th June 1953. There were special services in the churches, and a drumhead service on School Common at 4.00 p.m. on Sunday 31st May. On Coronation Day, 2nd June, many people, either in their own homes or with friends and neighbours, were able for the first time – by television – not only to hear but also to see this momentous event as it took place. Street parties were organised for the children. Later in the day a procession formed on School Common, and at 6.30 p.m. moved off down the hill to join the official Caterham and Warlingham Urban District celebrations in Whyteleafe Recreation Ground. Prizes were awarded for different classes of decorated float, and

10th June 1953. Residents of Sunny Bank and friends gather for a Coronation Party held in the field by the British Legion Club. Note the buses behind the group.

for the children's fancy dress competition. There were various sideshows, dancing, and a grand firework display. Other items in Warlingham during the week included sports for the children, music and dancing on the Common, a gymkhana, the ever popular Comic Cricket Match, and tea and entertainment for the older residents. The Pilgrim Players presented their first production *Quiet Weekend*. Finally on Saturday 6th June Warlingham and District had a procession to which all local organisations were invited to contribute a float. This assembled at Hamsey Green, and via The Green, Farleigh Road, Sunny Bank and Limpsfield Road, toured the district, arriving at the Common for a Grand Finale.

Since 1953 there have been numerous fêtes, fairs and fun days, held variously in the Sports Club ground, on School Common, in the vicarage field, and more recently in the grounds of the Blanchman's Farm Community Wildlife Area, off Limpsfield Road. In 1975 the tercentenary of the almshouses was marked by a week of events, both indoors and out, and an exhibition of local items of historical interest set out in the Mission Room. In 1985 the two-day parish festival *Our Village* was staged in the church hall and in All Saints' Church. On the Saturday, music – vocal and instrumental – was performed throughout the day in All Saints' Church. Amongst the performers was Harry Leppard, playing a *Floral Medley* on the organ.

1958. Warlingham May Queen in the Caterham & Warlingham Carnival Parade. The float won a First Prize in Class B.

Organisations which started in the later 1940s and 1950s include the **Over 60s Club**, founded in 1949, the **Warlingham Residents Association** which was formed in June 1952, and in 1953 the **Warlingham Boys' Club**, of which Police Sergeant Charles (Nobby) Spiers was one, if not the, principal founder. For some years now membership has also been open to girls. The **Floral Art Group** of the Horticultural Society dates from 1965, and more recently, in November 1988, the **Hamsey Green & Warlingham Probus Club** was established. The parish directory, *Our Village*, has often been published in lieu of the August parish news.

Personalities

Henry Maurice Leppard, always known as Harry, first contributed to music in Warlingham when aged only eight. In December 1920 his name appears on a school concert programme playing a piano duet with Louise Harwood. It was not long before he was advanced enough to play on the church organ occasionally. By early 1925 he had passed both lower and higher division examinations on the organ. Music was Harry's lifetime hobby, his daily work being with the merchants Hall & Co. He had a musical background, his father being secretary of the Warlingham Brass Band, and no doubt a player, and his grandfather one of the small band of musicians who played in All Saints' Church in the 1850s, before the acquisition of a barrel organ. Harry had his own dance band for many years, and an organ to play on at home.

Harry Leppard (Piano) and his Spots, in the 1950s. *Photo courtesy of Graham Leppard*

He was church organist at St Leonard's, Chelsham, from May 1926 to early 1942, when he moved to All Saints', the organist there, E G Ingrams, having resigned. At the end of June 1959, he moved again, this time to St Francis, Warlingham Park Hospital. In 1986 Harry completed 60 years as a church organist, and he continued to play organ or piano almost to the end of his life, dying in November 1994, aged 85.

Two men who contributed greatly to the parish earlier in the century, and in a different way, were **Charles Herbert Goodman** (1848–1937), and **Charles Langton Lockton** (1856–1932). Both were churchwardens at All Saints', the former people's warden from 1896 to 1911, the latter vicar's warden from 1901 to his death. Both came to Warlingham in the 1890s. Charles Lockton's house 'Teeton' stood opposite the top of Hillbury Road. There had been a small thatched cottage on the land which he bought. Now, in its turn,'Teeton' has given way to more modern property. Charles Goodman bought a plot much further down Westhall Road, and his house had the name 'Bryn Cottage'. More recently it has been known as 'St Heliers', and then 'Little Bromfield'.

They both had a considerable interest in the village and its history. Charles Lockton painted many views, buildings and scenes now long gone. One or two were constructed from early photographs, change having already taken place. A number of his paintings, which were given to the Parish, can be seen in Warlingham Library. It was Charles Lockton who started the Warlingham museum, a collection of items of interest now housed in the East Surrey Museum. Charles Goodman was a photographer, and keen on every aspect of local history. He delved into every accessible document he could find, and searched out many details about our district in the past. He started his monthly contribution *Parish Notes* in the Warlingham and Chelsham Parish Magazine in 1898. He also made use of the magazine to record current events and items of interest which occurred in the village. Although he moved to West Hoathly in Sussex in 1911 he continued the monthly *Parish Notes* until 1925. The Surrey Archaeological Society holds a set of these notes in paste-up form with illustrations.

Ambrose Keevil (1893–1973) and his wife Dorothy were much involved in local affairs in Warlingham during a span of just over 40 years. They came to live at 'Bayards' in Westhall Road in 1931, and over the years a number of fund-raising events were held in their garden. Colonel Sir Ambrose Keevil, as he was to become in 1952, had a distinguished career, the first recognition of his worth being the awards of the Military Cross and an MBE after World War I. He worked in the food industry, and during World War II held important positions in the Ministry of Food and in connection with the Home Guard. His book, published in 1972, relates the history and development of his firm, Fitch Lovell, of which he rose to be president. His other business achievements were many and varied. In Surrey he was a Deputy Lieutenant, and High Sheriff in 1956/7. He was first chairman, then president, of the East Surrey Conservative Association during the years 1945 to 1971. More locally he held a prominent position on the board of governors of Reedham School, Purley, and in Warlingham he was for many years treasurer of Warlingham Church Council. He was president of several local organisations, including the Village Club, the Pilgrim Players, the Sports Club, Warlingham and District Horse Club, and the local Pony Club. Sir Ambrose was a very able man, an organiser, who fitted an enormous amount into his every day. Lady Dorothy Keevil moved to Limpsfield, where she lived a further five years. 'Bayards' was demolished, and the 8½ acre site redeveloped. Only 'Temple Belwood', converted from the original stabling/garage premises with four-room staff flat over, remains from the original development.

The opening of 'Salute the Soldier' Week, Saturday, 1st July 1944.   General Sir Hastings Ismay, KCB, DSO; Cllr Dr Harold Trafford, and – on the right – Ambrose Keevil MBE, MC.

It is appreciated there may have been omissions in this chapter as not every event can be included, nor every person who has given their time and capabilities for the benefit of the community.

SOURCES

Personal collection of programmes re events.

Press cuttings.

Warlingham and Chelsham Parish Magazine, including *Our Village*.

Chapter 21

Technical Progress Brings Change

Nowadays we grumble if there is even a brief power cut or break in water supply due to essential repairs, and it is difficult to imagine life, even as recently as only 100 years ago, when many of the aspects of modern living conditions and of communication which we take for granted were not present in rural Surrey. Several, indeed, were not yet even invented. Life was slower, and generally much quieter, in the era of the horse.

Transport

The valley road, which came under the Surrey and Sussex Turnpike Trust, passed through the edge of Warlingham parish, and was well used, but travellers were few on the route across the hilltop. The Limpsfield Trust was created in 1770, and one of the trustees was Thomas Wigsell, attorney, (son of Mary Atwood and Nicholas Wigsell of Greenwich) who was lord of the manor of Sanderstead and Warlingham at the time.

> 'An act for the repairing, widening, and keeping in repair the Road leading from Eaton Bridge Turnpike Road at Cockham Hill in the parish of Westerham in the county of Kent, through the village of Limpsfield, to the village of Titsey, over Botley Hill, Worms Heath and Willingham Common to the turnpike road leading from Croydon to Godstone in the County of Surry.'

There were tollgates at Botley Hill, where the house remains though enlarged, and at Hamsey Green. The original route beyond this latter gate towards London was across Hamsey Green common and out on to Riddlesdown to join with the valley road. By about 1830 it seems the route used was along through Sanderstead and down the hill to Croydon. Expenditure on repairs, wages etc proved to be almost twice the income received from tolls. No interest was paid on the £2000 borrowed initially – nor, it seems, was this capital ever repaid. Trusts were renewed every 21 years. This one was not renewed in the 1850s, and the turnpike gates were removed. It is known that a daily coach passed through Warlingham in the later 1840s, but this was probably one of the routes set up in a vain attempt to outdo the railways, and soon ceased due to lack of passengers.

In 1851 it is recorded that the carrier, Luke Scott, was making the journey to London and back every Tuesday, and various carts must have gone down to Croydon market. The better-off rode horses, or had carriages; otherwise people walked to their destinations.

The opening of the Caterham branch railway line in 1856 made little immediate impact on Warlingham on the hill. The line through to Oxted, which opened in 1884, did bring about considerable change. For a few years, in the early 1900s, John Bashford, job master, had livery and bait stables by Upper Warlingham station, and advertised regular times for his local horsebus and carrier service. The stops included *The White Lion* and *The Bull* on Chelsham Common, and on Tuesdays and Fridays some journeys went out to Tatsfield.

It was August 1921 before the new, single deck, motor buses came into Warlingham, run by the East Surrey Traction Co Ltd of Reigate. A comment in the September parish magazine indicates that not everyone welcomed this connection with Croydon, and beyond on the Kent side to Westerham and Sevenoaks—

> '...always some have wanted to see the transport connections made and some have dreaded or disliked the prospect. Both used to say the hills would be prohibitive. But now the ornamental blue buses, inside only, are actually on the road, and negotiating the hills, and Warlingham is no longer a place rather out of the way and protected by its hills, but is just one stopping place on a route. There was a good deal of feeling before the buses came, and even public meetings on The Green. Perhaps there is something to be said even for those that opposed them. If the gain is

great in convenience there may be some loss in seclusion. But the buses are a fact, and the changes that ensue remain to be seen.'

Following the London Traffic Act 1924 routes in the Metropolitan Police area were renumbered. East Surrey operated S (south) 3 on behalf of the London General Omnibus Co, and this became 403. The Garage – known as Chelsham but actually in Warlingham – opened in 1925, and closed when the lease of the land expired in 1990. Over the years various routes, such as 408, 470, 453, and varieties of 403 have come and gone. The long distance Green Line service, operating in the 1930s but suspended during World War II, restarted in June 1946. These coaches, 706 and 707, ran from Aylesbury through to Westerham and Oxted. As more people obtained cars passenger numbers dropped, and these coaches were withdrawn in 1977. Deregulation from 1986 has brought change of ownership of routes. For a short time the 403 was a red bus, then it reverted to the green of the London Country routes. Currently the routes passing through Warlingham are numbered 403 and 411.

The Southern Heights Railway

This project, put forward in the 1920s, was for an electric-powered light railway just under 15½ miles in length, leaving the main railway at a point near Purley Downs Golf Course, and passing through Warlingham, Chelsham and Tatsfield, to terminate at Orpington in Kent. The promotion was headed by Lt Col H F Stephens, who had been involved in the construction of several light railways. A station was proposed at Hamsey Green, and another on the further side of the parish, to be called Chelsham. A two-day inquiry was held at Orpington in March 1926, attended by representatives from all the various councils and landowners affected and from Surrey County Council, gas, water and telephone companies. There was a lot of opposition to the project, and much delay caused by extended queries and disagreements.

The Ministry of Transport agreed to the proposed light railway in May 1928, and the Southern Railway was prepared to back the scheme financially, provided it received 75% of the gross receipts. However, the two year starting time ran out before anything had been done, and the promoters could not get an extension. The London Passenger Transport Act (1933) which would involve pooling of all receipts in the London area was looming, and the Southern Railway withdrew its support. By May 1933 the scheme was quite dead, no doubt to the relief of the clerk to Coulsdon and Purley Urban District Council, whose file on the matter remains to provide a fascinating insight as to what might have been.

Water and Drainage

At the beginning of the 19th century the population of the parish was under 200, so the natural water supply in the various ponds was probably adequate in normal conditions. In 1846, when John Epps who practised homeopathy came to live in 'Meadow Cottage', there were about 500 residents, and he became concerned at the way humans and animals shared the same water supply. At his instigation a new pond was created in 1847, fenced around to exclude animals. This was at the junction of Bond Road with Limpsfield Road. Since 1931 the council yard has been on the site. In 1861 Dr Epps left Warlingham.

Five ponds on the common land, including Dr Epps' pond, were detailed in the 1866 Enclosure Award. These were handed over to the churchwardens and other parish officers who were to keep them in good order.

Warlingham was included in the designated area of the Caterham Spring Water Company which came into being in 1862, but the first piped water did not arrive until 1868. It was pumped, at considerable cost, to the brickfield by Limpsfield Road. In subsequent years piped water became available to most properties. Crewes and Kennel Farms had wells. From time to time the part of the parish in the valley suffered when the Bourne was in flood. Well Farm was so called because of the deep well there, never known to be dry.

Above: June 1903. Dr Epps' pond, which was at the Limpsfield Road end of Bond Road. The household waste depôt now occupies the site.

Left: The work of installing main drainage in Warlingham started in December 1930. This photograph was taken in Warren Park.

As the population increased so did the problem of sewage disposal. A long forgotten cesspit or soakaway is even now occasionally uncovered near older properties. In 1929, when Warlingham was moved from Godstone Rural District to join Caterham Urban District, a new main sewer was being laid along the valley to Purley. A sewer was laid through the Westhall area, but the initial work of laying 24,100 yards of drains was concentrated on the village area. The contractors were Howard Farrow Ltd and the cost – some £53,178 – was covered by a loan to be repaid over 30 years. The work started late in 1930, and was expected to take 18 months. A comment in the February 1932 parish magazine brings to mind the conditions created by the recent cable laying in the district—

> '...One of the choicest spots will be found at the bottom of Church Road where things are in such a state that to go to church on a Sunday evening is quite an adventure. The gas lamp is generally not working, so that the darkness is complete which adds much to the fun. Those who go regularly are best off because in course of time they learn which are the shallowest pools. For motors Church Road is a splendid test of car springs, but then the joys of having main drainage brought to Warlingham have made all our roads like that. But cheer up, everybody. Someday, somebody will do something to put things right, and those who have survived will get the benefit of what we are so happily enduring. All the same, future generations of Warlinghamites will owe much to the patience of this generation. It has been, and still is, a very trying, wetting, and shaking experience.'

The houses in Hamsey Green Gardens, constructed in 1932/33, were the first in Warlingham to have gas, electricity, water and drainage laid on.

Post and Telephone

In the early 19th century there would have been very few letters to or from Warlingham. In 1851 George Brooks had a receiving office in his grocer's shop situated on the edge of the common.

The letters were brought up from Croydon, expected daily at 9.15 a.m. and outgoing post was taken away at 1.50 p.m. With the influx of new residents from the 1880s onwards, and the opening of the railway line providing a station in Whyteleafe, the post was routed via the train and received a Whyteleafe handstamp. In the 1890s William Brown, baker and grocer at Mill House, was sub-postmaster. In 1899, when Richard Joseph Ringer came up from Croydon to Warlingham and took over Ebenezer Wilson's general stores, the post office was moved to his shop. It remained on this site for the next 40 years until Cullen's had the premises rebuilt, and it moved to the present location.

A public telephone was installed in Ringer's stores in 1909, linked to the Purley exchange. World War I probably delayed the installation of telephones to an extent, but by 1924 a local exchange was needed. A house for this purpose was built in Redvers Road, designed so that at a future date it could be a normal domestic property. By 1931 there were 335 listed subscribers, about a third of whom were business and professional people. The telephone was still very much a luxury.

More house building in the 1930s meant more letters, and in 1938 a Post Office Sorting Office was built on Limpsfield Road frontage of the glebe allotments field. This building was in use until 1993 when staff were moved to Caterham. The building was demolished, and replaced by the Norwood

The Post Office Sorting Office, which opened in 1938, had this plaque, placed above the clock and letter box.

Aquarium warehouse. Advances in technology, coupled with increased demand, brought about the end of the manual exchange, much regretted by many residents who missed the friendly personal contact. Cables went underground, many telegraph poles were removed, and in the early 1960s the present exchange was built alongside the sorting office. In 1988 the familiar red telephone boxes were replaced by modern kiosks. Warlingham 'phone numbers have been 'all numbers' for some time now, the code 01883 and prefix 62 still indicating those Whyteleafe subscribers who were attached to the former Upper Warlingham exchange.

Fire Brigade

Village fire brigades were composed of volunteers who worked locally. In the early 1900s the Captain of the Warlingham and Chelsham Brigade was John Quittenton. The vehicle and horses were kept at Chelsham Place Farm. There were two or three hydrants sited around the village, and useful items such as a length of hose were kept in the parish fire box which was on the corner of the common nearest to The Green. A quote from the parish magazine states—

> '...In addition the Voluntary Brigade have a handcart with hose etc. stationed at the Vicarage stables. This does not necessarily mean that the Vicar is the proper person open to receive calls. These should be given at once to any member of the Brigade whose names have been clearly painted on the appliance box. Then the fire bell at Mr Chissell's farm should be vigorously rung until the Brigade appear.'

July 1905. The Fire Brigade about to enter the gate into the churchyard. It formed part of the annual church parade preceding the service held on behalf of the 'Pride of Warlingham' Lodge of the Oddfellows.

The sound of the bell would have carried a considerable distance in those more peaceful days, but there must have been quite a delay before the Brigade actually arrived at the scene of a fire.

Aside from fire-fighting, the brigade took part in many local events, such as church parades and fetes. In the 1920s the captain was Mr Webb. The horses, Dolly and Babs, were kept in the field adjacent to 'Box' – better known as 'Webb's' – Cottage in Farleigh Road, opposite Bond Road. In 1929, when Warlingham was moved from Godstone Rural District to Caterham Urban District, a fire station was built by the Soper Hall in Caterham, and the local volunteers were disbanded. In the later 1980s the fire brigade moved to premises near the M25 at Godstone.

Gas and Electricity

By 1890 there were several new properties in the Westhall area of Warlingham, and more in process of building. A representative from the Caterham and District Gas Company, established 1869 in the valley near *The Rose and Crown*, canvassed the new residents and found several were interested in having gas laid on. In 1892 a main was laid, bringing gas up Succombs Hill and along Narrow Lane to the junction with Westhall Road, This brought gas to, amongst others, W S Church at 'Keilawarra', William J Stuart at 'Dorincourt' and Timothy Neems at 'The Laurels'. A branch main was laid along Southview and Westview Roads. By April 1898 Homefield Road had gas and the laying of the main progressed steadily towards Warlingham village.

In 1899 a public meeting was held to decide whether the village should have gas street lamps. Not all were in favour, but eventually in December 1899 a contract for five years was signed, and the first seven lamps were erected. By the end of 1902 the gas main had reached Croydon (Warlingham Park) Mental Hospital, via Limpsfield and Chelsham Roads. In March 1903 the clerk to Warlingham Parish Council wrote to the Gas Company to complain of unsatisfactory service. Subsequently 1% was deducted from the street lighting bill for the quarter around Christmas 1902.

Above: **The top stretch of Succombs Hill in 1969. This is the ancient route from Westhall into the valley.**

Left: **Narrow Lane, in 1969, linking Succombs Hill with Westhall. Originally called the Parish Road, both gas and electricity were brought up Succombs Hill and along here to Westhall Road. This lane was widened in 1970.**

This photograph, taken in May 1903, shows that Westhall Lane (Road) was hardly wider than the Parish Road (Narrow Lane) which goes off to the right. The gas and electricity supply route continued along here towards the village.

In 1904 when gas was connected to 'Southlands' in Chapel Road the first cables bringing electricity to Warlingham were already being laid. Caterham Power Station was built in 1903 on a site purchased from Richard Ramsay Bond who had inherited land and property in Caterham and Warlingham when his father died in 1891. The route for electricity was similar to that used for gas. The take-up was generally rather slow, being considered a luxury. Many cottagers were tenants, and landlords were not willing to go to the extra expense. The Church Hall, by the Green, completed in 1914, had both services laid on. Houses built from the late 1920s were all wired for electricity. Gas street lamps were used throughout the district, but from the 1950s these were gradually replaced by electric lighting, starting with the main roads. In the South Eastern Gas Company's area the process of conversion from town gas to natural gas started in 1969. Warlingham was one of the very last places to be converted in the mid 1970s.

The Doctor

There was no resident doctor in Warlingham until towards the end of the 19th century. If necessary a doctor had to be fetched from Croydon. Around 1880 Dr Henry Dearsley came to live at 'Meadow Cottage' in Farleigh Road. He was followed in 1886 by Dr Henry Ross Todd, who married Miss Marriott, the vicar's sister. During his residence alterations were carried out, and the house renamed 'The Meadows'. Dr Richard Gordon Pollock came to Warlingham in 1898. In 1901 Dr Ross Todd, who specialised in nervous complaints, left the village to take up a position in London. Dr Pollock moved to 'Hilminster' in Westhall Road, and Dr William Robert Etches came to 'The Meadows'.

Dr Pollock remained at 'Hilminster' for several years. Meanwhile in 1903 Timothy Neems, owner of the house, died and it was sold by auction to Dr Thomas William Shore of Dulwich for £775. Dr Pollock then obtained a nearby site, part of the original plot on which 'Clovelly' stood. His new house, named 'Brightside' and completed in 1910, included a surgery. Having a widespread practice, he found the most efficient way to get about was on horseback. In 1907 the Warlingham, Chelsham and Farleigh District Nursing Association was formed. For a small subscription, in 1925 one penny a week, subscribers were entitled to the help of the local resident nurse, free of further charge except for maternity cases. In 1931 No.7 Warren Park was registered as a nursing home for confinements. This house, renumbered No.13 in 1938, was home to Nurse Bill, Nurse Witty, and then Nurse Baillie. The subscription was raised to twopence in 1944, lasting until 1948.

After almost 30 years Dr Pollock retired in 1927, and Dr Harold Trafford took over the practice. The local architect, Briant Poulter, designed 'Grafton House' in Westhall Road for him. For a while 'Brightside' was a small nursing home. Some years ago the house was renamed 'Cluny'. First Dr Oliver Ive, then Dr W S Russell Thomas worked in the practice with Dr Trafford. In 1937 Dr J A C Burridge came to Warlingham. A new surgery opened at Hamsey Green with Dr J Brittain after World War II following another spate of house-building. The Trafford/Burridge partnership ended in 1970 when Dr Trafford retired from general practice. Apart from a very busy life as a doctor he had been an active local councillor from 1931 to 1953. He was chairman of Caterham & Warlingham Urban District Council for the year 1939/40. He was made an Honorary Alderman of Tandridge District Council in 1992, just a few months before his death at age 90 in 1993. His many small helpful deeds when a doctor, often of a financial nature, have passed unrecorded but will not be forgotten by those who benefited. After many years in Warlingham Dr Burridge retired in 1973. Others whose length of time in the district varied include Doctors Herrick, Hennessy, Mawer, Phillips and Morrison. Currently Dr David Beckitt, Dr F Allenby and Dr P C V Ramage have all been in the area over 20 years.

As regards dentists some may recall Harold Fox, also C T Francis and his son R C Francis. The latter retired in 1982 after completing 40 years in his Warlingham practice.

SOURCES

COULSDON & PURLEY URBAN DISTRICT COUNCIL – Papers regarding Southern Heights Railway.

Directories.

Enclosure Award 1866.

GOODMAN, C H *Parish Notes*.

HUITSON, M *Caterham Gas Company*.

KING, J T & NEWMAN, A G (1965) *Southbound from Croydon*.

PIPE, J (1997) *Electricity Supply in Caterham and District* 1900-1992.

SPENCE, J – Notes regarding Southern Heights Railway.

Warlingham & Chelsham Parish Magazine.

Chapter 22

Sport in Warlingham

by Roger Packham

Sport is recognised as being an important strand of village life and at Warlingham it has long held a place in the fabric of the locality. There is a reference to archery for 1539 and in 1553 the Warlingham manor court imposed fines on Robert Nightingale, John Wooden, William Ownsted, John Taylor and others for playing bowls in secret. In the 19th century another sport which frequently came under the scrutiny of authority was boxing and on 18th June 1819 Warlingham Common was the scene of a contest between Cy Davis of Bristol and Ned Turner.

Fox hunting was popular from at least the early 19th century but undoubtedly, in common with several neighbouring villages, it is cricket which has played the most important part in Warlingham's sporting history.

Cricket

The earliest reference to Warlingham cricket is a match in 1751 when players from the village combined with those from Croydon, Cheam and Addington to oppose Ripley, Thursley and London in the celebrated Artillery Ground in London (the Lord's of its day). The names of the Warlingham players are unrecorded, but it is likely that one or more of the brothers Frame were included.

The most famous of the four brothers was John Frame who was born at Warlingham in 1731. His great skill as a bowler led to appearances for England and he was enticed to Dartford to play cricket for that town. There is a poster in the British Museum advertising the Dartford v All England match in 1759 in which Frame opened the bowling for Dartford. He remained in the town for many years and became mine host of *The Eleven Cricketers* on East Hill. John Nyren, in his classic of cricket literature, remembered Frame as 'an unusually stout man for a cricketer'.

In 1833 Warlingham's match against Westerham was entirely unsatisfactory—

'...it having been considered that the Westerham brought an unfair eleven, the match was not played. The parties then proceeded to *The Leather Bottle*, and partook of some of the host's "good things of this life", after which two elevens were chosen on the Green, but the Westerham party ordered their horses with the intention of leaving. The "Blacksmith's daughter", however, had been put on the stable-door by the hostess of *The Leather Bottle*, which was not taken off until the 'mopusses' were forthcoming, as a recompense for the woeful havoc made by the Westerham party at the luncheon; but from which many made a dinner. The party departed amid the hootings of the crowd, among whom were some of their own players.'

The next recorded Warlingham match is that against Coulsdon in 1838 when the Warlingham eleven was: Sales, G and J Smith, Saker, J & W Brooke, Gatland, J Atkins, Baker, Burt and Morley. This is the first known team and it includes many well-known local names. However, there was more acrimony -

'...the darkness of the evening put a stop to the game. Notwithstanding the Coulsden (team) had but eight runs to get, and six wickets standing, their opponents refused to give up the match. This caused much dissatisfaction and the evening was not spent in the most harmonious manner.'

The two matches with Limpsfield in 1856 provide the present club with its foundation date and in the succeeding decades matches appear quite regularly in the newspapers. Opponents included Blindley Heath, Caterham Association, Deptford Unity, Croydon Amateurs, Oxted United, Sanderstead, Sutton New Town and Sutton Phoenix and the Warlingham team was sometimes styled Warlingham Alma (1861-80) or Warlingham & Chelsham United (1883).

It is evident that Warlingham cricket received a considerable impetus in the late Victorian period through the energetic vicar, the Revd F R Marriott (1888-1900). His photograph has recently been published with the 1891 team and this was certainly no gentlemen's eleven. His notes in the parish magazine provide a detailed record of the cricket and he repeatedly urged the players to exert themselves in improving the ground on School Common - 'Therefore let us roll.' His scores of 114 not out and 121 not out in 1893 testify to his ability and his departure to Wootton near Woodstock was generally regretted.

SPORT IN WARLINGHAM

In 1906 successful efforts were made to find a private ground—

'Whit Monday was a memorable day in the annals of Warlingham cricket, for on it the new private ground was opened. The Common did very well for a long time and the level of cricket maintained there in Mr Marriott's day will not easily be passed...But it has gradually become evident that a new ground was needed. First, that ever-widening footpath; then the increased traffic across and around the Common and the building which seemed to make it shrink, and the ever-multiplying children all made it merely a matter of time for the Common to be closed to adult cricket. An ideal position was found in one of the Glebe fields, money was quickly subscribed to fence it and level and re-lay a portion sufficient to play on, it being hoped that gradually the whole may be levelled; a pavilion was quickly run up by members...and as though a fairy had waved a wand and made a transformation on June 4th 1906 Warlingham Cricketers moved to a beautiful private ground...The first ball of this historic match was bowled, as was meet, by Mr Lockton.'

This new ground was the glebe field, Little Nine Acres, (mentioned in Chapter 5) sited near the top of Westhall Road on the Tydcombe side, and adjacent to Lockton's property in Ridley Road. It was though to be a short-lived move because the land was sold to the East Surrey Water Company in December 1912. It is uncertain if the cricketers were obliged to move again before World War I, but after the war, the formation of the Warlingham Sports Club in 1919 led to a permanent move to the present home in Church Lane.

The inter-war years were dominated by the imposing figure of C A V Slade, who captained the club for 23 years and he is remembered by a memorial gate on the ground.

Early in World War II a cricket match was interrupted by an air raid and during the blitz a bomb fell close to the cricket table. The pavilion was taken over by the army and an anti-aircraft gun appeared on the field.

After repairs had been effected, the Club meandered towards the advent of league cricket in 1971, occasionally hosting matches for Surrey beneficiaries; a match in 1946 for the Oval Centenary Fund saw the appearance of two very distinguished visitors - Arthur Mailey, the famous Australian bowler of the 1920s and the England captain, E R T Holmes.

Today the Club, replete with overseas players, thrives in the Surrey Championship and maintains a long established Wednesday eleven.

Association Football

The comparatively modern game of association football has never made a real impact in Warlingham. It was slow to take off and in October 1896 it was reported that—

'An earnest attempt is now being made to start a Football Club. There is not the least reason why we should not have one, and a good one. We have lots of material – many young men who, doubtless, would be able to play the game well if only they would make a start and get over the preliminary training in a knowledge of the rules of the game...'

Subsequently, the first match took place on Saturday, 16th January 1897 when Godstone Swifts were the visitors. The result was a 1-1 draw 'which was very creditable seeing that this was our first match and that the majority of our team began football this season.' The report of the match highlights the game's inherent problems—

'W Lancaster of Warlingham snapped his collar bone and it is possible to imagine pleasanter opponents'.

A visit to Caterham Village a year later, when Warlingham lost two men to injuries prompted the following—

'It was not a pleasant game. Our opponents seemed to forget that football is merely a game and ought to be played in a friendly spirit.'

After promising beginnings, no doubt encouraged by the captain (Revd Marriott) and vice-captain (Revd Macaulay), enthusiasm declined, matches were scratched and only two members were present at a general meeting in 1899.

"SOUVENIR SUPPLEMENT" drawn by Skipper C. C. Haynes.

"A GREAT WINNING TEAM OF LOCAL LADS."

WARLINGHAM F·C

TAKE THIS WITH YOU TO THE NEXT MATCH AND COMPARE THE CARTOON WITH THE ORIGINALS WHO ARE ALL WORTHY OF YOUR SUPPORT AND ENCOURAGEMENT.

Inserted in the "Warlingham Parish Church Magazine" by courtesy of the Vicar.

School Common proved unsatisfactory, mainly 'on account of the path, which cuts across the ground in whatever position the goals are placed' and so, in 1900 a move was made to Mr Bond's meadow off Farleigh Road, opposite the forge. This was not a permanent move, however, and in 1913 it was reported that the club was experiencing difficulty in finding a ground, having had to give up a pitch half way through the 1912-13 season and making temporary use of another field. For the new season it was decided to return to a ground occupied a few years ago (possibly Mr Bond's meadow).

After World War I, the football club became a founder member of the Warlingham Sports Club, competing not very successfully in the Edenbridge & District League Division I – in 1921-22 eleven successive defeats were recorded. The club also competed in the Caterham league but had to drop out before the end of the 1925-6 season, only to return five years later in Division II.

Despite competition from the neighbouring Farleigh Rovers, whose ground is in the Parsonage Field, off Harrow Road, Warlingham FC celebrated its centenary in 1996. Chairman Gary Buckett appeared in the *Croydon Advertiser* receiving a centenary award from Surrey County FA's representative, Les Smith.

Warlingham Golf Club

Members outside Warlingham Golf Club – early 1900s

Warlingham Golf Club was opened in 1897 but its location was outside the parish at Manor Park, Whyteleafe, where it is still possible to see some of the tees and greens off Burntwood Lane. A plan of the course appears in *Local History Records* 26 together with a view of the clubhouse, formerly known as Caterham Manor, from the first green *c.*1930 and an Edwardian tea party at the golf club in 1904. In *Bygone Caterham* there is a magnificent photograph of the lady golfers outside the clubhouse in 1911, all with splendid hats and proudly displaying their clubs. In 1904 some of the great names in the history of golf appeared—

'The members of the Warlingham Golf club had a special day on Saturday last, arrangements having been made for a professional competition between James Braid (champion), Harry Vardon (ex-champion), J H Taylor (ex-champion) and John Hill, who is employed by the Warlingham Club. The weather was showery and not favourable but Vardon played a grand game, and won first prize with a total of 77, the score being 37 in the first round and 40 in the second. Taylor was second with a score of 78 and Braid third with 79, he having lost a stroke through approaching out of bounds. Hill was fourth with 81. In the afternoon, when the weather was fine, Braid and Taylor were opposed to Vardon and Hill. The former won, going round in 75, the score of the latter being 77. The numerous visitors were entertained at the clubhouse which is on the ground.'

A description of the course, where par was 72 playing twice round, can be found in the above *Local History Records*. The club came to an abrupt end when, on 28th August 1940, a string of bombs fell along the bottom of the park, destroying the house almost completely. The golf club did not survive the war and the whole area soon became derelict.

Rugby Union

Warlingham Rugby Football Club commenced in 1922, using part of the Warlingham Sports Club field and the season of 1922-3 was its first full season. In 1923 the Club visited Coventry.

In 1925 the captain and honorary secretary was Arthur Skull of 'Warren Lodge' and both the first and A fifteens were reported as doing well.

An important move to the present venue at Hamsey Green Field, at the rear of Hamsey Green Gardens, occurred in 1928, and in March 1930 the Warlingham Rugby Football Ground Ltd was formed to acquire the freehold of the 14-acre field.

Warlingham currently plays in the London Two South League. By 1990 it had embraced Hillcrest Netball Club, Warlingham Archery Club and in 1992 provided a new home for Selsdon Cricket Club.

Lawn Tennis

In 1893, the parish magazine recorded the first attempt to establish a lawn tennis club in Warlingham. It would appear to have been strictly for the families of gentlemen and membership for ordinary village folk would have been most unlikely—

> 'WARLINGHAM LAWN TENNIS CLUB
>
> With so many houses springing up in the part of the Parish commonly called Westhall, it is only natural that there should be a Lawn Tennis Club. Its successful start is mainly due to Mr Ashwell. In August last he called a few friends together to discuss the question; a committee was formed and he consented to act as secretary. Promises of donations and members' annual subscriptions were numerous enough to justify the committee in hiring a piece of ground, levelling three courts, drawing up a set of rules and definitely starting the Club.
>
> There are now thirty-three members, and others have expressed their intention of joining. "We propose", the honorary secretary writes "to put up a small pavilion, hold tournaments, and, if possible, a Club-day, when ladies will take turns in providing tea. It is hoped these meetings will bring people together and give pleasure to many residents". We heartily wish the Club success.'

The driving force behind the club was the Ashwell family of 'Hazlewood': in April 1894, the Misses Ashwell organised an entertainment at the School for club funds and 'Mr Ashwell, in his negro character, was most amusing.'

The club was in Homefield Road and eventually built on and it was not until after the formation of the Warlingham Sports Club on its present site that public courts became available.

In 1930 tennis was flourishing on two grass courts at the Sports Club and these were later made into hard courts. On 11th November 1939 an official opening took place of three hard courts from funds provided by the Urban District Council and the National Playing Fields Association and in April 1985 three shale courts were converted to all-weather, making a total of five.

Archery

An interesting reference to archers in Warlingham and Chelsham is found in 1539 at the time of the quarrel between the Pope and Henry VIII. Typical family names in the muster were: Ward, Ownsteed, Comport, Wodden, Hayward and Bassett – all well known in local history as churchwardens and sidesmen. It was proposed to form a tableau depicting these men in the pageant for the Warlingham & Chelsham Festival of Britain celebrations in 1951. In March of that year a meeting was held at the Warlingham Sports Club which led to the formation of the Warlingham Archery Club, which held its first meeting in the Vicarage Field on 12th April the following year.

Colonel Ambrose Keevil was the club's first president and W L Morgan its first chairman. Despite the venue for the inaugural meeting, the club did not become part of Warlingham Sports Club and in 1990 it was using the premises of the Warlingham Rugby Club, though it now appears to have lapsed.

Members of the Archery Club in action — in the Vicarage Field, 1952.

Rifle Clubs

Warlingham Rifle Club was formed at the end of 1907 and a miniature rifle range was built in Mint Walk. This was an indoor range of 25 yards costing £175 and it was opened on 9th January 1909 by which time the club had 60-70 members.

It is not certain whether the club survived World War I and in 1935 a new club was formed - the Warlingham & District Miniature Rifle Club. When a general meeting was called in 1936, the club was open to ladies and gentlemen over 18 years.

Athletics

In 1913 the second Spring Warlingham & District Races were held at Hamsey Green Farm but unfortunately attracted some unwanted attention—

'Many of the residents are complaining that it attracts a large number of undesirables to the place. Quite a rough element turned up last week and were rightly refused admission to the ground, but they loitered about the villages of Warlingham and Whyteleafe and a considerable group was observed in one thoroughfare playing pitch and toss, with men each end watching to give warning should the police appear. There was also a somewhat disorderly scene at the railway station in the evening when these race meeting followers wanted to board trains without paying fares.'

Motor Sport

There were proposals for a motor racing track at Warlingham outlined in *The Surrey Mirror* for March and May 1903. The scheme is discussed by J P S Martin in the Bourne Society's *Local History Records* Volume 35 but with the advent of Brooklands a few years later, it was never constructed. 'Purley Bury House' would have been the clubhouse and the track was due to cut across Riddlesdown to Hamsey Green where there would have been a grandstand.

Swimming

In 1950 a local newspaper carried a headline: 'Two Pools - but only one place to swim' and carried photographs of the Warlingham Scouts' popular pool (which attracts enthusiasts from as far away as Purley and Croydon) and the 'Mountain Pools'. The photograph of the latter shows it unpeopled and desolate with a 'For Sale' notice prominently displayed. 'Before the war it was a popular Lido, but now, following a long period of requisition, it is closed and derelict.' The Mountain Pools were on Godstone Road, Whyteleafe and were the subject of an article by Judith Faulkner in *Local History Records,* Volume 27.

Fox Hunting

Warlingham has a long association with fox hunting and there is a photograph of the meet of the horses and hounds outside *The White Lion* and *The Horseshoe* c.1903 in *Warlingham in Old Picture Postcards*. The following is taken from a sporting newspaper for 1823—

'Surrey Fox Hounds meet Monday at Hamsey Green; Thursday at *Rose & Crown*, Riddlesdown. Sanderstead Harriers meet Monday, Wednesday and Saturday at kennels.'

Warlingham Sports Club

The present Warlingham Sports Club was formed in 1919, a natural successor to the pre-war Village Club Sports Association, which had its origins with the Village Working Man's Club (opened 1902) and with C L Lockton.

The official opening of the present ground took place on 30th April 1921 and it was agreed to offer shares to buy the ground 'which would be vested in trustees to hold for use as a sports ground by the people of Warlingham for

WARLINGHAM SPORTS CLUB.

President - • *R. A. PRICE, Esq.*

CRICKET.   TENNIS.   FOOTBALL.

Open Letter to the Residents of Warlingham.

Why not join us ? Become a Member of any of the above sections, and help our Management Committee to build up the best Sports Ground in Surrey. We have the space (14 acres) situated in ideal surroundings; the organisation, the equipment, and everything necessary for healthy recreation. Our great need is more Members, real enthusiastic Playing Members, whose zeal will greatly assist us to carry out various ambitious schemes of Ground improvement, New Pavilion, Bowling Green, &c. The minimum Subscription for Tennis or Cricket is only 10/6 per annum, and Association Football, 5 - per season; a figure within the reach of all. Our Hon. Treasurer is always open to accept more, if you are willing to give more. We particularly need Cricketers and Tennis Players for the best of our National Summer Games. Do join without delay, and perpetuate the glorious traditions of Village Sport.

....

Make your application now to

Hon. Cricket Secretary:	Hon. Tennis Sec.:	Hon. Football Sec.:
H. N. WITTS,	LESLIE HONOUR	F. JARVIS,
CICETER, FARLEIGH ROAD,	CROYDON ROAD,	BUGHILL ROAD,
WARLINGHAM.	WARLINGHAM.	WARLINGHAM.

Hon. General Sec.:	Hon. General Treas:
H. P. HAYNES,	G. F. SNELL,
KINGSWOOD COTTAGE,	HOMESTEAD,
HAMSEY GREEN.	WARLINGHAM.

WE NEED YOU ! !

Advertisement for Warlingham Sports Club in Warlingham Parish Magazine, June 1932.

all time'. In 1929 the honorary secretary of the Sports Club was able to report that the past year had seen the fulfilment of the Ground Acquisition Scheme. The immediate aims were hard tennis courts and a bowling green. During the past year the association football section had been re-started and a ladies' hockey section had been formed. Another feature was the institution of indoor cricket made possible by the conversion of the rifle range and was very popular. The opening ceremony of the latter was performed by H D G Leveson-Gower.

In April 1940 the 21st birthday of the Sports Club was celebrated and it has since developed into one of the best appointed sports and social clubs in the district. The pavilion and bar have been enlarged, new sections have been formed (e g squash) and the disastrous fire of 1995 has been overcome.

SOURCES

ASHLEY-COOPER, F S (1900) 'Cricket 1742-51' in *Cricket* 19th April.

Bell's Life in London 1823, 1833, 1838.

Caterham Weekly Press 1913, 1929.

Croydon Advertiser, 1869, 1871, 1873-74, 1877, 1879, 1880, 1882-3, 1946, 1996.

Croydon Chronicle, 1856, 1861, 1862, 1868.

DUNNING, J (1996) 'Warlingham C C'. *The Surrey Championship Year Book* pp 63-5.

Edenbridge Chronicle 1923.

FOOKES, GWYNETH (1987). 'The History of Manor Park' Bourne Society *Local History Records* **26**.

GOULSTONE, JOHN (1978). 'The Frames of Warlingham'. *Sports Quarterly Magazine* **9**.

GOULSTONE, JOHN (1978). 'The Golden Era of Dartford Cricket', *The History of Cricket in Dartford.*

Kelly's Surrey Directory 1927.

MARTIN, J P S (1996). 'The Purley Race Track'. Bourne Society *Local History Records* **35**.

MILES, HENRY DOWNES (1906). *Pugilistica: the History of British Boxing*. John Grant. **I**: 385-7.

NYREN, JOHN (1833) The *Young Cricketer's Tutor*. Effingham Wilson.

PAYNE, JACK (unpublished, *c* 1996). *Memories of Warlingham Sports Club.*

Surrey Mirror 1904.

TOOKE, JEAN (1988) *Bygone Caterham* Phillimore.

TUTT, DOROTHY Miscellaneous notes on Warlingham (unpublished).

TUTT, DOROTHY (1988) *Warlingham in Old Picture Postcards* **I**. European Library.

Warlingham & Chelsham Parish Magazine, especially 1893-1900, 1906.

Chapter 23

Birds and other aspects of Natural History

by Brian Thomas

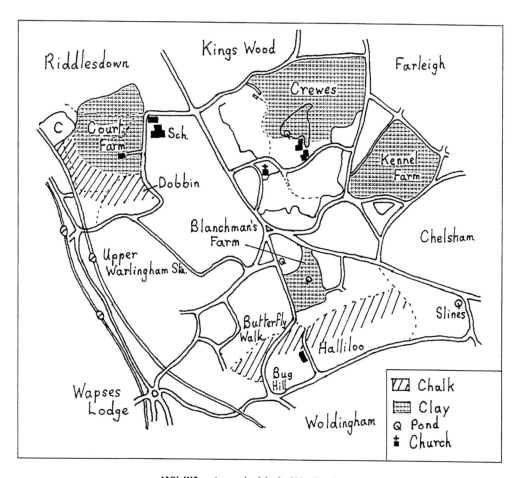

Wildlife strongholds in Warlingham

THE BEADELL HERITAGE

Just as Caterham was extremely fortunate in having the pioneer bird photographer Richard Kearton living in the district from 1898-1928 painstakingly recording for posterity everything of natural history interest; so Warlingham was similarly lucky in having its very own wildlife recorder – Arthur Beadell (1872-1957).

Beadell was not even a national let alone international celebrity like Kearton and he never made a pictorial record, but in his *Nature Notes of Warlingham & Chelsham* published in 1932, he bequeathed a unique and wonderful record of the past. Whether it is crawling through beds of stinging nettles impervious to the pain so as not to disturb a bird; leading a gamekeeper a merry dance around the woods for the very fun of it; walking 30 miles to see a butterfly, or waiting four years to identify a rare orchid through all the vicissitudes of cattle trampling and people picking it, the book's intimate detail and fascination shine through. Without it, who would believe that there were very few carrion crows and no magpies for 30 years but that hooded crows were regular winter visitors including an amazing flock numbering 60. We learn that the red squirrel was scarce here even before the grey arrived during World War I and how the little owl also appeared at this time.

An admirable reissue and update of the flowers section of Beadell's notes, published in 1982, followed some 40 years of local study by Raymond Clarke (1904-1982) and quite justifiably states – 'It is difficult to imagine any English rival to this area in respect of recorded knowledge about plants'. The same thing can be said about the birds of the district since, apart from Beadell and Kearton, renowned Surrey ornithologist Howard Bentham recorded birds in the county from 1906 until his death in 1968, including several notes on the Warlingham area, particularly in the early part of the century. Last but by no means least, mention must be made of Hubert E. Pounds, whose book *The Birds of Farleigh and District and the North Downs* (1952) is a meticulous historic compilation incorporating personal records spanning some 25 years.

CHANGES IN THE LANDSCAPE

Even in 1932 Beadell tells us – 'Warlingham is fast being built upon; all the interesting woods and fields are disappearing' though 'Chelsham retains its rural character'. He would have been saddened by the further losses such as the locally treasured flower and butterfly rich 'Top Field ' where Crowborough Drive was developed in the late 1950s and the numerous infill developments in the Westhall area including those at Hillside Road in the old lime quarries.

Despite these and other losses to suburban housing, schools, sports and recreation grounds and commerce, and the fact that a high percentage of the open fields that remain have been given over to horse grazing and/or 'improved' so as to be of limited wildlife value, tracts or pockets of considerable wealth have persisted or 'resisted' with the assistance of a Green Belt policy or Set-aside. These areas are principally on the periphery of the parish and are well served by public footpaths/bridleways. Two of these, the Halliloo Valley/Bug Hill area and the Dobbin are chalk downland; the remainder – Kennel Farm, Crewes Valley and Blanchman's Farm – are situated on the clay-with-flints plateau.

Chalk Downland – *Halliloo Valley/Bug Hill*

The deep trough-shaped dry chalk valleys running from the precipitous escarpments of the North Downs along Woldingham Ridge, meander northwards to Warlingham. One runs under the 800 ft peak of Nore Hill, Chelsham, before turning westwards into the Halliloo Valley to form the southern boundary of the parish. The valley bottom has recently been developed as Duke's Dene Golf Course, but was formerly Fuller's Farm. Further west at the source of the Bourne and under the attractively arched Mumbles railway viaduct, it is joined by the Marden Park Valley and further west still it meets the main Caterham Valley before moving north-west through Whyteleafe to the Dobbin and Riddlesdown, so forming the western parish boundary.

From the western end of the Halliloo Valley, the elevated Butterfly Walk footpaths afford a wonderful vantage point to view part of the North Downs Area of Outstanding Natural Beauty with the beech hangers of Slines and Nore Hill to the east and Marden Park in the south; Marden Park famously described by Sir John Evelyn 300 years ago as being 'in such solitude among hills ... not above 16 miles from London, seems almost incredible'.

Corncrakes nested in the valley close to Bug Hill Farm at the turn of the century and it was probably here in Tippets Piece that Beadell discovered the very rare Lady orchid. Typical chalk downland flora is still in evidence, particularly on the bank fringes, including rock rose, scabious, yellowwort and marjoram, with broad-leaved helleborine and the scarce stinking hellebore in shadier corners. The palm tree that once graced the chalk hollow half way up Bug Hill has long since gone, but the hedgerows are a beautiful sight even in the winter with the chalk-loving wayfaring tree, wild clematis (wiffey wood – old man's beard – traveller's joy or what you will) and the pink flash of spindle berries very much in evidence.

Katie and Sam on the Leas above the Halliloo Valley, 1996.

The top of this bank is a good location for glow-worms on a summer evening, though possibly in insufficient numbers today to provide enough of the wonderful greenish-blue light for a Thomas Hardy type card game!

Kestrels and even more so sparrowhawks – recovered from their 1950s pesticide-related population crash – regularly hunt the valley. With luck common buzzards – which are currently undergoing a range expansion – may be encountered passing through particularly in spring and autumn. With recently proved breeding for the very first time in the area of that elegant falcon, the hobby, the chances of seeing this superb flyer taking a butterfly, dragonfly or small bird on the wing are far from remote.

Common Buzzard

The slopes of Halliloo Leas (pronounced *leys* by locals) have regretfully long since lost the adonis and chalkhill blue butterflies (although the latter retains a perilous foothold at Nore Hill on its horseshoe vetch food plant). Surprising as it may seem Beadell only saw one comma butterfly in Warlingham during his lifetime, no speckled woods nor gatekeepers and in his eagerness to encounter the marbled white butterfly, he made a 30 mile round trip on foot to Shoreham and subsequently cycled there on two occasions before succeeding in his quest. This species has been moving steadily eastwards from Box Hill and also away from the Downs in recent years and has been regularly encountered since 1996 at nearby Nore Hill. Similar good news concerns that beautiful woodland butterfly, the white admiral, which was seen for the very first time in the area in 1997 and again in 1998.

– *The Dobbin and Court Farm*

The southern extremity of Riddlesdown beyond the disused chalk quarry is just in the parish. It is this area – known locally as the Dobbin – and the fields adjacent to Court Farm, that produce the best birdwatching in the area.

Looking towards The Dobbin and Court Farm in 1905. The path on which the people are walking started by the railway bridge at the bottom of Hillbury Road.

On the raptor front, kestrel and sparrowhawk are regular, hobby and buzzard are occasional possibilities and on 30th January 1987 there was a hen harrier quartering the lower slopes above the recreation ground. It is, therefore, a question of looking to the sky here – or should it be *Reach for the Sky,* since it was here that part of the 1950s film of that name, starring Kenneth More as Douglas Bader, was shot? In the middle of the last century Workhouse Lane (now Hillbury Road) ran up a virtually treeless valley. In the 1950s, as the cricket match shots in the aforementioned film witness, the Dobbin was still relatively open downland with a few scattered yew, ash and whitebeam trees and only low clumps of hawthorn scrub.

BIRDS AND OTHER ASPECTS OF NATURAL HISTORY

It was at this time that myxomatosis was first introduced into the country (at Bough Beech in Kent). With the rapid demise of the rabbit and none of the flocks of sheep left to graze the herb-rich pasture as they had done for centuries, there was nothing to keep the vegetation in check. Scrub such as hawthorn, dogwood, blackthorn and ash rapidly choked our flora-rich hillsides. Looking up at the Dobbin today the transformation is complete – thick secondary woodland scrub dominated by hawthorn with a very bare understorey often covered only by a bed of ivy.

The Conservation Volunteers established in the 1950s continue, in conjunction with District and County Councils, to clear large tracts of scrub often with amazing and rapid botanical and entomological results. It is often the second year after clearance that optimum results are achieved. Areas of the Dobbin have very recently been cleared – in early 1998 – and perhaps the best known plants of the chalk, the orchids, with their very complex needs will appear in greater numbers. Among the more common plant species the aromatic marjoram, birdsfoot trefoil, knapweed and milkwort can be expected to benefit along with numerous invertebrates. Badgers, squirrels and slow-worms seem to do well here whatever the conditions, but you need to be lucky to see adders or lizards.

Returning to the birds, historically the area was significant for numbers of red-backed shrikes (the butcher bird) and the wryneck. Both bred on these Downs, the wryneck up until the late 1960s, while ironically the very last shrike bred on the Kearton Reserve at Caterham in the early 1970s. Both birds were sadly extinct as breeders in the UK in 1995.

Meadow Pipit   **Blackcap**

Today summer visitors such as the common and lesser whitethroat, blackcap, chiffchaff and willow warbler all breed here. The scarce grasshopper warbler shows a liking for the grass scrub. Residents such as meadow pipit, skylark and yellowhammer breed as do tawny and little owls. Wheatear, whinchat and stonechat are regular passage migrants, the latter sometimes wintering.

The best chance of hearing a nightingale is at the foot of the Dobbin; the last bred in 1978 but one was heard again as recently as 1996, albeit briefly. In the winter months flocks of skylark, linnets, redpolls, yellowhammers, reed buntings and meadow pipits frequent the Set-aside or feed on linseed stubble and in the weedy hedgerows.

If the above is not proof enough of the Caterham Valley and the prominent Dobbin with its chalkpit acting as a magnet to migrants, consider the fact that ring ouzel and even that aquatic species the sedge warbler have been found here recently. In the quarry itself, there is a colony of the rare small blue butterfly as well as over 50 nesting pairs of jackdaws. If this does not whet the appetite, venture a little to the north to witness the benefits of managed sheep and cattle grazing on the City of London Corporation's land where round-headed rampion, chalkhill blue butterflies, glow-worms and much besides can be seen.

The Clay-with-Flints Plateau – *Kennel Farm Area*

The fields immediately to the west of Kennel Farm on the north-east of the parish were at one time farmed with arable crops, principally barley. Before this, however, we know from Beadell's records that they have been hay meadows, since he recalls how in 1926 a corncrake (now extinct as a breeding bird on the UK mainland) called continuously from here at night whilst he was lying in bed in his Sunnybank flint cottage. Even up until the 1960s coveys of grey partridge and numbers of hares were a regular sight here. The former, which have suffered a catastrophic national decline, has been extinct as a breeding bird in the area for many years, and only in the wilder parts of Chelsham can hares still be found.

Although not botanically rich, with several hedges having been uprooted in the past making it effectively one huge field, the area has been Set-aside for several years now with obvious benefits to wildlife. When it is considered that over four million skylarks have been lost to the British breeding population since 1976, to see them here still in good numbers, together with meadow pipits, yellowhammers, linnets and goldfinches, is wonderful.

Red Kite

KCO

The thick tussocky grasses have in recent winters attracted roosting snipe and even a beautiful migrant red kite flew over in 1996. Roe deer, which Beadell never saw here, occasionally stray into the area in the early morning from the safe cover of Holt or Great Park Woods, Chelsham. Rabbits are present but they are not nearly as numerous as at nearby Worms Heath.

Green Hill Lane with its rosebay willowherb, bracken-lined verges and tall hawthorn hedgerow, together with the adjoining vacated allotments overgrown with bramble and other scrub, is an excellent area for breeding whitethroats. Passing migrants include wheatear, stonechat, whinchat, common and black redstart, willow warbler and chiffchaff. Last, but by no means least, the once very common house sparrow can still be seen here and in the adjoining roads to the south. In this connection the British Trust for Ornithology's Garden Birdwatch for the winter 1997/98 showed an all time low for this species and the song thrush.

Stonechat

Song Thrush

BIRDS AND OTHER ASPECTS OF NATURAL HISTORY

– *The Crewes Valley*

Just a short walk from All Saints' Church with its ancient yew tree, the tranquillity and rural scene that awaits in the sweeping clay-topped chalk valley of Crewes never ceases to surprise. Still actively farmed in part, with cattle and horses grazing in the fields, it witnessed an amazing event on the evening of 5th September 1958 when a torrential thunder and hailstorm moving north-east across Surrey, transformed the valley bottom into a huge lake the like of which had never been experienced in living memory.

Unlike nearby Sanderstead with King's Wood and Selsdon with its Bird Sanctuary, Warlingham cannot boast large tracts of 'ancient semi-natural woodland' (i.e. managed over the centuries and continuously wooded since before 1600). However, this area does possess small remnants in the form of narrow shaws and copses, the best example lying near Kingswood Lodge on the bridleway to Farleigh.

Like our valuable hedgerows the longer a wood is in existence the greater the benefit from a conservation standpoint with additional species establishing themselves and so increasing ecological diversity. Coppicing of deciduous woodlands by our forebears (often of hazel or sweet chestnut) enabled more daylight to penetrate; this encouraged many woodland flowers to flourish and in turn helped a number of insects and other creatures. Ancient woodland indicators include bluebell, primrose, crab apple, wild cherry, holly, wood anemone, wood sorrel, dog violet, goldilocks (woodland buttercup) and wood mellick. The treat of seeing the annual carpet of bluebells or wood anemones in these fragments of woodlands or the magnificent white splash of the particularly fine blackthorn hedgerows is not to be missed. Crewes Wood itself, despite the ravages of the Great Storm in October 1987, has several splendid specimens of pedunculate oak as well as a small pond and, of course, the bluebells.

Lords and ladies (or Wild Arum, Cuckoo Flower, Long Purples) is numerous throughout the district and Cecil Prime, who wrote a book entirely devoted to this single plant, lived for many years not a stone's throw away on Farleigh Common.

Barn owls have been seen recently in the area as well as at Blanchman's Farm, though they are most probably of captive bred origin from a Woldingham release site. Bullfinches love the blackthorn thickets and all three species of woodpecker can be seen with the lesser spotted by far the rarest.

- *Blanchman's Farm Community Wildlife Area.*

This area south-east of the Green and with access from Leas and Limpsfield Roads, is owned by Tandridge District Council and is specifically managed by local residents and the Downlands Countryside Management Project (DCMP) with wildlife in mind. Thousands of trees have been planted comprising 30 different native species including black poplar. The old farm pond on the site has been re-created, grass meadows on the very heavy clay soil have been sensitively managed, and coppicing, hedging and path construction – including all-weather access for wheelchair users – are just some of the tasks undertaken to date. A very popular annual fete is held on the old rugby field.

The abundant supply of berries has attracted good numbers of thrushes (fieldfare, redwing, blackbird, mistle and song) in the winter. As well as a good range of resident breeding birds, spring and autumn migrants are drawn to the improved habitat – probably by way of the nearby Halliloo Valley – either to stay and nest or to feed up for their onward journey. The local branch of the RSPB (East Surrey Group) conducts a guided spring bird walk for local children every year and apart from other flora and fauna, participants were rewarded in 1998 with the wonderful spectacle of a whimbrel flying over calling on its way north to Arctic breeding grounds.

Arthur Beadell bemoaned the fact that the district had lost seven ponds. He would have been delighted therefore to see what has been done at Blanchmans and to learn that Willy's Pit Pond has been restored (by the DCMP on behalf of Tandridge Council) so to become in his words 'a thing of beauty to our village'. The roadside pond at Slines is unfortunately the repository for many unwanted, invasive garden pond plants and even unwanted animals. In recent years several terrapins have survived and are to be seen basking in the sun.

Warlingham. Worms Heath.

Slines Pond, alongside Limpsfield Road, in the early 1900s

WHAT OF THE FUTURE?

It is a sobering thought that nine out of 10 of the hottest years on record globally have occurred since 1983. In England the five warmest years since 1659 have all been post 1975. In the last 25 years some 20 common British breeding birds, including the wren, chaffinch and magpie, have been nesting earlier – nine days on average. It is not now unusual to see bluebells out in mid-March. What more proof is needed of global warming and greenhouse gases? This is, of course, only the tip of the iceberg, and an iceberg that is melting fast. We must hope that Man gets his act together speedily and that the wonderful resiliance of nature will be able to cope or adapt in the meantime.

Despite protection under the Wildlife & Countryside Act 1981, Britain's most treasured wildlife sites – our Sites of Special Scientific Interest (SSSIs) – can and are being damaged; one in five has been so affected in England nd Wales between 1991 and 1996 and recent research shows that almost half are in poor condition. withstanding the major losses of habitat and species since the turn of the century, it is encouraging to reflect hilst Arthur Beadell was considered childish and a freak to be engrossed in nature study, there are today e million members of wildlife organisations in the UK. Many of the gardens in Warlingham, bear these different attitudes and an awareness of 'green issues'. The 'wild areas' left at the bottom of the garden, the small ponds and bird feeders, whilst never a substitute for what has been lost, are nonetheless very important natural reservoirs – our own SSSIs in fact. We do need, however, to be ever vigilant in protecting against further destruction, erosion or mismanagement of the wilder places. We surely owe nothing less to the memory of Arthur Beadell and Raymond Clarke and for the future to our children and children's children. For what will their lives be worth 'if full of care, they have *no time nor place* to stand and stare?'

SOURCES

BEADELL, ARTHUR (1932) *Nature Notes of Warlingham & Chelsham*, Croydon Advertiser.

BRITISH BIRDS (1998) **91** Nos. 1, 2, 8 & 10.

CLARKE, RAYMOND (1982) *70 Years of Nature Notes in Warlingham & Chelsham.* Privately published.

DAVISON, MARK & CURRIE IAN (1990). *The Surrey Weather Book.* Frosted Earth.

DREWETT, JOHN (1987) *The Nature of Surrey – Surrey Wildlife Trust.* Barracuda Books.

GADSBY, JOY *[Ed.]* (1998) *Village Histories – 3. Sanderstead.* The Bourne Society.

JEFFCOATE G, GERRARD B, & ENFIELD M (1997) *Butterfly Report for Surrey Branch, Butterfly Conservation.*

PARR, DONALD (1972) *Birds of Surrey 1900-1970.* Northumberland Press.

POUNDS, HUBERT E (1952) *The Birds of Farleigh & District* College Press.

Illustrations of birds in this chapter are published by courtesy of Ken Osborne

THE BOURNE SOCIETY

The Bourne Society was founded in 1956 and takes its name from the underground streams which follow the lines of the A22 and A23 roads, meeting in Purley to flow northwards and form the River Wandle, which flows into the Thames at Wandsworth.

The objects of the Society – England's largest local history society – are to extend the knowledge of local history in Caterham, Chaldon, Chelsham, Chipstead, Coulsdon, Farleigh, Godstone, Kenley, Purley, Sanderstead, Whyteleafe, Warlingham and Woldingham, and to ensure the preservation of records and objects of historical interest. The Society's Membership Secretary, Mrs. J. Emery, 118 Coulsdon Road, Coulsdon, Surrey CR5 2LB, will be happy to provide details of membership and subscription rates. The Society's telephone number is 01883 349287.

The Bourne Society is a registered charity, and as well as general work it has active special-interest groups in archaeology, industrial archaeology, landscape history, photography and pub history. Regular meetings, events and outings are arranged. A wide range of publications are produced, including a quarterly **Bulletin** and annual *Local History Records* which are sent free to members. For prices and current availability contact John Tyerman, Publications Co-ordinator, 60 Onslow Gardens, Sanderstead CR2 9AT, telephone 0181 657 1202.

Some recent publications —

Books:

Village History Series. Vol. 1–Purley, editor Andy Higham (1996); Vol. 2–Caterham, editor Gwyneth Fookes (1997); Vol. 3–Sanderstead, editor Joy Gadsby (1998); Vol. 4–Warlingham, editor Dorothy Tutt (1999); Vol. 5–Coulsdon in preparation for publication in 2000; Vol. 6–Chaldon in preparation.

A Centenary History of the Chipstead Valley Railway (Tattenham Corner Branch Line, 1897-1997).

The Way We Were - A Bourne Society Book of Days by John D. Matthews.

A Surrey Childhood in the 1930s and 1940s by Muriel Neal.

Leaflets:

Getting to know our Downland Villages – No. 1. Sanderstead (1997); No. 2. Godstone (1998); No. 3. Caterham in preparation.